Jim Laker

The 'All Ten' Test Match.

At Manchester, Fourth Test Match, July 26 to July 31, 1956. England v Australia.
England defeated Australia by an innings and 170 runs and retained the "Ashes".

ENGLAND − First Innings
P E RICHARDSON c **Maddocks** b **Benaud** .104
M C COWDREY c Maddocks b Lindwall . . 80
Rev. D S SHEPPARD b Archer 113
+ P B H MAY c Archer b Benaud 43
T E BAILEY b Johnson 20
C WASHBROOK lbw b Johnson 6
A S M OAKMAN c Archer b Johnson 10
• T G EVANS st **Maddocks** b Johnson 47
J C LAKER run out 3
G A R LOCK not out 25
J B STATHAM c **Maddocks** b **Lindwall** 0
Extras (b2, 1b5, w1) 8
Total 459

Wickets fell at: 174, 195, 288, 321, 339, 401, 417, 458.
Australian bowling: Lindwall 21.3-6-63-2. Miller 21-6-41-0
                    Archer 22-6-73-1. Johnson 47-10-151-4.
                    Benaud 47-17-123-2.

AUSTRALIA − First Innings
C C McDONALD c **Lock** b **Laker** 32
J W BURKE c Cowdrey b Lock 22
R N HARVEY b **Laker** 0
I D CRAIG lbw b **Laker** 8
K R MILLER c **Oakman** b **Laker** 6
K MACKAY c **Oakman** b **Laker** 0
R G ARCHER st **Evans** b **Laker** 6
R BENAUD c **Statham** b **Laker** 0
R R LINDWALL not out 6
• L MADDOCKS b **Laker** 4
+ I W JOHNSON b **Laker** 0
Total 84

Wickets fell at: 48, 48, 62, 62, 73, 73, 73, 78, 84.
England bowling: Statham 6-3-6-0. Bailey 4-3-4-0
Laker 16.4-4-37-9. Lock 14-3-37-1.

AUSTRALIA − Second Innings
C C McDONALD c **Oakman** b **Laker** 89
J W BURKE c **Lock** b **Laker** 33
R N HARVEY c **Cowdrey** b **Laker** 0
I D CRAIG lbw b **Laker** 38
K R MILLER b **Laker** 0
K MACKAY c **Oakman** b **Laker** 0
R G ARCHER c **Oakman** b **Laker** 0
R BENAUD b **Laker** 18
R R LINDWALL c **Lock** b **Laker** 8
• L MADDOCKS lbw b **Laker** 2
+ I W JOHNSON not out 1
Extras (b12, 1b4) 16
Total 205

Wickets fell at: 28, 55, 114, 124, 130, 130, 181, 198, 203.
England bowling: Statham 16-9-15-0. Bailey 20-8-31-0.
                Laker 51.2-23-53-10. Lock 55-30-69-0.
                Oakman 8-2-21-0.

+ CAPTAIN   • WICKETKEEPER

The Surrey off-break bowler JC (Jim) Laker, having taken 9 for 37 in the first Australian innings and 10 for 53 in the second innings, created the following records:
• 19 WICKETS in the match, the most in any First Class game.
• 10 WICKETS in an innings, for the first time in Test cricket history
• 10 WICKETS in an innings twice in one season for the first time.
(Laker also took 10 for 88 for Surrey against the Australians in 1956).

Jim Laker
9 for 37 and 10 for 53

Jim Laker

a biography by

Alan Hill

ANDRE DEUTSCH

First published in 1998 by
André Deutsch Limited
76 Dean Street
London WIV 5HA
www.vci.co.uk

André Deutsch is a VCI plc company

A catalogue record for this book is available from the British Library

ISBN 0 233 99151 4

Typeset by Derek Doyle & Associates
Mold, Flintshire
Printed and bound
by WBC, Bridgend

To Betty,
for her splendid support in this spell
on a spinner's pitch

CONTENTS

ILLUSTRATIONS

Acknowledgements and thanks for the use of photographs and other illustrations are due to the following: Mrs Lilly Laker, Surrey County Cricket Club, Roy Ullyett, Pamela Wilkinson, Arthur McIntyre, Bert Flack, Robert Downie, Elizabeth Paczek and Peter Iles.

FOREWORD
by Richie Benaud OBE

Jim Laker was a part of my cricketing life, not always an enjoyable part, mind you, because he was responsible for many Australian batsmen shortening their careers, though not necessarily of their own volition. The story I have never forgotten, nor did the Queenslander concerned in his own lifetime, was to do with Ken 'Slasher' Mackay who had a certain number of problems with Jim on the pitches in England in 1956. At the end of that series it seemed Ken's career could have been finished but, when Ron Archer was forced by injury to pull out of the Australian tour of South Africa, Slasher was chosen to do battle with offspinner Hugh Tayfield. This produced a certain amount of hilarity in the UK but not with Jim, who backed him to make runs, which he duly did, and plenty of them.

I had observed him closely during the 1956 tour and when, in Madras, I remodelled and reduced my run-up, it was Jim's style and patience I had in mind. He and I worked together for BBC Television over a number of years and at that time there were a lot of new things happening in the television world with young producers like David Kenning and Nick Hunter taking advantage of various technological advances. Commentary boxes are like cricket teams with varied personalities; it would be very boring were everyone to be cloned. It worked well that each of us had a certain economy of words within our own styles and we blended well, although I suppose not everyone listening felt compelled to applaud the use of an Australian voice and one from Yorkshire. Jim had an acute knowledge of the game and what was being done to it and with it at any given time, and he had scant regard for those who tended to look at other people

xi

from a loftier than deserved perch in life. In that, he was a hard and humorous marker!

He had his own experience of being marked hard after the Ashes match against Australia at Headingley in 1948. Although credit was given to the Australians for winning an extraordinary contest, blame was apportioned mainly to Jim for not bowling them out and it certainly cost him places in Tests and in touring teams, notably the 1954–55 side which toured Australia under Len Hutton's captaincy. The selectors on that occasion were able to look back on victory and the retention of the Ashes against a side unable to handle the pace of Frank Tyson and Brian Statham. Back-up on that tour was successfully provided by Bob Appleyard. It has though always seemed to me unfair to blame Jim for the Headingley problems. He was playing in only his seventh Test match and, in a game where over 1,700 runs were scored for the loss of only 31 wickets, Alec Bedser was the one outstanding bowler in the side chosen by the England selectors, the others in the bowling attack were useful performers. It took Jim a long time to live down the Headingley perception of failure but the England selectors of the time did him no favours. It would have made Old Trafford 1956 even more pleasant.

Alan Hill has captured him well in these pages, setting out the man, his setbacks and his many triumphs, which were always noted with a delightful touch of dry modesty. Jim was a great bowler and a splendid character and this biography will deservedly add to his stature.

INTRODUCTION

'This above all – to thine
own self be true;
And it must follow,
as the night the day,
Thou canst not then
be false to any man.'

It can be said of few people that they followed the code of constancy so unswervingly as Jim Laker. The precept of Shakespeare's wise counsellor was the lodestar of his cricketing life. The teachings of his mother, the irrepressible Yorkshire matriarch, bequeathed a legacy of revulsion at injustice.

His rebellious attitude did not make him the easiest of travelling companions. Richie Benaud, his former Australian rival and fellow television commentator, recalls that Jim had a good memory for snobs. 'I doubt that people would have got far with him had they tried to pull rank or title in a high-handed manner.'

The course of the crusading radical was strewn with traps at a time when cricket's administrators ruled supreme. To step out of line was to invite punishment. Laker pursued what he considered was an honest quest for truth. He never deviated in his opposition to the existing amateur–professional divide. It was an affront to the dignity of his trade. His deeply held convictions were expressed in a book on his retirement. They led to the withdrawal of coveted MCC and Surrey privileges.

Friends and observers, including John Arlott and Jim

Swanton, believed that the tilt at authority could be attributed, in part, to Laker's resentment at his exclusion from two Australian tours in the 1950s. It was unquestionably a wounding slight with no apparent justification. Trevor Bailey is adamant that Laker had been a magnificent off-spin bowler for at least five years before he finally toured Australia under the captaincy of Peter May in 1958–59.

Laker's famous achievement against Australia at Old Trafford in 1956 did bring about a belated recognition of his gifts. It destroyed the ridiculous canard that he was just an 'Oval bowler'. More satisfying still was the revenge exacted by a bowler, then a self-confessed greenhorn, who had had to shoulder the burden for England's humiliating defeat at the hands of the same opponents at Headingley in 1948.

Achieving the true measure of a highly emotional man, who was almost embarrassed by success, has been a tortuous but rewarding task. The deceptively aloof manner concealed a warm heart and a generous man. My voyage of discovery has been immeasurably lightened by the unstinting support of his widow, Lilly. I am deeply indebted to her for placing at my disposal a variety of scrapbooks and photographic materials in support of the project. She has also enlisted the help of her immediate family and other relatives as well as important new contacts.

I am pleased to acknowledge the fond reminiscences of Jim's daughters, Fiona and Angela. Throwing other light on often puzzling matters were his nephew, Robert Downie, and nieces, Elizabeth Paczek and Caroline Therrien. Their own recollections and family researches have made major contributions to an intriguing portrait of Jim's mother, Ellen, and the boyhood years in Yorkshire.

Ron Buffham, Pat McKelvey and Pamela Wilkinson have been my guides in tracing Jim's apprentice years as a cricketer at Saltaire in Yorkshire, where he came under the earnest supervision of his first mentor and club secretary, the late Alf Burgoyne. The description of the transitional post-war interlude, bridging Yorkshire and Surrey periods, has been enhanced by conversations with former Catford club colleagues, John Clegg and Arthur Cooke.

I must also gratefully acknowledge the courteous assistance of the British Newspaper Library staff at Colindale, London, and Jeff Hancock, the Surrey CCC librarian. My thanks are also due to Paul E. Dyson, a new recruit in my cause, for his comprehensive statistical work.

Testimonies to Jim's faithfulness in friendship throughout their lives have come from fellow pupils at Salts High School, Fred Robinson, Bill Burgess and Jim Sutton. All have attested to his loyalty in their relationships and the ease they found in his company.

The presentation of Jim's qualities as a bowler – and his generally accepted stature as the premier off-spinner of his time – has been given substance by the tributes of former Surrey colleagues, Alf Gover, Michael Barton, Micky Stewart, Dennis Cox, Raman Subba Row, Peter Loader, Arthur McIntyre, David Fletcher and Sir Alec Bedser. Other key witnesses have included England and county contemporaries, Trevor Bailey, Doug Insole, Tom Graveney, Godfrey Evans, David Sheppard, David Allen, Peter Walker, Roy Tattersall, Bob Appleyard, Arthur Phebey and Bert Flack, the former Lancashire CCC groundsman.

Michael Barton, Laker's county captain in the late 1940s, reinforces the image of an intelligent cricketer. 'Jim was a clever man, very definite in his views, who thought more about his cricket than most other players.' Micky Stewart and Trevor Bailey both counter accusations of a remote attitude as a misleading interpretation. 'Jim kept his emotions under control', comments Stewart, 'by adopting a rhythm in his movements. His unhurried approach to cricket gave an impression that he didn't care. But, in fact, he was the most caring of men.'

Peter Iles, a former New Zealand friend now living in California, USA, has provided a glowing account of Laker's influence as the Auckland player-coach in the early 1950s. Jim's special rapport with the people of New Zealand was established in wartime and two other Kiwis, Bert Sutcliffe and Tom Pritchard, whom he first met in services cricket, have added their voices to the chorus of praise.

Jim Laker won pride of place as a benefactor to a host of aspiring young players at The Oval in later years. His work then, as Surrey's cricket chairman, made full amends for the earlier estrangement. It effectively sealed his reconciliation with the club. There was, in addition, the launch of a new career in cricket in which he claimed the attention of another generation as a respected television commentator. His association with Richie Benaud, who has kindly provided the foreword to my book, gave their privileged viewers a rarely matched distillation of knowledge and expertise.

Jim was, in the view of another valued collaborator, former BBC Executive Producer, Nick Hunter, a 'natural in vision'. This has been endorsed by two other broadcasting associates, Peter West and Peter Walker. There was the assurance of a born communicator, a further inheritance from his mother. Jim did not betray, behind the microphone, the highest standards which he had upheld as a cricketer.

Tony Lewis confirms the dedication to this goal. 'Jim brought clarity of recall to his cricket commentaries. He knew what true cricket quality was; he had seen it and remembered it.'

ALAN HILL
Lindfield, Sussex,
February, 1998

1

WEAVING HIS FIRST SPELL

'Jim is a boy of much charm for whom liking will increase as knowledge of him becomes more intimate.'

George Parkin, Salts High School headmaster

There was a formidable company of women waiting to greet the arrival of a boy who was destined to become a famous cricketer. The assembly included four sisters, two of whom were his senior by more than twenty years. Heading the reception was the proud mother, thrilled beyond measure at the birth of her first and only boy. At the age of 43, Ellen Kane, the indomitable Yorkshire matriarch, could now invest all her hopes in a new and exciting challenge.

For 'Aunt' Ellen, as some accounts mistakenly refer to her, the birth of Jim – or Charlie as he was known as a child – was a defining moment. He was born at 36 Norwood Road in the district of Shipley on 9 February 1922. From the start he was doted upon with the fervour of someone receiving an unexpected blessing. The care and devotion of Ellen was not misplaced. Rewarding her labours in middle age was the progress of a boy who was to become handsome, musical and brimming with sporting potential.

Ellen Kane, of Lincolnshire stock, hurtled through life as if carried on a roller-coaster at the fair. She was one of four children and born at Blackerhill, Worsborough in the mining hinterland of South Yorkshire. Her father, Fred Oxby, was a railway worker in this area of Barnsley. As an uncertificated schoolteacher, Ellen was to bequeath a legacy of acute

1

intelligence and pride to Jim and his sisters. She was staunchly independent, closing and reopening the pages of her perilous story with scarcely a backward glance.

At 20, she had married James Henry Kane, a journeyman printer from Bradford. Mary, or Mollie as she was called, was the first of her children, closely followed by Margaret, and then Doreen six years later. Then came Kane's departure, only seven or eight years after the marriage, which must have shocked the young mother to the marrow. It undoubtedly propelled her, however painfully, into an attitude of self-reliance. Kane, then aged 34, was judged guilty by his family of a serious misdemeanour. What provoked their drastic sentence is unknown, but the erring husband was peremptorily dispatched to Australia as a 'remittance man'.

His passage was paid, and he was sent regular monthly allowances; but other than that he was banished by the family. The later history of the disgraced man is unknown. The consequence of the furtive leavetaking was to reduce Ellen to near penury. Divorce from Kane was not considered practicable. Ellen's response in this hour of adversity was to show, as one neighbour said, the resolution of a born winner. She embarked, with admirable promptitude, on a career as a teacher. She may have been pointed in this direction by her elder sister, Emily, herself a teacher. Ellen's own venture revealed a discipline in line with her nature to make the best of any situation. She was never one to cry over spilt milk, however sour the taste.

It was a stoical campaign; a display of uncommon strength of character as she fought to provide for her abandoned children. Pictures in a family album reveal an unflinching lady: the eyes are bold and benevolent. The bespectacled gaze conveys an impression of a person in whose presence it was sensible not to throw down the gauntlet. As the years went by, Ellen assumed an opposition verging on scorn for authority. Socially, too, she defied the conventions of her class. All 'dolled up', in the Yorkshire phrase, she was the epitome of the thoroughly modern woman. She was an extrovert and paraded a glitter to match her personality. As one young

2

visitor to her home observed, the colour of her hair varied from day to day.

The image is presented of a huge personality with massive energy. As a teacher in mostly poor schools, she insisted that her pupils were given every opportunity to rise above their circumstances. The tireless Ellen spent days making costumes for local pageants; at various stages she passed on items belonging to her own children to others less fortunate. Another example of her generosity was the making and distribution of porridge each morning in the classroom. She well knew that many of her charges would have gone without breakfast. Ellen said: 'They cannot learn on an empty stomach.'

Mercurial in temperament, Ellen evinced a particular dislike for rigid rules. She had, though, within her vivacity, a strong and entirely personal moral code. It did not always coincide with that decreed by society. Injustice of any kind incurred her considerable wrath. Conversely, as with many dominant and attractive women, she was not invulnerable to the charms of men. Her independent status was put severely at risk when Charles Henry Laker arrived on the Yorkshire scene from Sussex.

A character in one of Chekhov's plays almost explodes with envy at the conquests of another contending male: 'The success he's had with women. Don Juan isn't in it.' Charlie Laker, over-flowing with bonhomie, possessed a similar magnetic quality. He was a philandering rascal with, it seems, a constant retinue of women claiming his attention. He revelled in his strong resemblance to Tom Mix, the film cowboy of the 1920s. There was a swagger in his stride as he walked the streets. Tall and handsome, he lassoed the local boys and girls with his charm. They were utterly convinced of his celebrity and would race alongside him and beg for his autograph. He did not attempt to dissuade them, much to the delight of his own children. The signing sessions became a running gag in the Laker family.

In Sussex, Charlie had achieved another kind of distinction as a runner with the Blue Star Harriers at Horsham. He was a descendant of a family of yeoman farmers going back to Saxon times. Early accounts place their residence in the present-day West Sussex village of Beeding, with the main branch of the family established at nearby Wisborough Green. 'Lakelands' in this village was the family home at one stage. The Lakers, as taxpayers, were clearly an influential clan in the late eighteenth century. Among their numbers was John Laker, a cricketer, who later achieved more lasting renown as one of the signatories of the Turnpike Act governing the route through this part of Sussex.

Charlie Laker and his brother, George, had both worked as bricklayers as young men in Sussex. By the time of his move to Yorkshire, Charlie had progressed to become an accomplished stonemason. It is believed that one of his first assignments was to work on Bradford Town Hall. In later years, he was employed by Sir Amos Nelson, a cotton tycoon, who lived at Gledstone Hall, near Barnoldswick in North Yorkshire.

Ellen Kane took another ill-fated path when she entered into a liaison with Charlie Laker. But there was the consoling outcome of a second family. Susie was their first child, followed by Jim six years later. Ellen's relationship with Charlie was brusquely terminated when he deserted her in 1924, when Jim was only two years old. It was another irrevocable break and Ellen – and the elder Kane children – hastily ringfenced the matter. They instantly decreed that the absconding partner should be considered dead. Jim, as a child, naturally accepted this announcement as the truth. In his own later writings he said that he had no recollection of his father and had never even seen a photograph of him. He did discover, in the early 1980s, evidence of his father's existence after the supposed death.

The discovery was made by Peter Parfitt, the former Middlesex and England cricketer, who then ran a country club at Eslack, near Skipton. Parfitt had engaged Jim to speak at a sportsmen's evening at his club. The announcement produced a call from a local cricketer and accountant in the neighbouring town of Barnoldswick. Told that Jim's father was buried in a nearby local churchyard, Parfitt drove to view Charlie Laker's grave. Charlie had died at Barnoldswick in 1931. The head-stone also revealed that beside Charlie were two women by the names of Annie Sutcliffe and Elizabeth Ellen Halstead. Mrs Sutcliffe had lived on until 1959. She was thought to be a lady with whom Charlie had lived 'over the brush' in the local idiom. The other occupant of the grave was assumed to be their daughter.

Parfitt, in a subsequent telephone conversation with Jim, cheerfully offered his news. He was more than a little embar-rassed when Jim replied: 'I never knew my father.' Jim was intrigued but did not display any special interest in the revela-tion. On the day of the dinner, Parfitt escorted his guest to the grave. Jim, then past his sixtieth birthday, must have had mixed feelings in this peaceful sanctuary. He was standing by the last resting place of a man who, though vexing in the extreme, was still his father. 'I gather he was quite a lad and a character,' he told Parfitt. The death of Charlie Laker at the age of 54, it was later found, had been partly a consequence of his occupation as a stonemason. Exposure to dust and chippings had severely undermined his health.

In 1924, Ellen Kane once again had to pull together the broken threads of her life. The new reverse did, in fact, bind ever more strongly the ties between her and the youngest chil-dren, Susie and Jim. The older Kane sisters had now left home and comfortably fitted the roles of 'aunts' in the community. Ellen, though, had to take stock of her situation. In the 1920s, and the years of the Depression, married women stepped gingerly on the economic tightrope as teachers. They were, in those days, usurping the roles of men as family breadwinners. Ellen now had no other means of support; her livelihood would have been endangered had she not described herself as a widow.

So she had to decide how best to silence gossip-mongering and protect her sorely needed teaching post. The measure adopted to hide her identity was to assume the pretence of 'aunt', or, quite correctly, Mrs Kane, in the school classroom. It now seems a hideously complicated regime. Robert Downie,

Susie's son, describes one of the methods engineered to deflect criticism. It seems that Mrs Kane and Susie and Jim would often hitch a lift on a milk float for the journey from their home in Carmona Avenue, Frizinghall to school. They would leave their transport at a strategic distance and mother and children then went their separate ways to the school gates. So it was that both Jim and Susie, as they sat there beside their mother in class, were accomplices in the deception. They were perfectly aware of the subterfuge and unconcerned in their anonymity. For a few hours, as they recited their tables, mother was just their teacher. The pretence did not falter when Jim moved to junior school. On his first day there another teacher sought in vain to elicit his name for the class register. In obedience to his mother's strictures, he repeatedly refused to answer the question. Finally, after much persuasion, Jim said: 'I've been told by mother not to tell *my* business.'

Jim, in fact, entered his mother's class at Calverley Church School on the Leeds–Bradford boundary while still a toddler. 'Sit down, Charlie, and be good,' he was told. His own children, Fiona and Angela, recall the benefits of this early education. 'Dad was brilliant at maths, history and English grammar, of which he knew all the laws and rules,' remembers Angela. In the family archives there is one splendid example of Jim's handwriting when he was only four years old. The script is beautifully formed, demonstrating his attention and diligence at this early age.

Before the birth of Jim, Ellen had given evidence of her natural ability as a teacher. For some time she had taught literature and history and was then prompted to take charge of these subjects in a senior class. Her knowledge was deep enough for Jim later to benefit from her guidance. In his adult years he could recite from memory the soliloquies of Shakespeare and stanzas of poetry.

All outside the immediate family circle have, down the years, been confused by the circumstances of Jim's boyhood. Ronnie Burnet, a future Bradford League opponent and later Yorkshire captain, has referred to a guardian aunt and the family living above a grocer's shop in Station Road, Baildon. This is the firmest of recollections. Another report from that time places the family as living in a shop in Baildon Road near its junction with Cliffe Avenue. It is known that Jim, as a boy, used to help out in a grocer's shop in Baildon Road owned by one of his mother's partners. This is confirmed by a photograph of Jim standing outside the shop. Friends of those years are as confused about the situation as Ronnie Burnet. They remember that Jim, after school, would tell them on some days that he was going to visit his 'auntie' at the shop. It seems likely that the bogus aunt was one of his elder sisters.

Another concealing identity presented by Ellen Kane in Jim's primary school years was that of a widowed aunt, Mrs Emmett. Records indicate that a Lillian Emmott was briefly a supply teacher at Frizinghall Council School in the late 1920s and early 1930s. A close schoolfriend of Jim's at the Frizinghall School was freelance journalist Allan Warburton. Warburton has examined a photograph of Jim's mother and believes that she is almost certainly the Mrs Emmett, or Emmott, of his boyhood. Born in the same year as Jim, he remembers that his friend then lived in a small cul-de-sac off Valley Road, near Frizinghall. 'Jim was a straightforward, popular boy, above average intelligence, and a good sport.' Warburton recalls that Mrs Kane (alias Emmett) was a kind and patient woman. 'She owned a weekend hut, or caravan, out in the country at either Baildon or Hawksworth where Jim's friends were occasionally invited to play around on the field while she relaxed in a deck chair and knitted.'

Jim and Warburton, along with another boy, Charles Gardner, were tutored in cricket by the staff at the school. The encouraging elders were the sports master and deputy headmaster, William Walker, and Mr Feather, the woodwork and metalwork teacher. They were the leaders in the impromptu games on the tarmac playground. The wickets were either a portable one-piece set or painted stumps on one of the school walls. Jim, as the cricket captain, held sway in the mean landscape of Bolton Woods, the school playing fields. It was a grim setting for games. Over the grassless recreation area spilled out pungent fumes from the adjacent chemical works.

More wholesome were sporting excursions to Manningham Park or Northcliffe Woods during the long summer holidays. 'Every morning at nine o'clock,' wrote Jim in one of his books, 'I would set off for the Northcliffe playing fields, clutching my first precious bat (bought with sweet coupons) and a ball of some description. Then, with our jackets as stumps, we would play our imaginary Test match series with sessions that went on for hour after hour and day after day.' He concluded: 'It was, of course, the only sensible way to spend a holiday.' Holidays were, in any event, a luxury beyond his mother's modest budget. Throughout his boyhood Jim's life was restricted to little more than a ten-mile radius around Bradford. A trip to the Lake District and a few days at Filey on the Yorkshire coast were the only times he left the district until he was 16. The journey he then made to Eastbourne to stay with his sister, Doreen, was made even more joyful with a visit to the Saffrons to watch Yorkshire playing Sussex.

At the age of 10, Jim won a grammar school scholarship and a free place at Salts High School where, as he said, he was to spend seven of the happiest years of his life. The distinction coincided with the arrival of his mother's new partner, Bert Jordan. The resulting change in financial circumstances enabled the family to move to more pleasing surroundings at Baildon – and to a big, friendly terraced house in Kirklands Avenue. It still stands in the gracious tree-lined road adjacent to the village railway station. Neatly tended lawns lead up to the tall dwellings with their upper-storey balconies and decorative skylights.

Fred Robinson, a fellow high school pupil and lifelong friend, recalls his visits to Jim's home, which often included highly competitive table tennis sessions in the commodious cellar. Robinson remembers the welcoming atmosphere, which was reciprocated when Jim was a guest at his home, little more than half a mile away. 'Mrs Kane was a determined lady, quite a character, and she kept Jim up to the mark.'

8

Another memory of the time is provided by Elizabeth Paczek, Jim's niece, who also spent her childhood at Baildon. 'We used to walk across the fields to visit Grannie. Mr Jordan was there, neat and tidy in his plus-fours and smoking his pipe.' The impression lingers of a tightly knit family and a well-organised household in which Jim was secure and safe. It was also, contrary to the received view, not without important male influences. Norman Nelson, the husband of Jim's oldest sister, Mollie, was something of a father figure. Nelson, born in Texas, was a keen sportsman, a runner in his youth and a golfer into old age. His occupation was banking and he is credited with encouraging Jim in sport as well as using his influence in later providing an opening for his young brother-in-law at Barclays Bank in Bradford.

Jim, according to his sister, Susie, had aspirations to become a parson in his youth. The religious inclinations were doubtless part of growing up; but Susie attested to a phase of strong devotions. Jim was a chorister at St Barnabas' Church, Heaton, near Manningham Park, a suburb of Bradford. Vying for a time with his allegiance to Yorkshire cricket heroes Hedley Verity and Herbert Sutcliffe was the devotion accorded to Arthur Servent, a leading tenor in the church choir. Servent was later to achieve wider renown as a singer with the Carl Rosa Opera Company. Even, in later years, Jim and Fred Robinson were enthused to spend their Sunday evenings at the Heaton church, mainly to listen to Servent's imposing voice.

Jim was admitted to a boy choristership at St Barnabas' Church at the age of seven in December 1929. One report commented on his excellent record of attendance and a 'voice which will develop and improve'. Another, two years later, acknowledged his undiminished keenness: 'It is a long way from Baildon to Heaton for a small boy. He is beginning to show more interest musically. I notice his frequent enjoyment of music during practice nowadays.' As a valued 'corner boy' in the church choir, Jim was exhorted to maintain a proper example to others. Marring the progress of the 'splendid little chap' was a decline in his previously impeccable behaviour.

After his long journeys to church, his attention began to wander during services. 'I'm sorry to say that he is a very great nuisance with his incessant chattering,' ran another report.

Another schoolfriend, Bill Burgess, remembers Jim's talents as a boy soprano and soloist in the Salts High School choir: 'Jim enjoyed singing. He had a good, sweet voice.' One of the few times Jim faltered in a public assembly was at a speech-day ceremony at the Victoria Hall, Saltaire. A variety of entertainment included a choral work, and Jim was selected to sing a short solo of around ten bars. Burgess recalls: 'He just dried up with nerves. We were all overcome with a wave of sympathy.'

George Parkin was the headmaster when Jim enrolled at Salts High School in September 1932. 'He was quite strict, but he had a lovely sense of humour,' recalls Fred Robinson. 'Everybody respected him and we learned a lot under his supervision.' Jim displayed a special proficiency in arts subjects. His enduring love of the English language was also fostered under Parkin's tuition. In 1938, Jim was successful in the Northern Universities' School Certificate examination, emerging with five credits. His standing and influence were rewarded when he was appointed as a school prefect. Parkin commended a pupil with a 'high sense of honesty and truth . . . Jim is a boy of much charm and personality – a boy for whom liking will increase as knowledge of him becomes more intimate.'

The sporting prowess of the young Laker was also noted in Parkin's glowing testimonial. Salts High School, with a register of around 250 boys in the 1930s, was small in comparison with other schools in the area. But that did not place them at a disadvantage on the football field. Leading the charge, almost inevitably, was the lanky Jim at inside-forward. He was regarded as one of the two or three best footballers at the school. Jim, as in cricket, was not the swiftest of movers. He did, however, pose problems with his bewildering footwork. His body feints were disturbing and taunting for defenders.

One of his puzzled opponents was Phil Jowett. 'Jim would bring the ball right up to me and feint to go one way and then move in the other direction. I never knew which way he was going.' Jim's adroit ball control was designed to create openings for others. He was the 'playmaker', in the modern phrase, who eluded the tightest of marking and released space for the goal-scoring opportunists in the team. Kenneth Bales, another schoolfriend, said that if Jim had not excelled at cricket he would have become a first-class footballer. 'Jim was a natural ball player. He was never without an old tennis ball in his pocket, and this he spun, flicked and bounced at every chance.'

The aura of the claret and amber colours of Bradford City never palled for Jim. He later recalled that after school games, played on Saturday mornings, he would race down to the snug Valley Parade ground, cut out of a steep hillside, in Manningham Lane. There he would pay his sixpence to be ushered through the turnstiles into the schoolboys' section on the Spion Kop.

By the time Jim became a supporter, the club had long since surrendered its eminence. Admitted to the Football League in 1903, City was for some years a First Division club. In one season (1910–11) they occupied fifth position and only goal average cost them third place. In this glorious year they joined the traditional elite. The top six in the division were: Manchester United, Aston Villa, Sunderland, Everton, Bradford City and Sheffield Wednesday. City also won the FA Cup in 1911, defeating Newcastle United 1–0 in the replay at Old Trafford in a match watched by a crowd of 66,000, then a provincial record attendance. It was a triumph of double significance since they were the first holders of the trophy (the third actual FA Cup) which was designed by the Bradford firm of Fattorini and Sons.

Across the city, at Park Avenue, was another football club which had formerly enjoyed premier status. There was a sharp contrast in allegiances, none more so than in the friendly rivalry between Fred Robinson, a Park Avenue supporter, and Jim. At Salts High School they had been combined in opposition to a future England international, Len Shackleton, then a pupil at Grange High School. The wizardry of Shackleton was always vastly entertaining to watch, even if he did carry the

11

tag of an indulgent trickster. Bradford Park Avenue, to reduce their bank overdraft, sold him to Newcastle for £13,000 in 1947. Shackleton must have been a tormenting proposition as a schoolboy. Fred Robinson was nominally his direct opponent at right-half in the match against Grange High School. He was, by his own admission, subjected to a humiliating lesson. 'Shack' was at his most irrepressible, and Robinson was left floundering time after time. 'He really gave me the "run-around" that day,' he ruefully recalls.

Bill Bowes, an illustrious member of the Yorkshire bowling pantheon, once reminded Jim Laker of the occasion when his old school, West Leeds High School, bowled out Salts High School for three runs. Jim countered this accomplishment with an even more impressive feat. In one house match at Saltaire in 1937 his opponents were routed for just one run. Jim, as the 15-year-old Celts captain, took six wickets for no runs, including five clean-bowled. At the other end, Ken Sutton returned figures of four for one. Bill Burgess and another Sutton, Jim, were members of the Angles eleven so rudely dispatched to the pavilion. Burgess recalls this devastating onslaught. 'Jim was then a fast bowler; he used to tear up to the wicket and bang it down. But Ken, a left-arm slinger, was even more fearsome.' Recalling the carnage on a lively pitch, Jim Sutton says: 'My claim to fame is that I scored the run.'

One of Laker's sporting mentors in his youth was Harry Dolphin, the nephew of Arthur Dolphin, the former Yorkshire wicket-keeper. Harry, regarded as one of nature's eccentrics, was a curious choice of companion. It was probably an attraction of opposites; certainly, Jim looked up to Harry, who was twelve years his senior. He later signalled his admiration by announcing that Dolphin had played a leading part in his cricket education. Kenneth Bales confirmed this view. 'Harry was a colossal spinner of the ball. He would never play with a recognised team, but I think that his example and skills meant a lot to Jim at that time.'

Despite the age gap, Jim and Harry were inseparable friends. Jim recalled that Harry, a non-smoker and teetotaller, had a dread of any female entanglement which could interfere with his cricket. He preferred to study cricket form and tactics. Fred Robinson remembers that Dolphin was often pressed by Yorkshire to join them. Dolphin played for the Nomads, a local itinerant club. 'The three of us, Jim, Harry and myself, used to go on Sundays to the Butterfield cricket ground in Lower Baildon and bowl at each other.'

Dolphin, as a freelance journalist, once received £2 for an article in the Bradford *Telegraph and Argus*. The fee was spent on two ten-shilling day-return fares to London. He invited Jim to accompany him on what turned out to be a bizarre expedition. Jim recalled: 'We left Bradford station at 7 a.m., complete with bat and ball and stumps, and arrived just on mid-day at King's Cross. A bus took us straight to Hyde Park, where the two of us pitched stumps and played solidly through until we returned to Bradford on the early evening train.' As an exercise in craziness, it must have proved an engrossing diversion for the strollers in the park. Only two madcap enthusiasts could have spurned the sights of the capital in favour of cricket. There was a sad sequel to their keen friendship. They had looked forward to a wartime reunion in Egypt. Dolphin died, presumed drowned, when his troopship was sunk en route for the Middle East.

Ellen Kane was at her most typically forthright and generous in advancing her son's cricket cause in the years before the Second World War. Jim was adored and cherished; it was a quite wonderful life for a boy with a natural aptitude for sport. Susie, with whom he remained close throughout her life, was his regular companion at cricket practice. At Ellen's insistence, she was ordered out into the garden to bowl to her brother for hour after hour.

Jim and Susie, the inseparable couple, were also combined in another exercise which nearly had dire consequences for the pair of them. They had gone out sledging in the snow on Rombalds Moor at Baildon. A blizzard engulfed the moor and they were presumed lost. There was consternation in the village. Search parties, armed with torches, tramped feverishly

13

around the moor. Happily, the two children were found only yards away from the track leading from their home. Jim's keen sense of direction had not led them astray.

Jim's promise as a cricketer was ample enough to persuade Ellen to dip into her savings. 'She took me off to Herbert Sutcliffe's shop in Leeds,' recalled Jim. 'The best Stuart Surridge bat in stock was mine at a cost of 45 shillings. Then came the accessories – a pair of real buckskin pads, boots, socks, shirts, even a box and batting gloves. It is frightening even to contemplate what she had to go without herself to afford such extravagance on me.'

It was perhaps on this shopping outing that Ellen discovered that Herbert Sutcliffe held coaching lessons indoors at Headingley during the winter months. Jim was booked in with other young hopefuls. 'In most cities,' recalled Jim, 'it would seem strange to see a 16-year-old trudging through the snow at Saturday lunch time, with a cricket bat under his arm, but it did not bring a second glance in Leeds.'

The Headingley classes were actually run by Benny Wilson, who had played for Yorkshire before the First World War, and two other legendary county men, George Hirst and Emmott Robinson. Robinson was one of the game's characters and the subject of many stories, including those of the apocryphal variety composed by Neville Cardus. Jim Laker, as one of Emmott's pupils, could offer a true one and the most disarming of tales. During his army service in Egypt he received a letter from Emmott, over three pages long and without a single punctuation mark. His rambling thoughts were an expression of disgust that war had pulled down the curtain on cricket. 'Hitler has buggered the whole thing up,' wrote Emmott.

Others running the rule over the legion of beginners at the Headingley nets were, in unofficial capacities, Maurice Leyland, who became one of the kindliest of teachers after the war, and the octogenarian Alfred Wormald, who had represented the county before the turn of the century. It was a cast of tutors well deserving of the reverence accorded to them. 'All the young lads in those days were absolutely in awe of the people who were our coaches,' remembers Ronnie Burnet, another cricket apprentice of this time. 'They were great names and gods to us.'

Burnet remembers that Jim Laker bowled 'fast off-cutters-cum-spinners' in the pre-war period. But as others point out, it was Jim's potential as a batsman which drew him into the ranks of Saltaire. Yorkshire were clearly of the same mind when they recommended Jim to the Bradford League club. His mother, with some pride, rousingly endorsed the verdict, but her preference as a cricket nursery was their home village of Baildon. Jim had had one or two games with the club's second eleven.

Ellen Kane did, however, encounter another vigorous spokesman in Alf Burgoyne, the Saltaire secretary. Here was a dedicated enthusiast who was destined to go down in cricket history as the man who discovered Jim Laker. On this occasion Burgoyne received a call from the outraged mother. 'What's all this about our Jim playing for Saltaire? You know full well he's a Baildon lad.' Burgoyne did not quail before her indignation. He replied: 'Because we've picked him, that's why, missis.'

2

BAPTISM BY THE AIRE

'Jim's a good cricketer and he wants putting int' first team.'

Ellen Kane

The riverside setting of Roberts Park was where Jim Laker, at 16, made his first-team debut for Saltaire against Baildon in 1938. Asked in later years for a review of his cricket status as a boy, he replied: 'I batted a bit and, as a bowler, I was fast and nasty.'

The big hands, said one friend, could have been modelled for spinning; but Jim had then only the sketchiest notion of his cricketing goal. It was a time for experiment as he competed in schools' cricket on Saturday morning and league contests in the afternoon. At Saltaire Jim did not surge above his contemporaries to advertise his future renown. By his own admission, he was no 'budding world-beater'. In fifty games in the Bradford League, Jim scored 526 runs, including one century, and took just 79 wickets. One Saltaire veteran, J. C. (Charlie) Lee recalled: 'In the nets Jim bowled all sorts of stuff, off- and leg-breaks, fast ones, and generally enjoyed himself without ever appearing to have the makings of a great bowler.'

There were, however, glimmerings of county interest. A treasured memento of this period was a postcard from John Nash, the Yorkshire secretary. In March 1938, Jim was invited for special coaching at the winter shed at Headingley. The invitation, extending over three days, provided an allowance of ten

16

shillings per day plus train fares. He must have been thrilled beyond measure to bowl at his Yorkshire heroes in the nets. Len Hutton, on the brink of his record Test innings at The Oval, was one mounting guard against Jim for the first time. Jim was in a cricketing wonderland as he stepped into the company of Hedley Verity, Maurice Leyland, Arthur Wood and Cyril Turner. Presiding at the coaching sessions was the venerable Benny Wilson, who offered advice on grip and method as Jim rehearsed his off-spin.

Alongside Jim at Headingley were other aspiring recruits: in one colts' trial match in 1939 his team-mates included Harry Halliday, Willie Watson, wicket-keeper Ken Fiddling and leg-spinner Johnny Lawrence. Watson, Fiddling and Halliday all played for the county after the war, while Lawrence, a future mentor of Geoffrey Boycott, moved into fruitful exile with Somerset. Halliday, from Pudsey, was a schoolboy prodigy and played for Yorkshire at 18.

'They were in a different class to me,' recalled Jim. 'I went away convinced that I would never be good enough to play for Yorkshire.' But he did wear the prized Yorkshire cap, if only in jest, when it was offered to him by one county senior. There is a photograph of Jim, smiling broadly and with the cap at a jaunty angle, in a family album. Alf Burgoyne, who had summoned Jim to Saltaire, also took a muted view of the boy's county prospects. While acknowledging that Jim was a 'willing lad', he assessed his recruit as a 'fairly useful batsman'. If we accept this as a typically guarded Yorkshire expression, it was a largely representative judgement of Jim's abilities in the early years.

One compliment paid by the revered Herbert Sutcliffe presented a more glowing testimony. On holiday with his sister Doreen at Eastbourne, Jim had played in several games for the local club at the Saffrons. His stylish innings had earned commendation. Sutcliffe's tribute to Laker was relayed in a letter to Cecil Cook, brother of Tom Cook, the Sussex cricketer. Cook had ordered items of cricket equipment from Sutcliffe's shop in Leeds. In his reply, Sutcliffe pronounced: 'Laker will make a name for himself in cricket.' It was a bold declaration by a percipient observer. He was the man who had foretold future greatness for his protégé, Len Hutton. It was, as with Hutton, a big prophecy for a boy who had hardly rested his foot on the sporting ladder.

The Bradford League, peopled then by uncompromising taskmasters, was a rugged proving ground for Laker. But it also engendered affection among its practitioners. Exiles from the south discovered a fascinating drama, alien to their traditions, played out week by week. One of their number was Pat McKelvey, the former Surrey cricketer, who made his home in Yorkshire. McKelvey, who first played for Saltaire in 1966, came to recognise 'that affinity with the grey stone and sweeping moorland'.

Alf Burgoyne was undoubtedly imbued with a remarkable sense of belonging to Bradford League cricket. Born in Mansfield, near Nottingham, he came to Yorkshire in the mid-1920s to take up an appointment as sales manager at Salts Mills. He first played at centre-half for the Salts soccer eleven; then, as an aspiring seam bowler, he joined the Saltaire cricket club. In 1932 he took over as second-eleven captain. In fourteen seasons he took over 300 wickets. His figures included three hat-tricks, one of which in 1943 neatly coincided with the identical feat of Tom Goddard, the Gloucestershire and England off-spinner, on the same day in a first-eleven match at Eccleshill.

Burgoyne's playing exploits were modest in comparison with his work as an administrator. Everything revolved around him at Roberts Park, and he was fiercely protective of his kingdom. Ray Illingworth, then the England captain, was sternly admonished when he ventured to criticise the preparation of the wicket. He was roundly told that it was none of his business. Burgoyne served Saltaire as secretary, league representative and president. The position as secretary was accepted temporarily in 1929 but he continued, with unflagging zest, in this role for fifty years. His wife, Eva, the daughter of a pioneering local electrical contractor, often said that Alf spent more time at the club than he did at their Shipley home.

By 1964, Burgoyne's monumental endeavours had long established him as a major personality in the league. His dedication was acknowledged by the award of the Sir Leonard Hutton trophy. On his ninetieth birthday he was saluted again, amid much rejoicing. Jack Sanderson, the Saltaire chairman, said: 'Alf was the nearest you can get to perpetual motion. He never stood still. His position as secretary did not indicate the vast amount of work at the club, nor his wholehearted commitment to Saltaire.'

The birthday milestone was linked to an association lasting over sixty-three years. The day was celebrated by the presentation of a trophy bearing Burgoyne's name, which rewards the achievement of an outstanding feat by a Saltaire player each season. For those chosen performers it serves as a permanent reminder of Burgoyne's special pride in encouraging talented youngsters at Roberts Park. Shortly before his death, at the age of 95 in December 1996, Burgoyne had not forgotten one boy who had fulfilled his highest expectations. 'Jimmy Laker was a grand lad, always willing, and conscientious in everything he did.'

Burgoyne's lifelong cricket home at Saltaire sits in rural splendour on the banks of the River Aire. Above the village are the beckoning moors, a cherished playground for Yorkshire folk. On the terrace promenade above the Roberts Park cricket ground stands the statue of Sir Titus Salt, the great Victorian textiles entrepreneur. It was erected in 1903 to commemorate the centenary of his birth and the fiftieth anniversary of the opening of the 'finest mill in Europe'.

Salt, appalled by the squalor of nearby Bradford, had long dreamed of a Utopian settlement; and he brought his employees under his paternal umbrella in one of the first of the model industrial villages. As a mayor and magistrate in Bradford, he had called for additional efforts 'to promote the morality of the town'. The *Bradford Observer*, in one editorial, responded to Salt's reforming zeal. 'Let the poor be extricated from dark, damp and noisy courts. Home will then be sweet home and when the working man leaves his fireside for a walk in the park or an hour in the library or the music-hall, he will enjoy these advantages more because he possesses a house and not a hovel . . .'

On the green-field site, covering forty-nine acres beside the river, Titus Salt built his industrial community, offering, as he said, the basic necessities of a decent life. He built good, clean houses, ranging in amenities according to rank, for his work-force. The concept also included churches, schools, a hospital, a mechanics institute, sports facilities, baths, washhouses and almshouses. The blandishments of Salt's brave new world excluded alcohol, at least in the form of the reviled public houses. He wanted, he said, a happy and contented people around him but he wanted them sober and industrious.

The opening of the mills of Titus Salt preceded by sixteen years the foundation of the Saltaire cricket club. Salt presided at another ceremony when Roberts Park was officially opened in July 1871. Saltaire joined the Bradford League in 1905 and the first of their titles (won in 1917–18 and 1922) ran in parallel with the signing of one of the greatest bowlers in the history of the game.

An advertisement in the *Athletic News* brought S. F. (Sydney) Barnes, then aged 41, to Roberts Park in 1915. His laconic three-word reply – 'Will I do?' – was swiftly followed by agreement on terms and the start of a memorable association, lasting nine years, with Saltaire. It began with figures of eight wickets for eight runs on his debut in May against Bowling Old Lane. In his second match against Baildon Green, Barnes took 10 for 14 in six overs, including five wickets in five balls. His feats in Bradford League cricket have never been surpassed. As an indication of his supremacy during the First World War, he was opposed to a galaxy of celebrity batsmen who included Jack Hobbs, Frank Woolley and Wilfred Rhodes. A total of eight Test players, along with a large contingent of county men, played regularly for one or other of the league clubs.

Week by week Barnes was bowling against some of the best batsmen in England. Yet he started off with 92 wickets at an average of under four and a half in his first season at Saltaire. Four times, in succeeding seasons, his average was under five and only once did it rise as high as seven. His aggregate in nine seasons in league and cup competitions was a staggering 904 wickets at an average of 5.26. It included two other ten-wicket feats against Bowling Old Lane and Keighley. Almost inevitably he headed the league bowling averages in every season at Saltaire.

Barnes wrought havoc in the leagues and in Minor Counties cricket in his native Staffordshire. Apart from brief excursions with Warwickshire and Lancashire, he rejected the daily round of county cricket as too irksome. But he was not just a ruler in the shallows; his detours into Test cricket brought a yield of 189 wickets at an average of 16.43 in 27 matches against Australia and South Africa before the First World War.

A succession of bemused opponents had cause to endorse the testimony of Sir Pelham Warner. Speaking at a dinner in Barnes's honour at Stoke-on-Trent in 1927, Warner recalled the first time he had batted against the master craftsman in 1903. 'Barnes pitched me one on the leg-stump. It came off the wicket like a streak of greased lightning and hit the top of the off wicket.' Warner cited another example of the control of Barnes in a Gentlemen versus Players match at Lord's. 'He was literally cutting up the pitch with his finger spin, and the ball was flashing right across the wicket.'

This amazing leg-break, delivered with impeccable accuracy and at varying speeds, was the key weapon in Barnes's armoury. But it was also combined with off-breaks and swingers, and almost every variety of ball except the googly. The latter offended his instincts as a bowler; he did bowl it, but only in the nets. A telling story from his Bradford League years concerned one unabashed batsman. He vowed that he would not attempt any heroics against Barnes. His plan was to bide his time and wait for the loose balls. 'Th'll none ger ony runs today then,' retorted the next man in.

Barnes was undoubtedly the box-office attraction at Saltaire and he knew his worth. He was as shrewd a businessman as he was a cricketer and drove a hard bargain. Two examples of the magnet of his presence explain why he was able to command

21

unprecedented fees. The Priestley Cup final between Saltaire and Bankfoot at Park Avenue and the replay, after a tie, at Bowling Old Lane attracted a combined record crowd of nearly 24,000, with receipts of £642. The match between Saltaire and Bowling Old Lane in 1923, in Barnes's last season at Roberts Park, was watched by a record league crowd of 6,400 and yielded takings of over £176.

The wily money-spinner signed as a professional at Saltaire in 1915 at £3 10s (£3.50) a match and was also paid travelling expenses before moving to the area. Saltaire even footed a bill of £10 for his removal costs. Barnes's match fee was doubled in 1916 and by 1922 it had increased to £18 15s (£18.75). In addition, he was paid talent monies for his performances. Supplementing this tidy income were coaching duties at Bradford Grammar School. One Saltaire player remembered that the club stumbled into financial distress. The reason, so he understood, was that they had overreached themselves to pay for Sydney Barnes for a few years and win everything there was to win. The outlay was a generous concession but greatness has its price.

Another world war loomed before Jim Laker began his own, far more modest entry into Bradford League cricket. He could not have imagined that, in his later years as a Test bowler, his name would be listed ahead of Barnes in the record books. As a boy, he had listened in amazement to a conversation between George Hirst and Herbert Sutcliffe. 'They did not always agree with each other, but Herbert nodded his head approvingly when George pronounced that "Sydney Barnes was the greatest bowler there ever has been – and what's more the greatest bowler there ever will be." ' Hirst, with 200 wickets and 2,000 runs in one season, was also among the elite. So his was a judgement beyond dispute.

In his mature years, Laker also sang the praises of Barnes. He watched the old warrior on one occasion, guesting as a professional against Saltaire. 'He must have been into his sixties but his control was still remarkable.' He was also privileged to enjoy a long conversation with Barnes at Lord's.

'Never before or since have I met anybody with such genuine confidence in his own ability. So much so that he said it was nothing unusual for him to bowl an inswinger, a fast off-break and a leg-cutter in the same over.' Jim recalled the words of advice from the maestro: 'Keep trying something different.'

At Saltaire, Laker followed humbly in the footsteps of Barnes. One particular hero of those days was the Baildon Green professional, George Senior. As a 12-year-old, he had watched Senior in rousing battle with West Indian professionals, Martindale and St. John. Jim's first ball in league cricket was bowled at Senior, who then needed four runs for his half-century. 'He cracked my first ball for four, gave the collectors time to take the boxes round the ground, and then played outside a straight half-volley.'

It was a fine gesture, artfully managed to encourage the young bowler; but salvation was not available in another match against Baildon. It was a day of batting savagery. This is an enduring memory for Ronnie Burnet; and, in later years, it provided a conversational topic to gloat upon with Laker, one of the sorely troubled bowlers. Burnet recalls: 'I went in at No. 3, with the score 0 for 1, and finished up 152 not out.' There were four centuries in the match and 520 runs were scored in five hours. Saltaire, as Laker also cheerfully reminded Burnet, did have the last word. Chasing a target of 260, they were the victors by nine wickets.

Batting was undeniably Jim's strongest suit in his formative years at Saltaire. In 1940, he headed the club's batting averages in all matches with 357 runs, which included an unbeaten century against Bankfoot. He was, though, not without his prizes as a bowler. In 1941 Saltaire, with the Derbyshire pair Bill Copson and Alf Pope as their rampant spearheads, did not lose a match. They played in eighteen league games, won seventeen and drew one. After one humiliating reverse at Roberts Park, the Great Horton captain, Edgar Robinson, was set on revenge. 'Just wait till we get you to Great Horton. We'll show you how to play fast bowling.' For three days before the return match their pitch was drenched with water to expunge the pace. Alf Burgoyne recalled that Copson and Pope were absentees, their car having broken down at Chesterfield. As it happened they were redundant. The sun came out to bake the fortuitously saturated pitch; and Laker and G. A. Wilson, the slow left-arm bowler, relished an unexpected opportunity. They bowled out Great Horton for 103 and Saltaire won by 106 runs to complete the double over their rivals.

As in the First World War, the Bradford League revelled in the enlistment of distinguished Test and county players when another conflict intervened in 1939. The flood of professionals included the dynamic West Indian, Learie Constantine, considered by many to rank only second in appeal to Sydney Barnes for league followers. Constantine was described by the Saltaire veteran J. C. Lee as a man of education and character with whom it was a pleasure to consort. In one match for Windhill against Saltaire, Constantine arrived late after his journey from Lancashire. Lee was batting and he recalled the great cheer when the West Indian stepped on to the field to take his place in the gully. 'The next ball I cracked into this area at express speed. "Connie" threw himself at it and the ball lodged safely in his right hand.'

There were other notable men to excite attention in the years leading up to the war. At Saltaire, Sandy Jacques topped the league averages in one season, with 63 wickets at 10.90 runs apiece. These figures included all ten, clean-bowled (for 25 runs) against Bankfoot. Jacques played twenty-eight matches for Yorkshire and it was his proud boast that he was never on the losing side with the county. Edmund Hutton was one of Jim Laker's senior colleagues at Saltaire during the late 1930s. One of his finest innings was an undefeated century against Baildon Green in 1938. Sir Len, his illustrious brother, would have acknowledged this as a worthy exploit.

Arthur Mitchell was another stalwart who represented Saltaire before flourishing as a key member of the Yorkshire team in their great championship era in the 1930s. Mitchell was an iron-clad character, as forbidding, until you knew him, as the moors on a bleak winter's day. He was known as 'Ticker' in the Yorkshire camp. This was a derivation from the Indian word 'Tikka', meaning 'Well done', or 'Good lad'. While coaching in India, Mitchell had enjoyed friendly relations with the natives on the Patiala estate, who would call out 'Tikka' when he was scoring runs for the maharajah's team. Frank Dennis, associated with Mitchell on this coaching assignment, remembered the admiring tag of their Indian friends, and it was passed on to greet Mitchell in the Yorkshire dressing-room. Mitchell's proximity as a neighbour at Baildon exalted him as a giant for Jim Laker. The veneration prompted Jim to cast himself as the dour Arthur in a make-believe 'Roses' match. 'I made a classy 50 off a tennis ball as Mitchell while a young Lancashire lad toiled in vain as Cecil Parkin.'

J. C. Lee opened with Mitchell at Roberts Park. He recalled: 'We were playing one Saturday afternoon at Park Avenue. I went up to the ground with Arthur and others by tram.' Mitchell had not considered it necessary to inform his colleagues of an important ceremony he had attended earlier in the day. 'It was not until later that we learned that he had been married in the morning,' said Lee. 'It was just like him to keep it quiet.'

Jim Laker played in his last full season for Saltaire in 1940. There were signs of greater certainty in his cricket, but he had to act as an understudy to others of England renown. It was a formidable company of principals: a quartet of men from Derbyshire included the Pope brothers, Alf and George, Bill Copson, and Les Townsend, who also bowled off-breaks to supplement his strengths as a batsman. Bill Bowes, before his departure for war, was another towering presence, a bowler steeled in combat with Yorkshire and England.

It has been speculated that but for the tyranny of Adolf Hitler, Jim Laker might have looked forward to an honourable retirement after a lifetime with Barclays Bank. His cricketing reputation might have been restricted to half-remembered feats as a batsman in the Bradford League. Laker, like another great Yorkshire off-spinner, George Macaulay, started his adult career in a bank. Certainly, it was his mother's wish that security in the bank should take precedence over any cricket ambitions. Jim's schooldays had ended in 1939. Armed with credits in matriculation, he had succeeded in obtaining a post with Barclays in Bradford. It was, as he said, a tough introduction to the world of commerce. For a monthly salary of £5 he worked a nine-hour day during the week; and even on Saturdays balance time was never before 1.30 p.m. In addition, he had to attend Bradford Technical College five nights a week in the winter to study for banking examinations.

The clarion call of war was the catalyst for a startling change in his fortunes. Whether Jim was enticed by the prospect of exciting adventure, or simply the need, as with all young men, to flee the maternal nest, is matter for conjecture. His affection for his mother, who had striven so hard to give him a good start in life, was not in question. But there were new horizons to explore.

It is not difficult to imagine the turmoil which prevailed at his Baildon home when Jim, at the age of 19, volunteered for army service in 1941. Adding to his mother's distress was the fact that he had given a false age (gaining an advantage of five months by using his sister's birth date in July) to speed his call-up. Within weeks of his infantry training in Leicestershire he was issued with tropical kit and sent home on seven days' embarkation leave. This was the signal for a vigorous protest campaign mounted by his mother. 'Mother was distraught and, much to my embarrassment, spent half that week pounding the doors of every officer she could find complaining about the injustice of an under-age soldier being dispatched overseas with such haste,' recalled Jim. There can be cruelty, however unintended, in cutting filial ties, and Jim was relieved that his mother was repulsed in her efforts to change the decision. Before the summer ended he had bid farewell to an inconsolable parent.

Jim Laker embarked from Glasgow on the SS *Mooltan* late one evening. His wartime odyssey to the Middle East transformed his life. 'There were no coaches to help, no manuals to study as I became a self-taught off-spin bowler in the shadows of the Sphinx and the pyramids.'

3

DISCOVERY OF SPIN

'Laker used to play for Saltaire as a batsman. He should now walk into most county sides as a bowler.'
Peter Smith, Essex and England leg-spinner

'Laker skittles Australians' is an evocative headline. The banner astride the sporting columns of the *Egyptian Gazette* drew attention to what was in effect a trial run for the Yorkshire corporal. In the newly opened El Alamein stadium in Cairo, the fledgling off-spinner took six wickets for 10 runs in 29 deliveries. The Australian opponents were routed for 60 runs. 'His vicious spinners were practically unplayable,' enthused the *Gazette* correspondent. One watching Yorkshire serviceman reported: ' "Jack" Laker is busy keeping up the good name of Saltaire.'

Laker, withheld from the hazards of action in the Royal Army Ordnance Corps, discovered his cricketing vocation in the Middle East. 'To my utter amazement, I was soon turning the ball quite prodigiously on the coconut matting strips,' he recalled. Quite suddenly, Jim found he was moving the ball more than anyone else.

In his four wartime years, Laker earnestly sketched the first notes in his bowling repertoire. John Arlott remembered how, during this time, English cricketers were writing home to county secretaries to tell them of an unknown Yorkshire lad who was bowling off-breaks like a master. The gossip that leaked back to cricket circles also linked Laker with the New

27

Zealand batsman, Bert Sutcliffe, as players who looked good enough to measure up to first-class standards.

More than fifty years on, Sutcliffe recalls his first meeting with Laker towards the end of the war. It was the start of a close friendship. 'Troops from all nations stationed in Cairo and Alexandria were keen to cross swords on the cricket fields of the Maadi and Gezira Sporting Clubs.' At the Gezira club, as Sutcliffe relates, matches were played on coir matting over turf. 'Jim was then showing signs of his off-spinning abilities. His effect was variable, depending on the tightness, or otherwise, of the mat. He could be lethal on a tight one because he was able to get bounce as well as turn. His action seemed almost innocuous, but this was deceptive if you were at the business end.'

One Shipley soldier, who preceded Laker in his service in the Middle East, avidly perused Bradford League reports. These were contained in the *Mail in Egypt*, written by the sports editor, who adopted the *nom de plume* of 'Wanderer'. One account referred to Laker's debut with Saltaire. The Shipley man was delighted to meet his Yorkshire neighbour when Laker joined his army unit. 'At that time Jim was only a very moderate medium-to-fast bowler and first-wicket batsman. After he had been with us for about twelve months, Jim changed his bowling style to that of an off-spinner and from there he went right to the top in this category.'

Laker had first attracted attention as a footballer. He captained, from left-half, the Corinthians club in Tel Aviv in what was then Palestine in the winter of 1942–43. Before long he had won a place in the British Army XI, playing alongside England wing ace Tom Finney, Scotland's Willie Telfer, Harry Clifton (Newcastle United), Dave Massart (Birmingham) and another pre-war England star, George Male, the Arsenal full-back. Cricket loyalties were, though, insistent and gaining in priority. A flourishing services career was given impetus by his unswerving application. Tom Pritchard, the New Zealand all-rounder, who played for Warwickshire after the war, remembers one particular aspect of Laker's preparations. 'Jim spent hours pushing a cricket ball between his spinning finger and middle finger until he was able to spread them far enough to settle the ball at the base of these fingers.'

The measure of Laker's progress, then as a genuine all-rounder, was revealed in heartening exploits. In Cairo in 1943 he was opposed to the New Zealand Air Force, the Royal Air Force and various Army elevens. In seven matches he scored 500 runs. One Yorkshire correspondent referred to a fruitful cricket tour on leave in Alexandria. Laker had a haul of 25 wickets, all against top-class rivals. The 'Old Salt' returned figures of five wickets for 10 runs, including the hat-trick, against the RAF. In two months in 1943 Laker scored 600 runs, including three centuries, at an average of 45, and took 50 wickets at 7 runs apiece. 'This was a sure sign that Jimmy is keeping his hand in and fulfilling the expectations of his many friends at Saltaire and Roberts Park,' concluded the correspondent.

'The bowler with the nautical roll', as one reporter described Laker, forged on to impressive feats in 1944. There was a century and six wickets against the South African Air Force. Laker opened the batting and was last out, scoring 106 in ninety minutes. He then proceeded to take six wickets for 10 runs, as the SAAF team were bowled out for 29. Another zonal league match produced a return of seven wickets for 8 runs. In his second over Laker took three wickets, then two more in his fourth over. He finished his fifth over – and the last of the innings – by taking two wickets without conceding a run.

There was a telling conquest in the inter-zone match between Cairo City and Helwan at the Gezira Club. Helwan were captained by Dudley Nourse, the formidable South African batsman, who led his country in England after the war. Laker had a spell of five wickets for 7 runs. They included the wicket of Nourse, a scalp to be prized in his growing collection. Even more pleasurable was the tribute of Nourse, who said that Laker was an England cricketer in the making.

Laker's mounting stature as a bowler brought representative honours in 1944. His tally for the season was 221 wickets (average: 5.7) and 960 runs, achieved, as one observer related, 'in cricket of distinct county class'. In a two-day match at the Alexandria Club he represented the Cairo area. There were four wickets for Laker as Cairo won by 27 runs. The Alexandria ranks were heavily reliant on Peter Smith, the Essex leg-spinner, and J. H. Pawle, the Cambridge blue, their only players with first-class experience. Cairo had stronger forces at their command. Laker's colleagues included Nourse, Pritchard, Ron Aspinall (Yorkshire), George Perkins (Northants), Horace Wass (Derbyshire) and one of cricket's sunniest characters, A. E. ('Sam') Pothecary, of Hampshire.

Pothecary, an immensely popular figure in the Middle East, told one amusing umpiring story. In one match he appealed for a wicket. He was very surprised by the reaction. Instead of making a decision, the umpire made his own appeal to the astonished Pothecary. 'Well, you've had much more experience than I have, sir,' he replied. 'What do you think?' Pothecary perhaps remembered this unusual entreaty when his competence as an umpire was challenged in later years.

Umpiring – and the deviations of certainty in dismissals – also deeply concerned George Emmett, the Gloucestershire and England batsman, one of Laker's opponents in services cricket. Jim recalled that Emmett, in one match, was judged lbw, sweeping, with his left foot extended well down the wicket. In a later discussion, they debated the margin of error involved in such a situation. 'Well, there are occasions when you can be out that way,' explained Emmett. 'I remember once in an Army game abroad I was the victim of the most outrageous decision in my life. Some whippersnapper of an off-break bowler got me lbw with a ball that would not have hit a garage door, let alone a set of stumps.' Jim was forced to confess that he was the audacious culprit. Emmett did not check his indignation at the dismissal, which still simmered in remembrance. 'Well, you had an effing cheek for appealing,' he said.

In Alexandria, the local hero was Peter Smith, who was to tour Australia under the leadership of Wally Hammond after the war. Smith fervently advanced Laker's claim for recognition in first-class cricket, then and afterwards. In one wartime commendation he said: 'Laker, with his immaculate length off-breaks, used to play for Saltaire as a batsman. He should now walk into most county sides as a bowler.'

Towards the end of the summer of 1944, Laker savoured the spirit of a 'Test' match, keenly contested by English and Australian servicemen at the Alamein club. It was played in searing heat and watched by a vociferous crowd of about 10,000 troops. Jim was footsore and weary after a long day in the field. 'I made my way over Kasr-el-Nil back to my unit with an enormous pack of cricket gear on my back.' As he crossed the bridge, a dispatch car, bedecked with flags, roared to a halt beside him. He was hailed by a veteran brigadier, who displayed an unmistakable air of command. 'By that time I had reached the exalted rank of War Substantive Corporal,' recalled Jim, 'but I was amazed when he offered me a lift into town.'

Laker related the story of his subsequent confusion many times; it was one of his favourite anecdotes. Depending on interpretation, it does require some suspension of belief: the famous battle at El Alamein had occurred two years earlier. There was an urgent enquiry inside the car. Jim was asked where he had come from. In all innocence, he said he was just returning from Alamein. 'Tell me, Corporal, what's the position there now?' Jim replied too briskly for his own comfort; the words died on his lips even as he uttered them. 'Well, sir, Australia were 320 for eight at the close of play, but we did miss a few chances.' The brigadier was not talking about cricket. He was interested in a different kind of battle area. The car stopped abruptly. An embarrassed Jim was ordered out. He had to continue his journey on foot.

The unexpected boon of four weeks' leave in England in 1945 was linked poignantly with a sad departure. It had been a troubled war for Jim's mother. Bert Jordan, her partner, had died, and straitened circumstances had compelled her to move from her comfortable Baildon home. She had passed retiring age but had been retained as a supply teacher at the Thornbury

31

Boys School. She was now living in a side-street terrace house in Spring Gardens, Manningham, close by the Bradford City football ground.

Ellen Kane, at 66, still maintained her independence. But Jim thought she looked tired, if exhilarated at the return of her soldier son. The day before his arrival she had refereed a school soccer match. She did seem indestructible. One member of the family fondly remembers a woman 'who was full of life. She attempted to live every day and never thought she was too old for anything.' Only a short time before her reunion with Jim she had bought a motor-cycle. It was, she said, better than walking to school. Jim was, though, worried about his mother's declining health. He strove hard to make amends for his long absence. A few days before his leave ended, Ellen suggested that he should go down to Eastbourne to spend some time with his sister, Doreen. 'Perhaps she had a pre-monition because she insisted on accompanying me to the station,' said Jim. By the time he had reached the south coast, she had returned home, collapsed and died.

It was almost like an act of surrender following the joys of Jim's homecoming. A neighbour discovered her, sprawled across the bed in her tiny home; she had suffered a massive heart attack. Frugal to the last, and uncaring of her own needs, she had gathered together a handsome nest-egg for her adored Jim. In her will she bequeathed to him the whole of her estate, a sum amounting to over £1,000. Ellen was cremated at Scholemoor Crematorium in Bradford.

Jim was able, after protracted negotiations with the army authorities, to extend his leave for a further two weeks to attend to the funeral arrangements. Although he was shortly due for repatriation, he had to return to Egypt. The recall did coincide with his selection to represent the MEF (Middle East Forces) against the CMF (Central Mediterranean Forces) in a two-day inter-command match in Rome in August.

The record of the match indicates the wealth of talent on view as cricket happily took precedence over war. The MEF side was captained by Norman Yardley and included, in addition to Laker, Peter Smith, Ron Aspinall, Joe Horton (Warwickshire) and the New Zealanders Bert Sutcliffe and Don Taylor. It was a convivial reunion for the MEF senior players. The CMF eleven, stronger on paper and, as it proved, in action, boasted a full first-class counties' complement. They were led by the Hon. Arthur Grey Hazlerigg, the former Cambridge and Leicestershire captain. Among their ranks were Tom Pritchard; Bill Merritt, the New Zealand leg-spinner; Basil Allen and George Emmett (Gloucestershire); Frank Smailes (Yorkshire); Arthur Wellard (Somerset); Pat Vaulkhard and Bert Rhodes (Derbyshire); and Tom Dollery (Warwickshire).

It was a hostile wicket, the liveliness of the pitch heightened by matting stretched tight over the concrete base. Laker's team, submissive to the pace of Wellard and the spin of Merritt, were beaten by an innings and 13 runs. Sutcliffe was top scorer with an unbeaten 88 out of 139 in the MEF first innings. When they followed on, there was the consolation of a buccaneering innings, which included seven fours and a six, by Yardley. Laker, batting at No. 9, was undefeated on 21 in a vain bid to avert the innings defeat.

The match also afforded Laker the chance to examine for the first time the excellence of a man who would become a key accomplice in the years ahead. Sergeant Arthur McIntyre gave notice of his ability with two stumpings, one swiftly executed to dismiss Yardley, and two catches. McIntyre recalls the first meeting with Laker in Rome. 'Jim was a good bowler then – a little quicker than most off-spinners on matting wickets.'

Jim Laker did sometimes wistfully think that he might have played for Yorkshire. He once said that if he had been born two or three years earlier he might have fulfilled this ambition. But the choice of recruits then at Yorkshire's disposal was wide and the competition between them was daunting for all but those of the topmost rank. In Yorkshire, as Brian Close, one of the county's post-war newcomers, said, you did not win your spurs overnight. The award of a Yorkshire cap was the equivalent of a film Oscar. For bowlers, and especially spinning tyros, there was the near impossible task of measuring up to the standards of Wilfred Rhodes and Hedley Verity. Yorkshire-based cricket writers, like Jim Kilburn, were jealous guardians of tradition. Their voices were stridently raised to disclaim those young pretenders who fell below expectations.

There were so many likely lads. Laker, despite the plaudits he had gained in the Middle East, was still known primarily as a batsman; yet there were urgent demands for a renewed inspection of his burgeoning talents as an off-spinner. They included one intervention in November 1945. 'Knowing how close is the Yorkshire cricket network, I don't suppose that the Headingley intelligence service is unaware of the fact that Jim Laker, the Saltaire all-rounder, is home from service overseas,' suggested one newspaper correspondent. He concluded: 'Laker, who is 23, may be the answer to the county's prayer for a high-class off-break bowler.'

One Shipley serviceman, from the same Middle East unit as Laker, wrote to Headingley on his return to Yorkshire. His recommendation to consider 'a most promising cricketer' was spurned by the county authorities. He was somewhat abruptly told that Yorkshire were not interested in off-spinners. Laker was, of course, some way down the queue of those challenging for recognition.

Among the established seniors poised to resume first-class cricket were Frank Smailes, who played for England against India in 1946; and, crucially, Ellis Robinson, the bowler in possession of the off-spinning role. Robinson, purveyor of extravagant spin, was also an inspired member of Yorkshire's close-fielding cordon. He was close to Test selection before moving to Somerset in 1950. Ronnie Burnet remembers a time of plenty in Yorkshire after the war. Other available talents included the veteran slow left-arm bowler, Arthur Booth, who enjoyed a splendid swansong to head the national averages in 1946. Waiting in the wings were two other left-arm contenders, Johnny Wardle and Allan Mason.

Maurice Leyland, another of Yorkshire's old guard and soon to become the county coach, listened carefully to the overtures about Laker, but concluded: 'I'm afraid we haven't got room for him.' The soundings, falling deafly on Yorkshire ears, were a factor in Laker's decision to move south. But his exile, which was to yield abundant compensation, really confirmed a preference for the bright lights of London. He always remained a Yorkshireman in spirit and manner; but his roots in the north had been broken by his mother's death.

Laker returned to Yorkshire only briefly in 1945 before his posting in deep midwinter to Folkestone. It was a frustrating time as the process of demobilisation dragged on and on. He recalled a month of misery in the zero temperatures on the Kent coast. To his immense relief he was able to negotiate a transfer to the War Office. In London, he was given a friendly sanctuary at the Forest Hill home of a close army friend, Colin Harris. He was to stay there for five years, accepted, as he said, almost as a son in a tightly knit and welcoming household. The severance of his ties with Yorkshire was completed there. 'It was the happiest family I have ever encountered,' he said.

Laker discovered a refreshing camaraderie in this company; his services cricket in 1946 was combined with a productive period at Catford. At 24, though, he was still in the foothills as a cricketer. He deliberated long and hard on the path to be taken: Jim was always circumspect in his judgement. Occupying his thoughts was the advice of both his mother and his former headmaster, George Parkin. They had warned him against cricket as a livelihood. His design for living, they insisted, required greater security.

Banking was one of his options. His request to his pre-war employers at Barclays for a transfer to London had been granted. In addition, General Palmer, who was in charge of Army cricket, had recommended a career in the Regular Army; there was the promise of a permanent peacetime commission. Jim did sensibly juggle all the possibilities for the future. But it is the view of Fred Robinson, his Salts High School friend, that none of these ventures ever really came within his considerations.

Other persuasive influences were to catapult Laker on to a

momentous course. John Clegg, the former Catford president, recalls the introduction of the shy Yorkshireman to his club. Jim's companion on the visit was his friend, Colin Harris. There had doubtless been many fireside talks at Forest Hill before Jim was persuaded to present himself. 'A potential new member, still in the Army, was brought along to a special meeting in March 1946,' relates Clegg in the Catford centenary book. 'He described himself as an off-break bowler and a batsman.'

Watching Laker in a Sunday benefit match that season was Andrew Kempton, the Catford president. Kempton had been associated with Surrey cricket since before the First World War. His special pride was the encouragement of young cricketers. He was perceptive in his control of likely beginners. The kindly steward gave firm direction as Laker stood haltingly at the crossroads. This young man, he knew, should be shown the signpost leading to Kennington Oval.

4

FROM KENNINGTON TO THE CARIBBEAN

'The rise of Laker to the front rank in the West Indies represents a very big gain for England.'

E. M. Wellings

The route into first-class cricket did have one final diversion for Jim Laker before he presented himself at The Oval. Peter Smith, his wartime services companion, had told him in Cairo: 'I'll get in touch with you when this lot is over. There may be a future for you in county cricket.'

Smith did not forget his promise. While still in the Army, Laker was offered a trial with Essex. Immediately before this important date he had bowled many overs in a services match. The consequence was an ugly split to his spinning finger. It was the first of many such injuries which were to handicap Laker throughout his career. He was compelled to withdraw from the trial. It was, perhaps, no more than a disappointment for a young man, still uncommitted to the game and quite content to enjoy relaxed weekend outings in London club cricket.

At Catford, Laker moved into a congenial company. The warmth of the welcome at Penerley Road did much to make him feel at home. Former colleagues remember a 'very quiet man, bordering on the shy'; as Jim settled down, the barriers were breached. The droll quips and sallies charmed his southern hosts. John Clegg, one of Laker's Catford team-mates in 1946, recalls: 'We thought of Jim at that time as a batsman who could bowl.' Clegg opened with Laker in a Sunday match at Elmer's End. 'We reached 113 without loss before lunch,' said Clegg, but his part in the proceedings was fairly nominal. He occupied a supporting role as Laker nonchalantly stroked his way to 75 not out.

There were, however, instances of the spin which had worried and perplexed county players in the Middle East. One analysis to underline his repute was all ten wickets for Catford against Bromley Town. Laker's figures included a hat-trick; and he conceded only 21 runs in a spell of 12.3 overs. Eight of his victims were clean-bowled. It was an impressive feat but Catford, requiring only 96 to win, rather spoilt Jim's day. In another avalanche of wickets, they were beaten by 28 runs. Catford redeemed themselves in another match against Addiscombe. Laker's six wickets at a cost of 14 runs was this time rewarded by a five-wicket victory.

Laker's 'teasing medium-pace off-spinners' did, as one report noted, prove that the Bradford League recruit was quite an acquisition. During the period at Catford he began a lasting and valued friendship with Arthur Phebey, the future Kent opening batsman. 'Jim was obviously someone very special,' says Phebey. 'He had a good temperament and did not appear to get peeved if luck ran against him. Certainly, I would rather have played with him then at Catford than later against him at The Oval and Blackheath.'

Arthur Cooke, a former Kent second eleven player, gleefully recounts the story of Laker's return to Catford in later years. 'I persuaded Jim to come down and play in a friendly match. He bowled a few overs but I had to take him off, otherwise he would have ruined the game.' Afterwards, in the club bar, one of the chastened opponents remarked: 'That bloke you put on, he was spinning the ball like Jim Laker.' Laker, by this time, had changed and left for home. He would have appreciated the tribute, not to brag about his domination, but because he was able to bowl without being recognised.

In the brief interlude at Catford Laker added his name to a distinguished roll-call of players and opponents at Penerley

Road. The visitors included Les Ames, the great Kent and England wicket-keeper batsman. Ames was converted into a wicket-keeper by the Kent coach, Gerry Weigall, one of cricket's incorrigible enthusiasts. In 1924, Ames headed the Kent Club and Ground averages with 444 runs. His century against Catford in that season was in the cavalier mode. In a letter written shortly before his death in 1990 and published in the Catford centenary brochure, Ames looked back at his apprentice years. 'I was an 18-year-old who had never played in other than school or village cricket. It must have been my lucky day with good fortune prevailing, as I went on to score 125 at Catford.'

In the decade after the Second World War, two other Kent players, Arthur Phebey and Leslie Todd, represented Catford. Overseas recruits included Dick Cheetham, brother of the inspirational South African captain, Jack Cheetham, and Geoff Chubb, another South African. Chubb was described during the tour of England in 1951 as the 'Iron Lung' of South African cricket. At the age of 40 he was on his first tour, and he amazed everyone with his undiminished stamina and energy as a fast-medium bowler. Chubb took the most wickets for South Africa (21 in Tests and 76 in all first-class matches) in England that season.

Catford was the venue in the post-war years for Sunday benefit matches of great popularity against county elevens. One match in this sequence arose from a wartime friendship between the Notts and England opening batsman, Walter Keeton, and the Catford captain, Pat Thompson. A full Notts XI visited Penerley Road on August bank-holiday Sunday in 1946. Their ranks included Bill Voce and Joe Hardstaff, who were in the MCC party in Australia the following winter, Reg Simpson and Arthur Jepson. The fixture, which coincided with the annual county match against Surrey at The Oval, was repeated in the following year and continued for several seasons.

One abiding memory of those celebrity occasions was the majestic century scored by Joe Hardstaff in 1951. It is recalled with that drooling pleasure which greets all feats of enthralling batsmanship. Hardstaff later remembered the 'delightful Sundays' at Catford, but omitted to mention the toll exacted by the post-match revelries. 'The social side was incredible,' says John Clegg. 'The Notts players never used to go home on Sunday nights. Then they would have to report for serious duties at The Oval on Monday morning.' The lavish hospitality – and its consequences – did eventually lead to the abandonment of the Catford fixture, but it was great fun while it lasted.

Jim Laker had ample cause to remember the inaugural benefit match at Catford in 1946. In a closely fought contest Notts, captained by Walter Keeton, won by eight runs. Albert Penfold scored the first of his two centuries against the visiting county. Laker, batting at No. 4, hit 42, enjoying, as he said, the experience of playing against fellows who earned their living from the game.

Holding a watching brief was Andrew Kempton, the Catford president. Sir Alec Bedser remembers the veteran as a 'lovely man' who disdained amateur privileges during his long association with Surrey. It was opportune, if slightly ironical, that Laker should shine as a batsman and not as a bowler in the match at Catford. Nevertheless, his promise was communicated by Kempton to Andrew Sandham, the Surrey coach. The outcome was an invitation to a trial at The Oval.

Laker, along with another newcomer, John McMahon, the South Australian left-arm spinner, was inspected by the Surrey captain-elect, Errol Holmes. 'On this day,' recalled Laker with some relish, 'we caught him on a "turner". Both "Digger" and I found a gap between his front leg and bat a few times.' Holmes told the two spinning apprentices: 'Not many experienced county bowlers have made me look so foolish. There's room for both of you here.' McMahon, soon to be ousted by Tony Lock, was an especial favourite of Holmes. Geoffrey Howard, then Assistant Secretary of Surrey, relates that McMahon was initially preferred to Laker. 'McMahon bowled left-arm "chinamen" and spun the ball prodigiously.'

Laker made his debut for Surrey against the Combined

Services at The Oval in 1946. The services opposition included Donald Carr, John Dewes, Bill Voce and Reg Perks, all past or future England players. Laker's first wicket in first-class cricket was that of another man who would gain Test status. He was the then unknown Royal Air Force batsman, Don Kenyon, who later represented England against Australia and, with Worcestershire, became one of the most respected and prolific batsmen in the country.

Kenyon, caught by McIntyre in the first innings and bowled in the second, was twice included in Laker's return of six wickets at 20 runs apiece in the match. Surrey won by six wickets; but not before Army corporal Bernie Constable, another of Laker's scalps and his future county colleague, had scored a century. Constable and Alan Shirreff put on 186 for the seventh wicket in the Services' first innings.

Laker made two further appearances for Surrey at Kingston upon Thames in the inaugural festival at the ground in 1946. One was against another Combined Services XI and the other against Hampshire. The latter match brought him under the captaincy of Nigel Bennett, whose appointment was always considered to have been made by accident. Bennett was unheard of in first-class or even minor counties cricket. The widely held theory was that Surrey had intended offering the post to Leo Bennett, a top-class cricketer with county experience. By some mischance the invitation was received, to his immense surprise, by the other Bennett.

As may be imagined, the season under his rather erratic command had its hilarious moments, none more so than in the match against Hampshire at Kingston. Laker was handed the new ball and asked to nominate the end he preferred. Alf Gover and Eddie Watts, Surrey's regular opening bowlers, were puzzled bystanders. Laker was equally surprised; he had not bowled fast for years. Bennett at length detected the signs of indecision. 'What's the matter, don't you want to bowl?' he said. Laker replied: 'Yes, of course, skipper. But the fact is, I'm an off-spinner.' The sight of Gover's face, bearing unmistakable disbelief, brought the captain to his senses. Laker did not have to revert to pace; the new ball was thrown to Gover and he took up his accustomed role.

Surrey declared their faith in Laker as an off-spinner when they offered him a professional contract on his demobilisation in August 1946. Yorkshire, approached by Surrey, had agreed to his release. The terms were £6 a week in the winter augmented by match fees in the summer. There was jubilation at his promotion among Laker's friends at Catford. 'Catford will lose a fine player when he joins the Surrey staff,' ran one report. 'Everyone will wish this likeable Yorkshireman the very best of luck in his new sphere.'

Laker entered a more challenging domain at The Oval, where he encountered a regime at odds with his liberal nature. Errol Holmes, the Surrey captain in 1947, fell into the category of the old-fashioned snob. He was known to be jealous of his privileges as an amateur. He relished and thrived on his separate changing quarters and his different travel facilities. The social chasm existing in the early post-war years was an irritant for Laker at The Oval. As he related, he was not 'an impressionable teenager' when he first walked through the Long Room into the professionals' dressing-room. Like many returning servicemen, on their learning curve in the war, he had become cynical about the elitism in cricket and in other walks of life. Many of them, as mature men, were intent on breaking the pattern of servility. The sweeping mandate given to Clem Attlee's socialist government in 1945 was proof of the desire for change.

Laker did not accept – and never did as a professional cricketer – the need to skulk in deference to those amateurs who wielded power without skills comparable to those professionals under their command. Like his mother, he was agitated by injustice and saw the situation as an affront to the dignity of his trade. He was, in the words of one friend, disgruntled about the degree of class-consciousness at The Oval.

Adding to Laker's resentment, which simmered throughout his career, was the lack of recognition accorded to him by members of the Surrey hierarchy. For two years H. D. G.

Leveson Gower, then the county president, myopically referred to him as Laurie Fishlock. Fishlock, Laker's senior by twenty years, was a left-hand batsman, but Leveson Gower was late in making the distinction between them.

There were, however understandably, too many chips lodging on Laker's shoulders to permit ease in his relationships. Dave Fletcher confirms that his Surrey colleague was an anti-establishment figure: 'Jim was always his own boss.' Fletcher – and other professionals – took a more philosophical stance on the prevailing social scene at The Oval. It reinforced their independence. In no sense, according to Fletcher, did they feel inferior, despite the fact that the amateurs always stayed at first-class hotels. 'We used to think that they cost the club much more than we were paid as professionals.' Even young amateurs, green in cricketing years, quickly established themselves in the pecking order. They took their places, as by right, at the top of the lunch table.

The professionals, on the other hand, were obliged to meet from their match fees the cost of third-class rail fares, hotel bills, and to buy their own kit. Herbert Strudwick, then the Surrey scorer, did his best on limited resources with the hotel bookings. But, amid the groans, the accommodation was usually basic and often doleful.

Dave Fletcher was one of the new guard at The Oval. Alongside him in the Surrey Colts' side captained by Andrew Kempton were Derek Pratt, Bernie Constable, Geoff Whittaker, John McMahon and Eric Bedser. Another of the newcomers was a 'little sandy-haired boy' from Limpsfield. At 17, Tony Lock, according to Fletcher, 'was a fairish bowler, who cut the ball a little, bowled straight and on a length'. The Colts played weekly matches against prominent clubs in Surrey. In two seasons they did not lose a match. To mark this achievement, Andrew Kempton invited his boys to a celebration dinner at Richmond.

Surrey signalled their future supremacy by heading the Minor Counties championship in 1947. Yorkshire, likewise prophetically, were runners-up to them. Jim Laker, at 25, did not linger long in the second eleven. By July he had won a first-team place, confirmed when he took seven wickets for 94 runs in the narrow win over Essex. The final two months of the season exceeded his wildest dreams. In this time he bowled nearly 450 overs and took 66 wickets at 16.65 runs each to head the Surrey averages. The *Cricketer* reported: 'He spins the ball rather after the manner of Tom Goddard, but is faster than the Gloucestershire cricketer and at least one good judge considers he is already his equal.'

Tom Graveney recalls one early duel with Laker at Bristol. 'Jim was the up-and-coming bowler, and obviously going to make the grade.' George Emmett had told him: 'If Jim comes on, have a go at him because he doesn't like the stick.' Graveney attempted to follow his senior's instruction. 'Jim beat me in the flight; it would have knocked the lot over. The umpire gave me not out.'

Laker was blessed in that he chose the right time and propitious circumstances in which to develop his talents. He knew, instinctively, that his adopted county was on the brink of an eventful era. There was, also fortuitously, an inviting opening for his off-spin. This bowling, which could only be described as a back-up, was then in the hands of two top-order batsmen, Bob Gregory and Stan Squires. Squires was more highly esteemed as a batsman; his death from leukaemia, at the age of 40 in 1950, deprived the young men at The Oval of a wise mentor.

For Laker, there was also timely aid in the transformation of wickets at The Oval. It now possessed demons unknown in the pre-war groundsmanship of 'Bosser' Martin when the wickets were as unyielding as concrete. 'Result' pitches were to become the vogue; and for batsmen, as Dave Fletcher recalls, penetrating the lush, green outfield called for powerful hitting. 'You had to hit the ball quite hard so that it cut through the grass to the boundary.' Alf Gover, one of the pre-war campaigners, remembered the near impossibility of bowling out sides twice in the 1930s. Bert Lock, newly appointed as groundsman in 1947, tipped the scales in favour of the bowlers. 'He came in the year I finished,' says Gover. 'If I'd known how things would change, I'd have stopped on,' jokes a man who twice took 200 wickets in a season and was not flattered by any of them.

Errol Holmes, the 'playboy cricketer', still held sway in 1947. His approach to the game had a carefree gallantry at odds with winning championships. To his credit, he did endorse Laker's abilities as a spinner. It was, though, only because of Gover's insistence that Laker made an important advance against Northants at Peterborough. Gover referred to Holmes's clock-work routine as a captain. He would raise his eyes in mock horror when the Surrey captain asked him to take his sweater. This often occurred while the ball was still swinging in the morning mists, little more than half an hour after the start of play. At Peterborough, as Gover recalls, he and Eddie Watts opened the bowling. 'I had bowled Dennis Brookes to make a breakthrough. But Eddie was a little erratic and I said to Errol: "Get Jim on." ' It was a piece of timely advice. Laker was in his spinning element before heavy storms ended Surrey's bid for victory. He took six wickets for 55 runs in twenty-three immaculate overs.

Laker was even more dominant against Hampshire at Portsmouth in August. His return of eight wickets for 69 runs was achieved after Holmes had put the home side in to bat on what was reputed to be the greenest wicket in the country. So the portents were not encouraging for spin; and Laker was really the intruder on this day.

On the train from Waterloo all the talk had focused on the milestones within reach of Alec Bedser and Alf Gover. Both had taken 99 wickets but they had to wait until Hampshire's second innings before they each obtained the extra wicket. *Wisden* contrarily reported that the pitch took spin from the start of the match. In Laker's version, it was almost an act of desperation by Holmes that led to the ensuing rout. 'He eventually tossed the ball to me. Almost immediately, it began to turn and, after bowling Bridger through the gate, I went on to take six of the first eight wickets.' 'Laker bowled off-breaks in deadly fashion,' commented *Wisden*. 'Three times he took two wickets with successive deliveries.'

Arthur McIntyre was a key wicket-keeping witness in the match against Essex at Chelmsford. It was his first experience of keeping to Laker and the perplexities of the spin were an acute source of embarrassment. 'The ball was turning at right angles on a dusty wicket. It was lifting and bouncing over my shoulder. I didn't know where to stand.' His captain, Holmes, refused him the shelter of a leg slip. The concession of 33 byes, with the ball leaping away from his gloves, was a tormenting episode. The lapses did sharpen his wits and teach him a lesson. Thereafter, in keeping to Laker, he adjusted his position further down the legside and away from the stumps. Meanwhile Laker, in off-spinning tandem with Stan Squires, took seven wickets for 94 runs in 35 overs. McIntyre did find compensation in a rallying 70 with the bat, leading a late-order revival, and Surrey were narrow victors by two wickets.

Laker's return to Bradford afforded him considerable pleasure in this proving season. At Park Avenue, Surrey won by five wickets; and the 22-year-old Dave Fletcher won special praise with an unbeaten century. Fletcher carried his bat through an innings to cherish against Yorkshire and on a ground dreaded by opponents. His brilliant first season with Surrey yielded an aggregate of 1,857 runs. Fletcher announced himself as an England candidate. He was a worthy deputy for Laurie Fishlock, who was stricken with appendicitis and out of action for two months.

Fletcher's feat at Bradford was coupled with another undefeated century by Gerry Smithson for Yorkshire. Smithson, a handsome left-hander, was a stylist in the manner of David Gower of another cricket generation. His batting, in the words of Norman Yardley, invited comparison with young Australians. Smithson touched the hems of glory in his short reign with Yorkshire before moving on to Leicestershire. In 1947, Fletcher and Smithson were rivals for selection, won by the Yorkshireman, for the tour of the West Indies in the following winter.

There were also Test honours in the offing for Jim Laker, and his burgeoning skills did not go unnoticed against Yorkshire at Bradford. Laker shared a marathon off-spinning partnership with Eric Bedser. In Yorkshire's second innings they bowled a total of 69 overs for a yield of seven wickets. Attracting the attention of Bill Bowes, then in his last season with Yorkshire, was Laker's duel with Brian Sellers. Bowes recalled: 'On this sticky wicket Jim bowled an off-break to Sellers. It pitched on the stumps and spun viciously away down the legside. The next ball did the same but the one after that for some inexplicable reason didn't turn, but carried on after pitching and bowled Brian.'

Sellers had set himself for a pull over square-leg, anticipating a shot with the spin. He was bowled in some disarray. His eyes darkened with thunder at the dismissal. Afterwards, in the pavilion, Bowes asked Laker: 'Was it funny?' Jim replied: 'What Brian Sellers said was bloody marvellous!' He had enjoyed duping the Yorkshire captain. His triumph was sealed by the barrage of expletives, the words carrying the ring of a grudging compliment. The quieter commendation of Bill Bowes was just as pleasing. 'Jim likes us to know where he comes from.'

At Lord's against Middlesex, as John Arlott related, Laker faced the most searching examination of his short career. Denis Compton and Bill Edrich were in their pomp in the golden summer of 1947. They were chillingly merciless against off-spin. In the Middlesex first innings of 462 for 7 declared, Laker bowled more overs (32) than any other Surrey bowler and, for 105 runs, took the wickets of Denis Compton and Sid Brown, and had two catches dropped. As if to demonstrate the excellence of the wicket, he also made top score, 33, in Surrey's first innings and the highest but one, 60, in the second innings. Laker had surmounted his steepest hurdle: on 26 August he was awarded his county cap.

Laker played in only fourteen championship matches but they were sufficient for him to head the Surrey averages ahead of Alf Gover. He was rewarded with an invitation to play for

Sir Pelham Warner's XI against the South of England in the Hastings Festival. The match, as a spectacle, brought acclamation for Denis Compton in his achievement of a record season's aggregate of 3,816 runs. Laker's contribution, in what was in effect a Test trial match for him, carried him into contention for the impending tour of the West Indies. In the South's first innings he bowled 33 overs and took two wickets, those of Pawson and Robins: in the second innings, 33.2 overs for six wickets, including Denis Compton's, and a hat-trick – for 109 runs. To crown a remarkable first season Laker was a late selection for the MCC tour under the leadership of Gubby Allen.

John Arlott described the Caribbean venture as probably the most unnecessarily depressing tour in English cricket history. For the first time the MCC went through an overseas tour without a single victory to their credit. Of the four Tests the first two were drawn before the West Indies repeated their success of 1935 by winning the last two and the rubber. Arlott said the initial error lay in a selection which omitted Yardley, Hutton, Compton, Washbrook, Bedser and Wright. Hutton was later flown out to replace the injured Brookes; but this was an ill-equipped force to pit against a West Indian batting strength of Weekes, Worrell, Walcott and Stollmeyer on their own wickets.

The problems of an ill-fated tour began with an injury to Allen. He tore a calf muscle while skipping on board ship. At 45 he was, in harsh truth, too old; the valiant England stalwart had embarked on one tour too many. Among the other casualties was Notts bowler Harold Butler, who thrice broke down with injuries and bowled only forty overs in the Tests. As so often happens in adversity, the troubles came in profusion. Cranston, Tremlett, Ikin and Howorth were others afflicted by injury or illness.

Jim Laker, proudly wearing an MCC touring blazer for the first time, emerged from an uncommonly stressful tour as a major find. Embarkation day for the West Indies was 23 December 1947. The MCC party left Garston Docks, Liverpool in the Elders and Fyffes banana boat, *Tetela*. The prelude to the tour was not one for the faint-hearted. The train taking the south of England players was over an hour late. This delayed the ship's departure and she caught the tide with only twenty minutes to spare. Godfrey Evans recalled his vain resistance and how he finally succumbed to seasickness. 'I leaned over the ship rail and waited for the swallows to come!' Laker remembered the abysmal weather on a storm-tossed voyage. 'A 4,500-ton empty banana boat with cabin accommodation for 15 (if three shared a cabin) may have been fine for a Mediterranean summer cruise, but certainly not when lashed by 90 mph gales in the North Atlantic.' It was, as he said, a relief when the ship finally anchored off Bridgetown harbour, Barbados, overdue by a couple of days.

Laker later expressed the general forebodings about the forthcoming matches against their underestimated hosts. 'Our Test side on that tour, even if fully fit, in constant match practice and accustomed to vastly different conditions, would have been hard-pressed to contain the West Indies side. Without our established Test men, all unavailable, we had as much chance as an unseeded player at Wimbledon.'

In a postcard to his sister Margaret at home in Baildon, he wrote: 'These are the finest wickets in the world. I don't expect to do much out here.' Margaret thought this was a typical response by her brother. 'Jim was always that way about himself – never too hopeful, but always a trier.'

As a novice member of a party shorn of high quality, Laker honed his skills to refute his own pessimism. Among his seniors in the Caribbean was the Worcestershire slow left-arm bowler, Dick Howorth. At Howorth's dictation, he began to build his neat and compact action and obey the tenets of accuracy. In the colony game at Bridgetown, he earned the praise of Jim Swanton as a 'bowler of high promise'. Laker and Howorth, between them, bowled over 100 overs in the two Barbados innings; and the Yorkshireman emerged with match figures of nine wickets for 137 runs. By teatime on the last day, Barbados had scored 87 for three wickets. Then, in forty-five minutes, Laker and Howorth so exploited a worn pitch that five more wickets fell before Walcott and Hoad stood firm in the drawn game.

The purple patch, said Jim Swanton, occurred when the wicket at Laker's end showed a tendency to crumble and the swiftness of the crisis found the Barbadian batsmen temporarily unbalanced. 'But the primary cause was some fine bowling by Laker. Not often has a young cricketer made a happier introduction to the best class.'

The clamour shrilled ever louder to greet an outstanding performance in the first Test at Bridgetown. Laker, on his Test debut, took seven wickets for 103 runs in 37 overs. Charles Bray, in the *Daily Herald*, wrote: 'Jim Laker, last season's Surrey discovery, was the hero of an astonishing and unexpected collapse.' The West Indies, 244 for three overnight, were trapped on a lively pitch freshened by morning rain. They lost their remaining seven wickets in an hour for the addition of 52 runs. In nine overs, including three maidens, Laker took six wickets for 25 runs. Bray continued: 'Already he had shown he could bowl a good length and spin the ball. This morning we saw him use a helpful wicket, with all the guile of Tom Goddard. A sharp shower had moistened the top of this shirt-front wicket. The 26-year-old Yorkshire lad rolled up his sleeves and took full advantage of the conditions.'

Brian Chapman, another member of the press corps, enthused about a 'magnificent debut for a bowler, still only a recruit in county cricket'. Chapman recalled standing alongside the West Indies opening batsman Jeffrey Stollmeyer, who had earlier been dismissed by Ikin, when Laker began his destructive spell. 'Stollmeyer gasped with astonishment when he saw the break-back off the first ball. So probably did Headley, who had to deal with it. A couple of balls later, trying to pull, he swept the ball down on to his stumps.' It was the start of a procession of confounded batsmen. Gomez, wanting 14 for his century, was bowled off his pads; Christiani misjudged the spin and was lbw; Williams was caught by Ikin, and Ferguson and Gaskin bowled.

Jim Laker typically took a more measured view of his

exploits at Bridgetown. He was well pleased that England subsequently maintained their unbeaten record in Barbados. He did not dwell on his own statistics in the Test, nor did he wish to emphasise the fact that an obliging leak in the wicket cover made a 'very naive England off-spinner' the happiest and probably the most fortunate cricketer in the West Indies.

His recital of the events was concentrated on an escape when defeat seemed certain. England were set the monumental task of scoring 395 to win in the fourth innings of the Test at Bridgetown. Overnight they had lost two wickets for 60 runs. Brookes was absent with a broken finger, and on the following morning two more wickets fell cheaply. England's score, after less than an hour's play, stood at 86 for four, with Robertson and Place batting bravely on against a side scenting the kill. 'The hopelessness of the situation', he whimsically remarked, 'was endorsed by the sight of J. C. Laker and J. H. Wardle padded up with five hours still remaining . . . In subsequent years both Johnny Wardle and myself used the spinners' prayer mat to good effect, but our chances of dispensation were always much rosier at Park Avenue and Old Trafford than on a warm, sunny day in the West Indies. A couple of maiden overs followed. Then from nowhere at all, it seemed, two or three enormous raindrops fell on my forearm. I realised our prayers were being answered. Moving swiftly and surely in the direction of the Kensington Oval was an enormous black cloud. As though guided by help from above, its progress halted immediately overhead and the rains came.'

Within twenty minutes the wicket was awash and the ground was a lake. Several hours on, Laker walked from the pavilion to a waiting car. Leaning against the car was a little Barbadian boy, his ragged and torn shirt saturated, his shoes covered in mud. 'Worst of all', related Laker, 'were the great tears streaming down his face.' He asked the boy what was wrong and offered him a lift into town. 'For fully a minute no reply was forthcoming. The tears still streamed down. Then, finally, with a huge sigh, he wiped away his tears, and very

51

slowly replied: "Oh Massa Laker, de God sure is an Englishman."'

The paucity of England's resources, exacerbated by injuries, was recalled by the late Billy Griffith. Griffith had delivered his credentials as a wicket-keeper in the 'Victory' Tests against the Australian Services XI in 1945. In the second Test at Port of Spain, Trinidad, he scored 140 as an emergency opener. It was his maiden century in first-class cricket and, incidentally, the highest score made by any player on the tour.

At Port of Spain, England's regular opening pair, Dennis Brookes and Winston Place, were both injured. Allen ordered a net in an attempt to resolve the problem. In a bizarre situation, there were even suggestions that one of the attending press corps should be pressed into service. Ikin and Laker were selected, along with Griffith, for the practice session. The abundantly clear reaction of all three candidates was: 'Oh God, no.' Griffith disguised his feelings to summon the greater resolution and was given the job. He did not receive any compliments for his enterprise from the England captain. 'Just bloody well stay in,' said Allen.

The usually placid Griffith was perhaps affected by his captain's pessimism, for he ran out fellow-opener Jack Robertson to deepen the consternation. 'I had to stay in then; I was too frightened to go back to the pavilion.' Griffith scored 23 before lunch, advanced to 70 by tea, and soldiered on to reach 110 by the close of play. At the end there was a rousing innings of 55, including seven fours, by Jim Laker in a last-wicket stand of 56 with Butler. 'Laker hit a masterly half-century when runs were vitally necessary,' recorded Crawford White. 'By this action, he moved one more step towards a regular place in England's team.'

England were, though, indebted to Billy Griffith at Port of Spain. His marathon effort enabled his team to force a draw against all expectations. The arrival of Len Hutton to bolster morale, following an urgent cable by Allen to the MCC, relieved him of further responsibility. 'I am probably the only player to get a 100 in a Test and then be dropped,' said Griffith.

He did not play again in the series.

Jim Laker, despite the handicap of painfully damaged stomach muscles, bowled more overs and took more wickets (18) than any Englishman in the series in the West Indies. He was the most successful bowler, in aggregate and average, for all the first-class matches on the tour.

E. M. Wellings, in his postscript to the tour, sounded a warning note on future prospects. 'For a representative MCC team to go through a tour without a win in any sort of match is something new and depressing.' Wellings acknowledged that the 'bulk of our real side' was not on the tour and saluted the rise of Laker to the front rank. 'It represents a very big gain and my only fear is that he may suffer in the coming season from having been pressed into service when he was not fully fit.'

The biggest challenge of all lay ahead for the newly acclaimed Laker. He had returned home, still with less than a full season's cricket behind him, an accepted Test player. England, rebuilding after the long years of war, undoubtedly saw him as a matchwinner on the home stage. The Australians, led by Don Bradman, were about to cast a long shadow over this vision. Laker perhaps then knew in his heart that he was still short of the standards he recognised for fulfilment in this imposing assembly.

5

PERILS ON A HOMECOMING

'The guilt of Australia's famous victory rested heavily on England and, so it seemed, on Laker in particular.'

Alex Bannister

The inquests over the years have unjustly scorned Jim Laker for England's humiliation at Headingley in 1948. He was disavowed as a prospect; and plainly, as the selectors' whipping boy, held responsible for the defeat. The bright sails of the self-confessed novice were trimmed in a searing examination of his technique and nerve.

Laker was a hostage to fortune on a lamentable day. In an upheaval of rare magnitude, as *Wisden* described the eclipse, Australia coasted to an unexpected victory. Their target was 404 runs in five and three-quarter hours, and they won in a canter by seven wickets. Complacency, as Godfrey Evans, England's wicket-keeper at Leeds, recalls, was the major cause of the fiasco. 'We expected to win; no other team had previously scored 400 in the last innings of a Test.'

England were gripped by a fielding palsy which had the spectators shielding their eyes in disbelief. It was calculated that as many as seven chances were put down in an epidemic of fatal proportions. Bradman was missed three times and Morris escaped twice as catches were missed and stumpings not accepted. Australia, if truth were told, were not seriously looking for victory after Norman Yardley's early-morning declaration. England's lapses meant that they could hardly help winning the match. The astonishing upset enabled Australia to maintain a supremacy at Leeds which was to last until 1956.

Godfrey Evans points to an uncharacteristic lack of urgency against the traditional enemy. 'The Australians were padded up to No. 8; they anticipated a rout. Our attitude was such that we lost the initiative; and when that happens it is very difficult to arrest the decline.' Denis Compton recalled a later conversation with one Australian rival, Keith Miller. 'Keith said that the Australian team had already packed to leave the ground early because they thought the match would be over by four o'clock.'

Kenneth Cranston, also on England duty, remembers a perfect batting wicket at Headingley on which only a wrist-spinner could hope to achieve profitable purchase. England did not have bowlers of this calibre at their disposal. He agrees that Australia, at first, did not envisage victory. It appeared to be an 'impossible target'. 'They were so behind the clock that Norman was encouraged to introduce Hutton and Denis Compton into our attack. It nearly worked; both Morris and Bradman were missed off very easy chances.'

Laker's concession of 206 runs for his three wickets in 62 overs in the match was to have immense repercussions. The power of his spin meant that he suffered from dropped catches throughout his career. His critics, sadly including the selectors, preferred to overlook the faults of others which demeaned his reputation. Laker's bowling – and the fulfilment of his art – demanded fielding of the highest quality. It was not always forthcoming. 'Jim *knew* he was a good bowler,' says Godfrey Evans. 'But there were times aplenty when he wasn't allowed to be a good bowler because either the fielding was bad or it was wrongly placed.'

It was the ill-luck of a beginner that Bradman should thrice be reprieved at Headingley. As a boy, Laker had watched the great Australian in the execution of the first of his triple centuries at Leeds in 1930. On the occasion of Bradman's knighthood, he recalled his youthful wonderment and tendered his congratulations on the honour. Bradman replied: 'I didn't know before that you were a spectator at Leeds. But I do know that if Godfrey Evans had been a little more alert, I would have been a spectator in the fourth Test in 1948, and you would have been the cause of it.'

Before the indignities at Headingley, the Australians had announced their eminence against Surrey at The Oval. Barnes, Bradman and Hassett each scored centuries in a total of 632. Laker's only success – the wicket of Bill Johnston – cost him 137 runs: it was the worst analysis of his career. A fortnight later he played in a Test rehearsal for the MCC against the tourists at Lord's. 'Once more the Australians' batting rolled mightily,' related John Arlott. It was another merry extravaganza. Laker conceded 127 runs out of a total of 552. 'Miller mounted a powerful attack on Laker,' said Arlott. 'At one point, on the second morning after a shower had reduced the pace of the pitch, he and Johnson, between them, hit him over the short legside boundary for nine sixes.' It was a torrid experience for Laker and might have signalled the end for a less resolute cricketer. The Australians, with a contempt that was to linger in his memory, said: 'If this is Laker, let's have more of him.'

In 1948 they did exact a severe toll and the misgivings of the England selectors were not lessened by the assaults. In Laker's three Test appearances that summer he secured just nine wickets at a cost of 472 runs, with a woeful average of 52.44. It was a heavy expenditure even for a novice; and, as someone well versed in balance sheets, Laker must have been appalled to sink so deeply into the red at this stage of his career. He later accepted the liability, confessing that as an apprentice he had the cricketer's equivalent of the boxer's 'glass chin'. 'If I saw a batsman coming down the wicket to me, I didn't know how to stop him thrashing me. I became flustered, dropped my guard and was wide open to punishment.'

Arthur Morris was one of his Australian aggressors that summer. Morris was later to assess Laker as the finest off-spinner in his experience. His quick-footedness and emphasis on attack did, though, often give him the ascendancy against spin. 'On good wickets,' he said of his rivals, 'they have little spin and rely on accuracy. To push forward and allow them to dictate is to court disaster. They can bring fieldsmen in close to wait for the "bat pad" catch, so it is essential to go after them and not allow them to settle into an awkward length.' Morris contended that charges of off-spinners bowling badly did not take account of the fact that batsmen had disturbed their line and direction. 'It is not so much that a bowler has bowled badly but rather that the batsmen have called his bluff.'

Experience was to teach Jim Laker how to negotiate the hazards confronting all spin bowlers. Other bowlers, more practised than Laker, were just as daunted by the Australians in 1948. In a triumphant summer the tourists won half of their 34 matches with an innings to spare. The plunder was relentless: ten of the Australian batsmen, between them, hit 47 centuries.

Penetrating the gloom were cheering messages to greet Laker's selection for his first Test against Australia at Trent Bridge. They included a telegram from his sister Margaret and her husband Geoffrey; a letter on behalf of Salts High School was jointly written by the head boy and head girl; and another note of congratulations was received from his former head-master, George Parkin.

At Nottingham, Laker was beyond censure as a batsman, addressing the speed of Lindwall and Miller with a commend-able if outward show of calm. If he was, as one contemporary observed, 'a shade apprehensive' as a batsman, the gallantry of his driving averted a rout. England had lost eight wickets for 74 runs before tea. They appeared on course for less than the lowest score in a Test at Nottingham – 112 by England in 1921. The position was retrieved by Laker and his Surrey colleague, Alec Bedser, who more than doubled the score, adding 89 runs in 73 minutes. Laker was top scorer with 63 out of a total of 165. The pattern of a brave rally was encapsulated in one wry comment by Laker. 'Lindwall dropped one short at me. I went for the hook and the ball went like a rocket square on the offside for four. I was just a little late on the shot.'

There was also a measure of revenge for Laker as a bowler in Australia's first innings. At one stage he had taken three wick-ets for 22 runs in 12.4 overs. He dismissed Barnes to break the opening stand. Evans, with breathtaking anticipation, was his acrobatic ally. Barnes essayed a fierce cut and the ball struck Evans's thigh and bounced into the air. He thereupon wheeled round like a spinning top and, diving full-length, took the catch with one hand inches from the ground.

Laker's other wickets were those of Morris and, best of all, Miller for nought, deceived by his arm-ball and caught by Edrich at slip. Yardley then unaccountably discharged Laker in order to take the new ball, and Australia were able to reassert their authority. All that was left for England's satisfaction in defeat were the contributions of Alec Bedser and Denis Compton. Bedser achieved his third consecutive dismissal of Bradman, following his success in the last Test at Sydney in the 1946–47 series. Catches by Hutton in the leg trap brought Bradman's downfall. There were two more conquests for Bedser against Bradman to add to a proud tally in the next Test at Lord's.

Denis Compton never achieved greater distinction than in the gallantry he displayed against Miller and Johnston in near darkness at Nottingham. Partnered first by Hardstaff and then by Evans, he was the valiant master. His dismissal, with his score on 184, was a cruel end to one of his finest innings. Miller unleashed a lightning bumper which hurtled shoulder-high. Compton was set on the hook, then changed his mind and ducked precariously to lose his balance on the greasy turf and fall back on his wicket.

England continued to struggle at Lord's, where they were beaten by 409 runs. The match did include one intriguing duel between Laker and Bradman. The outcome of 'one of the best overs of my career' demonstrated that the Australian was never plagued by self-doubt. 'I was at the Nursery End, which meant that my off-break had to turn up the quite considerable slope of the wicket,' recalled Laker. 'Don played for the turn off my first ball and was beaten because it went the other way down the hill. The process was reversed for the next ball. He played for it going away and it broke back at him.' Bradman would have been trapped lbw, except that he achieved the faintest of edges before the ball struck his pads. The third and fourth balls, pitched with unerring accuracy, deepened Bradman's consternation and deserved a reward. Laker added: 'As I passed him at the end of the over, Don said: "Well bowled, Jim. Thank goodness, that's over. Now we can get on with some batting." ' He had acknowledged his discomfort, but it was now forgotten. Normal service was resumed in Laker's next over. 'Don belted my first ball for four and was never in trouble afterwards.'

Laker was dropped for the next Test at Manchester, but was then restored to the side for the ill-starred encounter at Headingley. England held the key to victory until the fateful last day. A vast Yorkshire crowd – the attendance figures of 158,000 amounted to a record for a match in England – nudged shoulders expectantly as the prize beckoned. What followed was a sad indictment of England's bowling resources. Australia feasted hugely on a diet of long-hops and full-tosses. For a glum Yorkshire assembly, proud in their memories of Rhodes and Verity, it was an act of abject surrender. Don Bradman, unruffled as if he had just completed an extended net practice, was undefeated on 173 in his farewell innings at Leeds. Bradman and Morris hit 301 runs in just over three hours. Sixty-six fours were struck by the rampant Australians.

Alec Bedser cites the omission of Jack Young, the Middlesex slow left-arm bowler, as the crucial error. 'We shouldn't have lost the game, but with Young in our side we would have won it.' Ken Cranston, the Lancashire captain and all-rounder, was preferred as Young's replacement. The selectors thus left the England captain, Norman Yardley, with an unbalanced attack. Dick Pollard, another Lancastrian, shared the new ball with Bedser. Cranston, Edrich and Yardley provided less than adequate support.

Laker, the raw beginner, was called upon to shoulder the main spinning thrust. By his own admission he bowled badly. The consequence was that Yardley had to place his hopes in the eccentric left-arm spin of Denis Compton and, briefly, in a pre-lunch gamble, in the leg-breaks of Len Hutton, who bowled only rarely for Yorkshire in the post-war years. In half an hour before the interval Bradman and Morris put on 64 runs.

'Norman did not need to turn to Len; there were other bowlers at his disposal,' maintains Alec Bedser.

The Cricketer was also astounded at Yardley's decision. 'What passage of thought, what evil genius induced him to do so is hard to imagine,' it reported. Off Hutton's four overs, which included five full tosses, all of which were hit for four, 30 runs were scored. It was a fatal decision and the catalyst for an afternoon of run-making gluttony. After lunch, two overs from Denis Compton produced 29 more runs. 'The need for a strong outpost line of fieldsmen to save the game was neglected,' continued the *Cricketer* correspondent. Yardley, often a valuable change bowler, did not enter the England attack until after tea. He then obtained his usual wicket. Morris, having put on 301 with Bradman, was caught by Pollard off the England captain's bowling.

John Arlott considered that the wicket had started to crumble by the last day. 'If it offered greater opportunity to the wrist-spinner than the off-spinner, Laker did, nevertheless, make the ball lift and turn.' Laker himself thought that despite Bradman's century, it was the left-hander, Morris, with a brilliant 182, who contributed most to the Australian success. 'The rough around his off-stump was made for me to destroy him, which would have made an English victory certain, but I failed hopelessly to take advantage of it.' These remarks were written more than thirty years after the match, and Laker's concluding sentence revealed the memory of his awesome vengeance. 'A few years later that great Australian side would have done well to reach 200.'

Arlott also stressed that Laker, equipped with more wisdom, would not have allowed Morris to score a century, or Australia to make 404 for three. 'Perhaps the tension and importance of the occasion threw him off balance. Bradman on the kill presented an insoluble problem to most bowlers of his time and Morris, riding the luck of his finest season, was a commanding hitter of the ball. The fact remains that Laker, trying to overcome the slowness of the pitch, lost control of both line and length. He was Yardley's main strategic weapon and thus carried the burden of the selectors' disappointment at the England defeat. He was not quickly forgiven.'

An important element in a vexed debate was the state of the Leeds wicket upon which, it has to be said, over 1,700 runs, including five centuries, were scored. Alec Bedser reiterates the general view that it was then the best batting wicket in England. 'It did turn on the last day, but it was still easy-paced.' Godfrey Evans, as a key witness behind the wicket, dwells upon its unpredictable behaviour. 'Three balls in an over would come straight through and then, when you were least expecting it, the ball would viciously turn and lift. It was completely out of character with what had happened before.' Evans believes that this handicapped the England bowlers. 'The ball did not turn regularly and, in consequence, it was difficult to power the spin, or control the direction of the ball.'

Evans relates that Arthur Morris reacted in a violent manner to the conditions. 'He took one look at the wicket and decided to go on the attack.' Morris, looking back over the years, presents a contrary view on the supposed evils of the challenge. 'Wouldn't it be easier and fair dinkum just to say that two good batsmen at the top of their form battled their way against good, tight bowling, and then took it by the scruff of the neck and made it possible for Australia to win?'

Morris recalls a slow turner at Headingley and counters Evans's comments on the wicket. 'Jeez, if that was the case, what about the two batsmen, let alone Godfrey!' The missed chances, according to the Australian, were restricted to just two during the course of an amazing day. 'Don was dropped in the slips by Jack Crapp, a difficult chance off Denis Compton's wrong 'un. The stumping chance was an impossible one for Godfrey who, from time to time, cops criticism. I had a peculiar shot (so I have been told), a scoop to leg from balls I figured I could reach on the full. I covered the ball completely with my body from Godfrey. I missed it, the bounce took it over the wicket and, as I turned, I saw the ball come back off Godfrey's chest. If anything, I should have been bowled, but the ball obviously hit a footmark on the batting crease. It soared like a jet taking off, admittedly in a slower manner.'

Jim Laker, at Headingley, was belittled by the fleet footwork of the Australians. His native good sense took him through this bad time. Even then his peremptory exclusion from the England ranks did not affect his constancy as a wicket-taker on other fields. In Yorkshire there was growing concern that he had eluded their attention. Fred Trueman recalled that in 1948 Laker was contacted by the Yorkshire president, Ernest Holdsworth, and entertained at a dinner in London. 'Jim was rather surprised by the invitation but went along to see what it was all about. It turned out that they were trying to persuade him to return and play for his native Yorkshire.' Laker thanked them for the offer, but said that he was quite happy with his adopted county.

Many years later, Sir Len Hutton confirmed the tardy recognition of Laker's assets. He remembered the Saltaire batsman who had been summoned to the Headingley nets before the war. Hutton said that Yorkshire did not know then, nor for that matter did Laker, that the batting recruit would in time possess skills to reduce the finest batsmen in the world to the level of bemused amateurs. In 1948, said Hutton, he was asked by a very prominent member of the Yorkshire committee to enquire, discreetly, whether Laker was settled in Surrey. The answer was in the affirmative. 'Yorkshire went on needing Laker badly,' lamented Hutton. 'We in the post-war Yorkshire team would wince when this gifted Yorkshire exile tied us in all sorts of knots in our matches with Surrey.'

In 1950, others exposed to Laker's developing spin winced in dismay. Surrey, now captained by Oxford blue, Michael Barton, shared the championship with Lancashire. Laker held exalted status among the array of spinners on the county circuit. He bowled over 1,100 overs and headed the Surrey averages with 142 wickets at an average of 14.54 runs apiece. He had to concede first place in the national averages to Roy Tattersall, of Lancashire, his principal off-spinning challenger. Tattersall, in his finest season, took 193 wickets. Laker's overall figures of 166 wickets were sprinkled with devastating performances. They included a match return of twelve wickets for 96 runs, including a spell of six for 16, against Gloucestershire at Bristol, followed by 10 for 98 against the same county at The Oval; 11 for 97 against Worcestershire; and a ten-wicket haul against Essex at Chelmsford.

Another important date in Yorkshire thrust Laker into the national spotlight in this season. The events in the Test trial at Park Avenue, Bradford were in stark contrast to his bruising Test baptism at Headingley two years earlier. Laker always said that he was hailed as 'Yorkshire-born' if he did well and as the Surrey bowler on less auspicious occasions. He unquestionably belonged in spirit to the broad acres after an astounding feat on a bleak morning in late May.

The intimate sporting basin of Park Avenue was likened by distraught opponents to the torrid environs of a bullring. Laker, in an article in the *Daily Express* written shortly before his death, remembered the enfeebling atmosphere. 'It was called the bullring because once you'd descended the three stone steps and gone on to the field, you saw brick walls all around and a circle of intent Yorkshire folk watching you.'

On the capricious Bradford turf upon which the post-war Australians and West Indian tourists had tumbled to near defeat, Laker spun a tale of triumph in taking eight wickets for two runs in a one-sided match. This magnificent feat overtook Ted Peate's return of eight for five at Holbeck, Leeds in 1883. One curious fact is that Peate's achievement against Surrey was surpassed by a Surrey player born in Yorkshire. The closest return in modern times is Derek Shackleton's eight for four for Hampshire against Somerset at Weston in 1955. Laker's figures were bettered statistically only by the nine for two of Gideon Elliott, once described as 'the fastest and straightest bowler in Australia', for Victoria against Tasmania at Launceston in 1857–58.

Laker had the memory of Headingley to erase at Bradford. He was on trial, just as much as the Oxbridge batsmen in the opposition. He had been omitted from the England team at The Oval in 1948, failed to gain selection for the tour of South

63

Africa in the following winter, and was chosen for only one of the four Tests against New Zealand in 1949.

John Arlott described the Bradford wicket as one of the most honest cricket pitches in the world. 'In normal circumstances,' he said, 'it was a fine wicket for stroke-making; but after rain, drying conditions will stir it into a true "sticky".' The potion, with the wicket left open to heavy rain for twenty-four hours before the match, could not have been more wickedly mixed for Laker.

His rivals facing interrogation in a perplexing tutorial were the hitherto flourishing university men. The Rest ranks included the Cambridge trio of Hubert Doggart, Peter May and David Sheppard, and Donald Carr from Oxford. Within an hour and a half, after the England captain, Norman Yardley, had put them in to bat, they were all out for 27. The match ended in their defeat by an innings before lunch on the second day.

It was a spectacular and sensational entertainment for the scattering of spectators taking shelter from the keen wind sweeping across the ground. But, as one writer disapprovingly observed, 'Here there was the smack of a first-class county side in conflict with a scratch Saturday afternoon eleven.' Billy Griffith, in *The Cricketer*, also declared that the value of the match was diminished by the conditions. 'The forward defensive stroke – almost a reflex action of a young triallist at the beginning of an innings – becomes the desperate means by which he hopes to get off the mark. To play such a stroke at Bradford against Laker was pure suicide.'

Laker bowled fourteen overs and each of the deliveries, a fraction faster than usual, turned with unpleasant sharpness. They included twelve maidens, as evidence of his taunting accuracy. He took two wickets (Doggart and May) in his first over and a third (Carr) before conceding a run. In his fifth over he dismissed four more before being edged for a single; and then brilliantly caught and bowled the last batsman, Les Jackson. The wickets sequence makes compelling reading: 1–1; 2–10; 3–10; 4–10; 5–18; 6–19; 7–20; 8–20; 9–21; 10–27.

John Dewes, another Cambridge representative, was spared embarrassment in the rout. It was, in his own view today, inexplicable that he should be in a different camp. Hubert Doggart, unsurprisingly, failed against Laker, while Dewes, less burdened in the England team, was able to score with comparative freedom. Yet Doggart won selection for the first two Tests against the West Indies that summer and then gave way to Dewes at Nottingham and The Oval. The selectors, believing that they had resolved the dilemma, picked Dewes – and another Cambridge partner, David Sheppard – for the following tour of Australia.

Dewes recalls that he and his Cambridge colleagues had to obtain leave for the Bradford trial during preparations for their university Tripos examinations. Those engaged in Laker's lesson must have had misgivings about the exchange of studies. 'The wickets in our day when it rained were bad,' says Dewes. 'And Bradford had an asterisk against it for being very bad.' Dewes recalls the humid conditions which often prevailed at the Yorkshire ground. 'In the heavy atmosphere, the ball for the seamers could deviate quite alarmingly. The great feature of Jim's day was the way the ball turned and lifted. He was faster and at the batsmen all the time.'

Dewes agreed with Billy Griffith that only batsmen of the calibre of Hutton (as he proved in a masterly exhibition in England's innings) or Hammond could have countered the conditions at Bradford. 'The great oldies had learned to drop their wrists so quickly to combat the spin. It did not always guarantee complete security, but they were much better than us who were only beginners.' Donald Carr also concedes that such defensive batting was beyond their capabilities at that stage. Another observer, ignoring the penalty of failure, believed that a more venturesome approach against Laker might have paid dividends. 'I did eventually decide to have a swish,' recalls Carr. 'The trouble was the ball went straight up in the air and I was caught.'

The slaughter of the innocents was complete in probably the greatest cricketing debacle ever seen in a major match at Park

Avenue. 'Laker pitched an attacking length with a precision George Macaulay and Hedley Verity would have applauded,' reported Bruce Harris. 'The ball, twisting and hopping all over the place, needed a fly-swatter rather than a bat to control it.' Jim Swanton, while deploring the futility of the match as a trial, said Laker utilised a quite hateful wicket excellently. 'He spun the ball prodigiously and dropped it on the spot every time.' Swanton added: 'If Laker has a rival as the best of his kind in the country, I do not know his name.' In his view, not the least remarkable feature of the match was that while Laker was in the ascendant, Hollies, normally proficient on the slowest of surfaces, was quite innocuous at the other end.

John Arlott said that Laker, having inspected the wicket before the start of play, quickly recognised its character and knew precisely what to do. Norman Yardley persisted with Trevor Bailey just long enough to dispose of Sheppard. He then called up Laker to bowl round the wicket to an eager legside field. 'Never a demonstrative cricketer, Laker was now in his element and at his most noncommittal. He strolled back to his mark at his characteristically constabulary gait, looked up to the sky as he turned and then jogged the approach he used artfully to vary, constantly changing the number of steps so as, often, to defeat the batsman's timing.'

Among the Rest batsmen only Don Kenyon shaped remotely convincingly against Laker. Kenyon batted for an hour for seven before submitting to a remarkable catch by Godfrey Evans. 'Don couldn't believe it,' recalls Evans. 'He played back to Jim; the ball lifted slightly as it glanced off his bat; and I whipped round in front of him and caught the ball just before it hit the ground.'

Of the two singles conceded in the innings by Laker, one was an inside-edged shot by Trueman. The other was courtesy of a full toss, charitably wheeled up to his county colleague, Eric Bedser. It was pushed in the direction of mid-on. Eric's brother Alec, stationed there, thoughtfully moved four or five yards deeper to concede the run. Alex Bannister jokingly reflected that Bedser, a fine off-spinner in his own right and often obliged to play second fiddle to Laker at The Oval, might have argued that this was the only favour ever granted to him by his fellow bowler. Trevor Bailey capped this sally with a memory of Laker's dry humour after the exploits at Bradford. Amid the compliments, Jim produced the perfect deadpan reply: 'Well, it would have been less expensive if I hadn't given Eric one to get off the mark.'

It is beyond question that Laker could not have bowled with greater accuracy or cunning at Park Avenue. He would have challenged the best of rivals. The verdict, whatever the opposition or circumstances, is that only a masterly exponent of spin could have come within touching distance of Laker's performance. It showed him in the ruthless, destroying vein that was to distinguish so many of his subsequent ventures.

The satisfaction that the hero of the day was a Yorkshireman was mingled with a regret that such a worthy bowler had ever been allowed to emigrate to Surrey. 'Why isn't he playing for us?' was the plaintive cry of the local partisans. The puzzlement was shared in a different manner by Alf Burgoyne, Laker's old mentor at Saltaire. There was a smile of disbelief on his face. After the applause welcoming Laker back to the pavilion had subsided, he explained: 'You see, when Jim was with us, we picked him out as a batsman. We knew he would make his name in cricket one day, but not as an 8 for 2 bowler.'

Afterwards Laker, relaxing with his sister Margaret at her home at Baildon, played down his triumph. There must have been a bubble of elation; but then, as in later years, he was almost embarrassed by success. 'There was nothing really special about it. It was just one of those days.' He had already had cause to rue the fickleness of fortune. 'It's a funny game, cricket,' he said. 'One day you are on top of the world. Next day you get nought for plenty.'

One delightful postscript to a memorable day maintained his grasp on reality. The innocent query of a cub reporter was relished beyond all adulation. The voice called out from the crush of admirers. 'Are these your best bowling figures, Mr Laker?'

6

THE BEST OF HIS MATCHES

'I thought English people were supposed to be fair. How
is it proper for eleven men to play against one?'
Lilly Laker on cricket

An artful matchmaker helped to tie the knot and provide the
spur for an enduring fixture. Among all his conquests, Jim
Laker never won a more faithful ally than the Viennese-born
Lilly. Six years after their first wartime meeting in Cairo in
1943, they hesitantly revived their friendship at a Middle East
services' reunion in London.

Jim and Lilly were at first reluctant to attend the function
until, through the agency of a mutual friend, they were each
given a compelling reason for their presence. The trap was
adroitly laid to beguile the unsuspecting couple. The message
conveyed to them was that they had both, unknown to each
other, accepted invitations to the dinner. So it was that they
came face to face again. It was an occasion in which joy was
mingled with relief. In a brief conversation they discovered
that no impediment existed to repulse thoughts of a continuing
association. 'How about dinner one evening?' asked Jim. 'No,
make it lunch,' replied Lilly. She gave him her telephone
number and requested a call to confirm the date. Jim took some
time to assess the prospects. Six months later, having fully
considered the position, he rang Lilly to take another step in
the courtship.

Lilly's vivaciousness was to prove an ideal foil for the shy
and retiring Yorkshireman. Her exuberance filled in the gaps

when Jim ran out of small talk, never one of his strongest suits. As a petite and attractive brunette, she was never without admirers; and it was largely due to her engaging influence that Jim eventually found some ease on social occasions.

Lilly had left her native Austria and was in the Middle East when war was declared. She joined up as an ATS in the British Army in 1942 and was based in Cairo for four years, attached to the Royal Ordnance Corps. Jim was serving in the same unit and they shared an office along with around eighty other service men and women.

The relationship between Lilly and Jim, amid the whirl of camaraderie, did not exclude other partners. They were, as the saying goes, just good friends. But they did step out for their first date in Cairo. The venue was the Gezira Club at which Lilly attended her first cricket match. Jim took the opportunity to explain the rudiments of the game. Lilly listened attentively but was puzzled by the apparent lack of equality in the sport. 'I thought English people were supposed to be fair,' she protested. 'How is it proper for eleven men to play against one?'

It can be said, with some certainty, that cricket was the least of the attractions which linked her to Jim. Others have said that her naiveté about the game made her all the more acceptable on the social scene where she could bring her bright mind to bear on different topics. Lilly very soon realised that she would never untangle the finer points of cricket. Those of us who have attempted to communicate on cricket matters to other, English watchers can sympathise with her. Her puzzlement did not deflect her loyalty to Jim; she sensed his hurt on disappointing days and rejoiced with him in happier hours. Sometimes, because Jim only offered a brisk comment on cricket proceedings, she failed to distinguish between the highs and the lows.

After one day's play at The Oval, Jim casually mentioned the figure 113 as his contribution. Lilly attributed this to a bowling concession and discreetly made no comment. On the following day, she checked her newspaper to find that Jim really deserved congratulations. He had *scored* 113, as a batsman for Surrey, his highest score in first-class cricket.

In broad terms Jim did, though, prefer to separate cricket from life at home. He was content, in his slippered ease, not to be asked to analyse the happenings of the day. With Lilly, not as knowledgeable as some cricketing wives, there was repose and comfort. After dinner they could talk of other things, or engage in word bouts in their favourite game of Scrabble.

The resumption of their friendship in 1949, delayed by Jim's belated telephone call, was marked by lunch at the Star and Garter hotel at Putney. Lilly was then working at Fulham Palace for the Bishop of London. It was a happy period of employment. Lilly started as a clerk but ended up as a girl Friday, with a wide range of duties. Her immediate chief was the secretary of the Reconstruction Fund, whose major task was the rebuilding of bombed churches in the aftermath of the war.

There was an amusing sequel to her lunch engagement with Jim, when he escorted Lilly back to her office. 'Jim was surprised and quite impressed at my lovely big room at the palace.' He thought it was like another palais, the dance-hall at Hammersmith. In later years, it became a stock item in his repertoire of stories.

At the Putney lunch, Jim really exceeded the bounds of gallantry with talk of the girls he had met on his first tour of the West Indies. It was a curious way to impress, if that was his intention, as was his revelation that he had actually presented engagement rings to three other girls. For a time, it seemed that he and Lilly would share no more than a fleeting liaison. But as the months went by and another cricket tour loomed in 1950, the dalliance assumed greater seriousness. 'In that summer we started going out together more often,' remembers Lilly. There were evening trysts at Lyons Corner House; a first visit to Lord's to watch Jim take eight wickets for Surrey in the victory over Middlesex; and regular outings to the cinema.

There was a spate of correspondence after Jim's departure on the Commonwealth tour of India. Jim was one of the English representatives in the multi-national team visiting the sub-continent under the leadership of Les Ames. 'He started to write to me from Port Said and then continued for every day afterwards,' says Lilly. The remembrances, jokingly alluded to by Lilly, of Jim's other attachments were dismissed as idle fancies. Marriage, if not strictly proposed, was now a declaration of intent. The suitor gave confirmation when he carried home a cargo of treasures from the East.

On his return from India, Jim made two rail journeys from his digs at Forest Hill to Lilly's home at Hampstead. 'One day Jim arrived with a big holdall containing his presents.' There were, in accord with his character, practical as well as romantic offerings. Inside the bag was a profusion of towels and linen (for her bottom drawer) and saris for personal adornment. On the next day he was on Lilly's doorstep again, carrying another bulging case. It contained an assortment of handbags and items of exquisite embroidery.

The siege indicated an unmistakable ardour. Lilly hoisted her hands in amazement, quite overcome with the blessings of the cricket traveller. At length, Jim smiled at her disbelief and explained: 'Well, I wasn't sure you would say "Yes".'

Sir Alec Bedser, with due grievance, has lamented the accent on unproven youth in Australia in 1950–51 and the decision to leave more experienced campaigners kicking their heels at home. Bedser once more shouldered a considerable burden in Australia. Rarely, if ever, has one bowler taken 30 wickets (at a cost of just over 16 runs each) and still finished on the losing side. Jim Laker, now approaching his peak as a bowler, was one of those who failed to gain recognition for the tour. His omission astounded many people, including Bedser and Trevor Bailey, another contemporary. Bailey attributes the bloomer to a pre-war mindset. 'It happened before anyone in England realised that off-spinners could take wickets in Australia.' That it was a folly was shown by the feat of Hugh Tayfield, the South African off-spinner, in the 1952–53 series. Tayfield took 30 wickets as Jack Cheetham's tourists unexpectedly tied the Tests with Australia. Laker, in his own appraisal of the situation, said that the legend that Australia was 'death to off-spinners' had not been substantiated. 'As we in England had rarely sent a decent off-spinner to Australia, anyway, it seemed to me that the policy came first and the legend followed after, like Mary's little lamb.'

Another fear nagging the irresolute selectors was that Laker might prove vulnerable on the faster Australian wickets. Arthur McIntyre, deputy to Godfrey Evans as wicket-keeper on the tour, presents this as a conjecture. But he does echo the general feeling in the team that it was a strange decision to leave out his Surrey colleague.

The England selectors, as Trevor Bailey again indicates, then pursued the traditional emphasis on leg-spin, with the slow left-arm bowler employed in the usual stock bowling capacity in Australia. Eric Hollies and Doug Wright, both in the MCC party, were among the last of the outstanding leg-spinners to command attention in the post-war period. In the 1950 series against the West Indies, England's spinners were Hollies and Roley Jenkins, another leg-spinner, at Nottingham; and Wright and Malcolm Hilton, the slow left-hander, at The Oval.

In Australia, Hollies proved to be ineffectual. Even more disappointing was the contrasting form of the enigmatic Wright. The Kent bowler was a finely tuned artist, a brilliant soloist when his extravagant spin was matched by unwavering length. Wright, on his last tour of Australia, veered from the masterly to the downright bad. His severest critics considered his effectiveness to be intermittent; but he was also in the opinion of many a magnificent and unlucky bowler.

As with Jim Laker, the pride of another Yorkshireman, Johnny Wardle, was bruised by his non-selection in 1950–51. Wardle was second only to Roy Tattersall in the 1950 season, with 174 wickets, and he also scored over 700 runs. The role of England's slow left-arm bowler was greatly coveted by Wardle, but it went instead to Bob Berry, the Lancastrian. Gubby Allen was a dissenting voice among the selectors. In retrospect, he considered the choice of Berry misguided. The distress of Wardle was such that he seriously considered leaving first-class cricket. He was tempted to accept a lucrative offer from a league club. The counsel of friends persuaded him to change his mind, and a Wakefield company came to his aid, providing him with a winter sales job to ease his fretful spirits.

The whims of the selectors drew a third Yorkshireman into the debate. At the heart of Laker's displeasure was the selection of the 19-year-old Brian Close. Subsequent events were to show that the prodigiously talented Close was betrayed by his immaturity. Anyone who saw him in his formative years with Yorkshire would point to his undoubted class. Laker, understandably, described the choice of this off-spinning rival as a 'wild hunch'. Close was given priority because of his all-round strengths, but the shuddering violence of his stroke-play was not then governed by the tenacity which won applause in later years.

Close belied his gifts on both counts in Australia. He scored only one run and took just one wicket in his only Test at Melbourne. His tally in all first-class matches was 231 runs (average 23.10) and 13 wickets at a cost of 36.53 runs each. Roy Tattersall, Laker's chief challenger in England in 1950, was flown out as a replacement. His 33 wickets, including four in the fourth Test at Adelaide, at just over 17 runs each, placed him at the top of the MCC bowling averages. Laker might have had less cause for complaint had Tattersall, then at the height of his form, been preferred to Close in the original selection.

Laker never dispelled his vexation at his exclusion from a coveted tour. 'I was, to put it mildly, disappointed not to be selected. Like a young man who has been jilted, I jumped at the next thing that came along, which turned out to be the Commonwealth tour of India.' His resentment at missing the Australian tour was compounded in a conversation with Les Ames, the captain of the Commonwealth team, on the voyage out to India.

He had earlier been intrigued by a rumour circulating on the selection of Brian Close. A protracted discussion by the selectors, so he had heard, had dwelt upon various names as off-spinning candidates. 'Someone, without much conviction, brought up the subject of Close.' It was not a serious suggestion and was about to be withdrawn until Freddie Brown, the England captain, jauntily pronounced in favour of the Yorkshireman. 'Close is just the man for me: I want him,' declared Brown.

Laker, during the stop at Port Said, sought the reaction of Les Ames to the story. Ames, as a member of the MCC selection panel, did not attempt to dispute its authenticity. He told Laker: 'Your story is quite true – but you shouldn't know about it.' Rubbing salt into Laker's wound was the success of another off-spinner, Jack Iverson, who was England's *bête noire* in Australia. He was a giant of a man, a six-footer weighing over sixteen stone. He took 21 wickets in the series at an average of 15.23. The delicacies of Iverson's spin contrasted with his physique. *Wisden* reported: 'He doubled back his middle finger under the ball, imparting sharp spin, and maintained a precise length. His flight and pace were not such to allow batsmen to leap out to him easily. His direction, at the leg stump, and carefully planned field settings permitted few liberties.'

Life always offers its compensations, even when it seems grimly set against ambition. For Laker, in his crisis, there was the succour of an invitation from George Duckworth to travel to India with the multi-talented Commonwealth team. It was considered superior to the MCC combination in Australia. Laker was privileged to unfurl his talents as a member of a superb spinning quartet. His companions were the West Indian Sonny Ramadhin, fresh from his exploits in England, and two Australians, George Tribe and Bruce Dooland.

Frank Worrell, thrust into the captaincy as deputy for the injured Les Ames, was the guiding star in a campaign without defeat. Worrell, the exemplar among the batting stylists from the Caribbean, hit 1,900 runs, including five centuries, on the tour. In addition, filling the gap left by the absence of another injured tourist, Les Jackson, he took the most wickets, 18, in the series of unofficial Tests. Preceding Worrell in the batting order were Harold Gimblett, Laurie Fishlock and George Emmett, three of the finest stroke-players in England. As an indication of the team's strength, six players – Gimblett, Fishlock, Emmett, Worrell and the Lancastrians Jack Ikin and Ken Grieves – all exceeded 1,000 runs in first-class games. Ikin, Laker's room-mate on the tour, had a spectacular Test aggregate of 625 runs in nine innings at an average of 89.28.

In Patiala, the home of the Sikhs in northern India, the tourists played on a plumb wicket rendered flatter by the power of an elephant, shackled between the shafts of the heavy roller. George Tribe, with his left-arm wrist spin, had to assert his considerable authority to impress a particularly resistant umpire. Each time, as he rapped various batsmen on the pads, Tribe was greeted by a bland Eastern smile and a shake of the head. The last batsman, the Maharajah of Patiala, endowed with his VIP status, seemed likely to bat on as long as he wished. A torrent of appeals against him for lbw, delivered with increasing vehemence, were spurned by the umpire. Nearing the end of his tether, Tribe shook the official roughly by the shoulders and cried out: 'Don't be such a bloody fool, have another look.'

The umpire, gazing first pleadingly at the batsman, then at the indignant bowler, took a deep breath and said: 'My word, Mr Tribe, you are right.' With a gesture of apology, he turned again to the beaming maharajah. His finger trembled as it moved, barely perceptibly, upwards. 'I'm sorry, Sir, but you are out,' he said.

Laker described an equally bizarre experience on another beautiful wicket at Poona. As he prepared to bowl, he was stopped in his tracks by the visitation of a huge rat, the size of a terrier dog. 'The rat had just reached a good-length spot when the drama reached its crisis. A big kite hawk swooped down, picked up the rat in its talons and took off again with its dinner.' The sudden descents of the scavenging birds were regarded as commonplace events among the cricket locals. Nonetheless, Laker, more used to the pigeon pursuits at The Oval, was so affected that his next ball bounced twice before being struck to the boundary.

The Commonwealth eleven drew three of the 'Tests', at New Delhi, Calcutta and Madras, and won by ten wickets at

Bombay and then, conclusively, by 74 runs at Kanpur to resolve the series. Illness curtailed Laker's tour but he still headed both the Test and the first-class bowling averages. He bowled 415 overs in India, including a marathon assignment in the torrid heat of Bombay in December. Fred Ridgway, the Kent bowler, took four wickets for 16 runs as India collapsed to 82 all out in their first innings. Six of the batsmen failed to score and only a ninth-wicket stand of 42 runs between Merchant and Nayudu averted a complete rout. The Commonwealth established a seemingly unassailable lead of 345 runs before toiling against the resurgent Indians.

'The fourth day,' recalled Laker, 'was like any other in Bombay, with soaring temperatures, but I never dreamt what was in store for me.' The wicket had eased after the liveliness of the first morning. India now paraded the true menace of their imposing batting line-up. The first eight places were occupied by Merchant, Mushtaq Ali, Umrigar, Hazare, Phadkar, Adhikari, Mankad and Manjrekar. Umrigar and Hazare both hit centuries in a magnificent rally. Their third-wicket stand yielded 225 runs.

Laker bowled almost throughout the day in the fiercest possible examination of his accuracy and stamina. His analysis in the Indian second innings read: 65 overs, 34 maidens, 88 runs, 5 wickets. The economy of his bowling was remarkable in conditions weighted heavily in favour of the batsmen. Laker always insisted that the gruelling demands of his Bombay achievement overshadowed all others. 'I do not believe, taking everything into consideration, that I ever bowled better.'

At dinner on the following day, Laker's endurance and success produced lavish compliments. Back home in England he was hailed as a hero. The headline in a London evening news-paper drew attention to his accomplishment. The words 'Tribute to Laker' were construed as a valediction by the intensely anxious Lilly. She knew about the sinus problem which was to hasten Laker's return home. Her worries were allayed when she scanned the newspaper report to learn that the tribute related to cricket deeds. It was a matter for joy, not sorrow.

The reassurance was sealed when Laker arrived home on Christmas Eve, his luggage laden with gifts for Lilly. The talk soon turned to their impending marriage. Jim, ever the pragmatic Yorkshireman, overruled Lilly when she suggested a wedding in September. He had gauged the financial advantages of an earlier date. 'We have to get married now because of the income tax,' he said. They were married at Kensington Register Office on 27 March 1951.

The honeymoon was spent in rain-swept Bournemouth. Jim, the shy bridegroom, went to immoderate lengths to avoid the congratulations of the other guests at the hotel. 'When we changed at the hotel,' recalls Lilly, 'confetti fell out of our clothing and Jim spent ages picking up every piece from the floor.' There was also his order that they should walk down separately to dinner. In the restaurant one man remarked: 'Isn't it awful – all these newly married couples in the place.' Jim inclined his head in agreement. His attempt at concealment did seem rather futile with all the London newspapers on sale at the hotel, each prominently featuring wedding photographs of the celebrated cricketer and his wife.

Jim was guarded with strangers; the undemonstrative man almost literally cowered in effusive company. This could have accounted for his desire for anonymity in the episode at Bournemouth. The characteristic of timidity has been passed down to at least one of his children and, in turn, a grandson with talent as a cricketer. Each of the generations, hugely confident and totally involved on sporting fields, could not and cannot abide fuss. The policy adopted by the family on one important tennis occasion, involving one of the daughters, was to hide in the bushes until play was over. For Jim, watched by paying audiences at The Oval, the distractions were not so easily negotiated. His defence was to shield his emotions, which led some people to accuse him of indifference.

In another, extended, honeymoon with Lilly, he was able to cast off his inhibitions in an oasis of friendly people. In the winter of 1951–52 he took up an appointment in New Zealand, as the Auckland player-coach. The visit, extending over five months, brought him into contact again with his wartime companion, Bert Sutcliffe. It also yielded other new and lasting friendships and forged an affectionate bond with the land of the Kiwis. Laker later recalled that in his playing days there was a strong patriotic pact between England and New Zealand. 'The heroism of the New Zealand troops during the war was still very much in people's minds when we set sail for Wellington on the SS *Rangitata* in September 1951.'

Travelling with the Lakers was a contingent of middle-aged Kiwis homeward-bound after their holidays in England. 'For many of them,' said Laker, 'it was the realisation of a lifetime's dream for which they had saved diligently.' The welcome for Jim and Lilly in New Zealand had an exceptional warmth. It expressed the pride of kinship with them and other travellers from England's shores.

Their hosts in Auckland were the parents of Don Taylor, the Warwickshire and New Zealand player and another of Laker's wartime allies. Lilly remembers that Taylor's mother – 'a very domesticated lady' – would not allow her to assist with the household chores. 'We paid her £4 a week for breakfast and dinner. She also cleaned our room and did the washing.' Idleness would not have suited the disposition of the industrious Lilly. She obtained a job in an insurance office, arranging her hours of work so as to be able to join Jim at the cricket ground in the late afternoon. The consequence was that the newly married pair had saved a tidy amount of money before their departure for home.

The hospitality in Auckland very nearly persuaded the Lakers to emigrate to New Zealand. The Auckland Cricket Association were prepared to re-engage Jim in the following winter. It was a tempting proposition, reluctantly declined because Jim felt that his cricket future lay in England.

Laker was just one of a notable assembly of Auckland coaches. Four of his predecessors, three of them Test cricketers, came from Sussex. They included the Edwardian all-rounder, Albert Relf, and Ted Bowley, whose renowned back-foot play was mirrored in a generation of Auckland batsmen. Another was the England slow left-arm bowler, Jim Langridge, who suffered from tuberculosis as a boy and, after a renewal of the illness, went out to recuperate as well as coach in New Zealand. A more vigorous Sussex personality was Bert Wensley. His hosts recalled Wensley 'with his broad shoulders and massive arm, toiling away through a scorching Auckland day, slaving to get some response out of the heartbreaking Eden Park wicket.'

Laker was another fine cricketing ambassador. He is remembered in Auckland for his bright, cheery outlook and impeccable conduct on and off the field. He was also assigned as coach to the university team, one of the weakest in the league but consisting of promising youngsters. There was excited gossip at his first net practice when the ball sang like an angry wasp as he delivered it.

Contemporaries in Auckland bear witness to Laker's scrupulously fair advice and the confidence engendered by the manner in which it was expressed. 'No one who sought Laker's help went away disappointed,' commented one observer. After one Plunket Shield match at Wellington, the Yorkshireman went into overtime to coach some of the home side's colts. 'This was only one of the many gratuitous acts that have made him so popular,' related another correspondent. The policy of even-handed attention won Laker commendation at school and provincial levels. His quiet enthusiasm brought the best out of his pupils. One future star emerging from his academy was John Sparling, who later captained Auckland and was, thought Laker, too sparingly used as an off-spinner on the tour of England in 1958.

Laker also sought to instil a strong code of discipline. He was appalled by the standards of dress in one junior-grade match at Eden Park. One Auckland selector said: 'There is no excuse even for juniors not wearing the right clothes when they play at the headquarters.' The disaffection was prompted by an 'extraordinary display of colour'. On the field the boys were a disparate bunch in multi-coloured sweaters, floral and other brightly coloured shirts, grey trousers, and even a felt hat. They were, in their motley garb, ahead of their time although Laker's admonishment could easily bear repetition today. Then he pondered on the indignant reaction at Lord's had the members there been subjected to such an exhibition. 'After all, it is an honour for boys to play at Eden Park. You might as well go in with half a bat as wear such costumes.'

Laker, as a member of the Auckland team, was undeniably the spearhead of the attack in his winter campaign. He took 24 wickets in four matches at a cost of 15.79 runs each in the Plunket Shield competition. It gained his selection as the Bowler of the Year in the *New Zealand Cricket Almanack*. Laker renewed his rivalry with Bert Sutcliffe in a low-scoring match against the reigning champions, Otago, at Dunedin. His bowling partner in the six-wicket victory was another Test off-spinner, Geoffrey Rabone, who had toured England in 1949. Rabone, newly transferred from Wellington, linked with Laker to form Auckland's

THE ENGLISH PROFESSIONAL J. LAKER, BOWLING FOR UNIVERSITY LAST WEEK MADE AN OTHERWISE WEAK ATTACK LOOK A DISTINCTIVE THREAT TO SENIOR BATSMEN.
(LAKER TOOK 15 WKTS. FOR 35 RUNS INCLUDING 6 WKTS. FOR 12 RUNS IN THE 2ND. INNINGS.) —NEWS—

"BY JOVE SIR, THIS LAKER CHAP'S A GREAT ASSET TO OUR BOYS DURING EXAM. TIME, WHAT!"
"AUCKLAND STAR"   SATURDAY 10th. NOV. 1951

Ellen, the indomitable Yorkshire matriarch, and her adored son, Jim, then aged two.

In his mother's class at Calverley Church School, circa 1924: Jim (seated, front row, fourth right); Susie (standing, second row, second right); and Ellen (standing, far left

m and his sister, Susie, the inseparable
ompanions.

The chorister at St Barnabas' Church,
Heaton, Bradford.

alts High School soccer group, including Jim (front row, second right) and lifelong friends
ill Burgess and Fred Robinson. Headmaster George Parkin is standing on the left.

School cricket XI, 193[?]

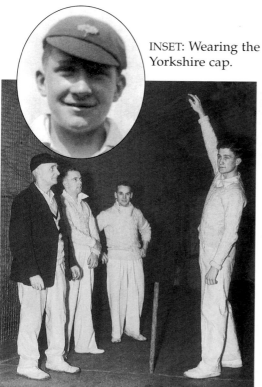

INSET: Wearing the Yorkshire cap.

At the Headingley nets with Emmott Robinson, the Yorkshire coach, and Johnny Lawrence (third left), later a Somerset player.

Alf Burgoyne, the Saltaire secretary and Jim's first cricket mentor at Roberts Par[k]

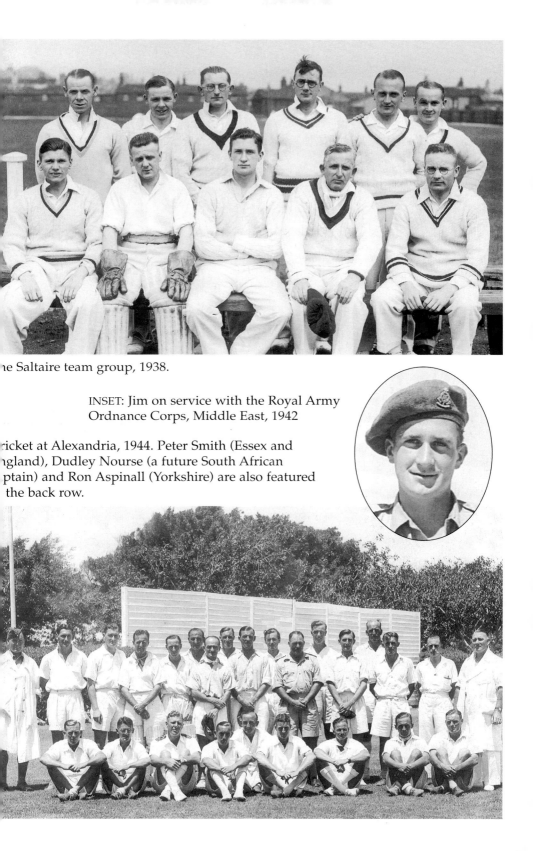

he Saltaire team group, 1938.

INSET: Jim on service with the Royal Army
Ordnance Corps, Middle East, 1942

ricket at Alexandria, 1944. Peter Smith (Essex and
ngland), Dudley Nourse (a future South African
ptain) and Ron Aspinall (Yorkshire) are also featured
the back row.

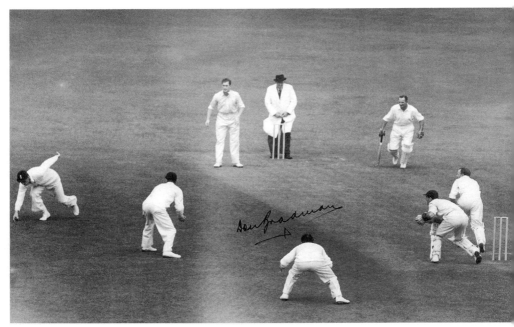

Bowling to Don Bradman in the first Test against Australia at Nottingham, 1948.

The England team (back row, left to right): Young, Simpson, Laker, Bedser, Hardstaff Compton, Evans. Front row: Hutton, Barnett, Yardley (captain), Edrich, Washbrook.

ark Avenue, Bradford, the scene of the 8 for 2 bowling feat in 1950.

Jew Zealand, 1951-2: Jim (standing, third left) and New Zealand Test player Geoff
abone (standing, second right) were key bowling partners for Auckland in the
'lunket Shield competition.

Lilly, his bride from Vienna.

Lilly and Jim on their wedding day in March 1951.

At home in Putney with their daughters, Fiona and Angela.

strongest bowling force for many years. They transformed an otherwise moderate attack into one of the best in the competition.

Bert Sutcliffe was top scorer with 88 for Otago in the match at Dunedin. His runs bolstered the meagre first innings total of 161. The enthralling duel between the two Test players and provincial coaches was described by 'Cantab' in the *Auckland Herald*: 'Laker and Sutcliffe, the wartime colleagues, had a great battle. Sutcliffe was palpably troubled by the spin, more powerful than I have seen at Carisbrook for the past 30 years. On three or four occasions, Laker missed Sutcliffe's wicket by the proverbial coat of paint. His splendid bowling was quickly appreciated by the spectators and there were frequent rounds of applause.'

Once again economy was the key to Laker's dominance. His five wickets in the Otago first innings cost him 44 runs in 25 overs. The second-innings return of three wickets for 48 runs was just as telling. He bowled 43 overs, 22 of them maidens. On his return to Eden Park he shone again with five wickets in the heavy defeat inflicted upon Central Districts. There was also a match aggregate of ten wickets in the victory over Wellington, in which he bowled 61 overs at a cost of 121 runs. 'Even on unresponsive wickets,' reported the *New Zealand Cricket Almanack*, 'his accuracy and control of spin were decided assets.'

The idyll in New Zealand finished all too soon. Jim and Lilly had many cherished memories, not least the delights of a holiday in Rotorua. 'We left Auckland in great style in a Teal Flying Boat and hours later made an equally memorable splash down in Rose Bay, Sydney,' recalled Jim. The journey home from Australia, in company with Ray Lindwall and his wife, was completed on the SS *Stratheden* via the Suez Canal. Jim later commented: 'Our round-the-world trip was surely one which must be the envy of all our modern jet-styled and highly paid international cricketers.'

Laker maintained his involvement with New Zealand cricket back home in England. In 1951 the London–NZ Cricket Club, a touring eleven, was formed. It consisted of former New

Zealanders, both permanent and temporary residents in England, as well as visiting players. The wide-ranging schedule included matches against the Cross Arrows at Lord's; the Surrey Club and Ground at The Oval; pre-season games at Cambridge University; and, in the lower echelons, games against club and village teams. For matches against stronger opposition, the LNZCC were reinforced by players of the calibre of John Reid, Bill Merritt and Tom Pritchard. Laker could not play because of county and other commitments, but he regularly attended and spoke at the annual dinners of the club. It was the means by which he renewed old acquaintances and was also an acknowledgement of the comradeship he had enjoyed over the years.

Jim Laker made just one more trip to New Zealand, in March 1983, to take part in ceremonies marking the centenary of cricket in Auckland. Joining him as a speaker at the annual Auckland Cricketer of the Year dinner was his former England colleague, Frank Tyson. Laker's chirpy humour illuminated this last meeting with old friends. The passing years had not shrouded his memories of a happy time. It was Jim at his anecdotal best, delving into his repertoire of jokes, and effortlessly the master of the revels.

More than thirty years earlier, one singular attribute had aroused especial comment in Auckland. It was his prodigious memory for names and faces and for placing people in context. His hosts had admired the unswerving democracy in his dealings with everyone, from parents of pupils, friends, and others more grand in the cricket establishment. Then, and now on his last visit, the modest, engaging man did not forget those who had opened their doors and royally entertained him.

7

ALL THE RAGE AT THE OVAL

'They were mortals who *did* command success; merely
deserving it did not interest them.'

Brian Chapman

Everyone who watched them in a very special time and place
exulted in the bright constellation of talents. It was a decade of
plenty for one of the finest attacks in the history of the game.
The master plan in the 1950s was to forge a winning advantage
by the end of the first day.

While the Surrey bowlers flourished in their awesome
conquests, the supporting batsmen lingered at their peril. The
consequences of tardiness at the crease almost inevitably
meant a brusque reprimand from the audacious ringmaster,
Stuart Surridge. Dave Fletcher, one of the sacrificial batting
subordinates under Surridge's leadership at The Oval, says:
'The glamour boys were the bowlers; we just went out there to
put up a score. Stewie told us: "Get out there, get some runs, or
let someone else have a go."'

In one match against Nottinghamshire at Trent Bridge, quick
runs were needed. Surridge sent out an order for more haste by
a dilatory batsman. It was unwisely ignored; the innings
proceeded at a snail's pace. Surridge was seething when the
players returned to the pavilion. 'Do that again and you're
finished with Surrey,' he told the offender. The attitude was in
keeping with Surridge's unquenchable desire to win. He
conducted his campaigns with one guiding principle. 'Go all

83

out for a win from the start. When victory has become impossible, but only then, play just as hard for a draw.' The bold
warrior laid down the gauntlet with unexpected declarations
to win matches against all the odds.

At the outset of his captaincy in 1952, Surridge had told an
astonished Surrey committee that his side was embarking on a
run of five successive championships. He was as good as his
word. After Surridge's retirement, Peter May maintained the
challenge to bring two more championships to The Oval.
Surridge and May, in his turn, always acknowledged their
indebtedness to a truly great team.

In one conversation, Surridge said: 'At the start my team
was a little *afraid* to win the championship. I had to give them
a few kicks up the backside. But once they'd won it, they didn't
want to lose it.' The sense of adventure, so unerringly dictated
by Surridge, caused consternation among the members as well
as the opponents. More often than not matches were
completed before the end of the second day. 'We would pack
our clubs and drive over to Wimbledon Park for a round of
golf,' recalls Dave Fletcher. 'Our members got rather peeved
because we were winning so quickly.'

The positive match-winning strategy earned the praise of
Neville Cardus. 'No county captain is more alive than Surridge
to a promising situation, none so swift as he to smell the moment
to strike home. A. C. MacLaren used to say that in every match
there comes a time when the tide turns, when victory is waiting
to be wooed and won. The great captain is he who does not drift
but is constantly sniffing the way of the wind.'

Alec Bedser, as one of the illustrious bowling ensemble, was
not alone in his bewilderment at Surridge's bravado. 'Stewie
had a will of his own and wanted things done his way. But
whatever our reservations, we always backed him.' Norman
Preston, the editor of *Wisden*, described the transformation of
Surrey under Surridge as little short of miraculous. 'His infec-
tious enthusiasm inspired the whole team.' Preston's
concluding words could serve as an epitaph for a great captain:
'Cricket was never dull under Surridge.'

One valuable maxim which Surridge communicated was the futility of coming second in any contest. It was a lesson which he had committed to memory. His own adviser had been Brian Sellers, the Yorkshire captain in their great years and briefly at the helm after the war. Surrey had held the initiative in one match against Yorkshire, only to lose in the end. Surridge, in some despair at an unexpected reverse, spoke to Sellers after stumps. 'You've won a match we had sewn up,' he said. Sellers replied: 'Well, mi'lad, there's no ruddy use in being second.' There was a certain irony in that Surridge took the adventurous route set by this inspirational leader. It was the basis of his conquests in his momentous era.

Brian Chapman said that Surridge, like Sellers before him, led from the front. 'He bestowed an aura of invincibility on ten better players who probably would not have scaled the heights so consistently without him. They were mortals who *did* command success; merely deserving it did not interest them.'

Arthur McIntyre has dwelt upon the percipient trait in Surridge's buccaneering leadership. 'No one read a game, or a given situation, as well as Stuart.' Surridge was never a slave to tactics. He disliked compiling safety-first scores. 'With 500 on the board, I wouldn't have known when to declare,' he said. He obeyed the old adage that you have to bowl out your opponents twice to win.

Doug Insole, as one of Surrey's opposing captains, says Surridge was unfailingly assured in his own battle plans. 'Stewie was a great character and some of his declarations were a little bizarre. He wanted to win matches in one day if possible. But he did have the standby of a second innings if matters went awry.'

One example of Surridge's whirlwind captaincy belongs to the championship year of 1953 when Surrey beat Warwickshire by an innings in a day. It had happened only once before in a first-class match at The Oval in 1857. There was a standing ovation by members to reward the team on emulating the feat. Warwickshire were dismissed for 45 and 52. Bedser took twelve wickets, including eight for 18 in the first innings, and

Laker performed the hat-trick. Twenty-nine wickets fell in the day.

Surrey once again triumphed through the brilliance of their fielding. This was demonstrated by the fact that not one of the visiting batsmen was bowled. Warwickshire, in their second innings, were all out in seventy minutes, five minutes fewer than in their first innings. Laker did not bowl in the first innings but his mastery was unfurled in the second innings. 'He was spinning the ball, and one which almost stood upright was a horror to behold,' reported one observer. Andrew Sandham, then the Surrey coach, said he had seldom seen such a pitch at The Oval. 'Certainly, I would not like to have batted on it.'

An even more daunting occasion at The Oval was the match against Worcestershire in 1954. The visitors, sent in to bat, were overwhelmed by the spin of Laker and Lock. They lost their last seven first innings wickets for five runs and collapsed to 25 all out. Lock took five wickets for two runs in 5.3 overs and Laker two for five in eight overs.

Disbelief was the reaction of the Surrey players to another seemingly outrageous throw of the dice by Surridge. Laker reflected on this and other gambles which so often turned out to be acts of genius. On this occasion, there was near panic in the Surrey dressing-room when Surridge made his declaration at 92 for three wickets. Peter May, to his astonishment, was called in, having scored 31. Those waiting to bat now had furiously to ready themselves to field. Alec Bedser echoed the general view of his team-mates. 'Skipper,' he said, 'you've got to remember that somebody else can play this game as well as us.' Surridge was dismissive in his reply. 'Nonsense. We've got enough.'

Surridge had, in fact, sagely taken precautions. He had checked and heeded the warning of a bad weather forecast. The lowering clouds at The Oval hastened his declaration. He speedily assessed that batting would become an untenable proposition. The match was only just completed before the onset of torrential rain. It lasted just over five hours and was concluded by 12.30 on the second day. Worcestershire were dismissed for 40 in their second innings. Surrey batted for only 24 overs, but still won by an innings. The aggregate of 157 runs was the lowest for any completed championship match.

Peter Richardson, one of the baffled Worcestershire batsmen, recalled the farcical conditions at The Oval. 'We shouldn't have been playing on that wicket. Everyone else was in disarray, edging, or gloving catches; but we never missed the middle of Peter May's bat.' Of his own dismissal, he says that he attempted to raise his bat out of harm's way. The ball kept climbing and it rose to such an extent that he was still caught at the wicket off Laker.

Passions, among the disparate personalities, often ran high at The Oval. It was an era of unremitting endeavour when every match carried importance as a championship stepping stone. It was patently not an environment for the faint-hearted. The less resolute of beginners cowered in fright on their introduction to the team. 'The Surrey team then was very loud, there was quite a lot of swearing,' recalls Micky Stewart. Stewart was often asked whether he enjoyed playing in such a highly charged atmosphere. 'It's lovely,' he replied. 'We win all the time.'

Jim Laker moved phlegmatically and unruffled in this volatile company. Arthur Phebey, as one close friend and a Kent opponent, remembers the barrage of expletives ringing in his ears. 'The Surrey chaps helped in their successes by geeing each other up. Bernie Constable would come strutting across the field from cover and call out: "Stewie, get your effing field right." ' Phebey would listen to the indignation of Eric Bedser and the groan of his complaint: 'He's got my brother on the wrong end again.' By his shoulder he would hear Surridge, in his customary short-leg position, pouring scorn on Tony Lock. 'Bowl bloody straight, Lockie, or Eric will be on.'

Laker was never drawn into this verbal jousting. 'It wasn't Jim's way; he wanted to concentrate on his bowling,' says Phebey. Just occasionally, as Peter Loader, one of the warring factions, ventured one cross word too many, Laker would express his vexation. 'Shut it,' would be the whispered command. Loader stresses that the blistering words – in the current phrase, 'industrial language' – did not mean they disliked one another. 'I always wanted to go one better than Alec and obtain a superior analysis. But our individual rivalries were in the interests of the team. This was the way we played and it worked.' Arthur McIntyre agrees: 'We had our rows on the field but afterwards they were completely forgotten.'

Laker was an undemonstrative man and so he occasionally appeared uninvolved. This probably fuelled a resentment among his more boisterous colleagues. He never rushed impulsively into situations. There was often the danger of an upset if others were less than co-operative. In true Yorkshire tradition, he would stand his ground very carefully before deciding on his course of action. His innate wariness led to his being categorised as a loner in The Oval camp.

On ability, he was of course welcomed as a worthy recruit. But his rapid promotion to the first team did, as he himself admitted, usurp the off-spinning role earmarked for Eric Bedser, who had come up through the Surrey ranks. There was undoubtedly a sense of unease which did little to quell his inherent shyness. There was also the ever-present risk that he would be charged with frailties if he failed to measure up to his tasks.

Laker was fortunate to discover a kindred spirit in Stuart Surridge. One of Surridge's best attributes as a captain was his man-management and his ability to apportion responsibilities and keep his team happy. Raman Subba Row was one of the younger school of Surrey cricketers at the time. He remembers Surridge as 'earthy' by nature and able to recognise the difference in people. 'Jim would not have been a happy performer with the kind of treatment meted out by Stuart to Tony Lock.' Surridge had great respect for Laker's judgement and was prepared to defer to his bowler because he knew that he was invariably right.

This is not to say that Surridge was prey to favouritism. Alf

Gover, then working as a journalist, cites the instance when the Surrey captain had to assert his authority. Laker was disciplined and relegated to twelfth man in a match at Lord's. The 'on the record' statement, relayed to Gover, was that Laker was injured. It was, as Gover knew, a public excuse designed to dilute the punishment. Surridge had taken the extreme step of demoting a great bowler to make it clear that he required greater effort. Laker, not unnaturally, felt humiliated. 'Jim was furious at the slight,' said Gover. It was a rare example of conflict, or breach of faith, between the two men. Generally, Surridge was sympathetic because, as others have said, Laker had the pride of an artist. He knew instinctively, more than anyone else, when he was not bowling well.

Laker did have to overcome his disappointment in the episode at Lord's. As an instance of Laker's control of his emotions in another context, David Sheppard cites the hostility on the field on his Test recall against the West Indies at Headingley in 1957. 'We had a very formidable and aggressive bowling side. Trueman bowled a series of bouncers at Kanhai and generally adopted his most aggressive stance. At the other end Loader gave Frank Worrell a mouthful of abuse. First change, Tony Lock came on and screamed one appeal after another. When Jim Laker came on, all composure and imperturbability, I couldn't resist going up to him at the end of the over and saying: "Jim, you really haven't got the right idea about this Test cricket!" '

Pat McKelvey, who was on the Surrey staff in the 1950s, remembers that Laker, without being aloof, generally kept his own counsel. 'Jim was capable of keeping himself to himself most of the day, especially if he didn't approve of something.' The dry wit would surface with a precision which belied his apparent indifference to the explosive exchanges of his colleagues. 'At the appropriate moment,' says McKelvey, 'Jim would utter his short observation upon whatever had been going on. The remark, disguised as a throwaway, would be succinct, caustic, very funny, and *always* bang on the nail.'

There are many instances of Laker's droll humour. One of

89

them was addressed to McKelvey after a demoralising experience at the hands of a great Surrey batsman. McKelvey, as a
slow left-arm bowler, was opposed to Peter May in a pre-
season practice match at The Oval. It was a depressing, cold
April day. There was continuous fine rain and the ball had
been reduced to the texture of a bar of wet soap. 'PBH was 32
not out and ready to have a fierce crack before retiring. I actually managed four or five tidy overs as the great man added a
dozen runs.' He began his next over with May on 46. 'The first
three deliveries were pushed through on a good length, just
outside the line of the off-stump. Peter played each of them
carefully into the covers.' His next ball was just as deliberately
pitched. May drove it back for a huge six into the members'
enclosure. 'Something different is needed,' McKelvey told
himself. His response was to try the arm ball. 'Holding the
seam up, I bowled a much quicker inswinger.' At first, May
appeared to have misjudged it, but then, adjusting his feet, he
hoisted the ball once again into the seats at the front of the
pavilion.

McKelvey next sought to deceive his rival in flight. He held
his sixth ball back, floating it up slower and with more width
outside the off-stump. 'He'll slice this to extra cover, I thought;
but there was another late adjustment of the feet and the ball
clattered on to the pavilion seats for another straight six.' Peter
smilingly took his leave. 'Thank you very much, gentlemen,'
he said, as he marched off to the dressing-room.

Despite the onslaught, McKelvey still felt that he had
bowled a tidy over. At mid-on, Laker thrust his hands into his
pockets and yawned. 'What do you do in a situation like that,
Jim?' McKelvey asked. 'It was a perfectly good over. What
could I have done to prevent that happening?' Laker gravely
considered the problem for a moment, gave the puzzled
bowler a sympathetic look, and then offered his advice. 'You
want to bowl in a bigger field,' he said.

Michael Barton, the former Oxford blue and Norfolk cricketer,
had presented appealing credentials when he succeeded Errol

Holmes as Surrey captain in 1949. Barton had an impressive start to his reign at The Oval, scoring three centuries in his first four games. Laker, as did all his colleagues, regarded him with the utmost affection. 'Mike was quiet, reserved and had a subtle sense of humour,' he said. 'His discipline was well organised and conducted in a manner which never offended.'

Barton, in his turn, confirms their harmony. Infringements, if they occurred, were always moderately negotiated. 'Jim was never openly disobedient but it would upset him if he felt he was being wrongly criticised. His sensitivity went together with his intelligence. He might lose heart quicker than some others.' He considers that Laker did require careful management to counter the bouts of depression. These were usually a reaction to futile bowling forays; a concern that he had fallen below his own exacting standards; and the glumness of a tired man at the end of a long day in the field. The bluff Yorkshireman was proud of his acumen as a bowler. 'Jim was a clever man, very definite in his ideas, who thought more about his cricket than most other players,' says Barton.

The Surrey captain was subject to charges that he made his bowling changes by rote. Laker wrote: 'He ruled by the clock, and I knew that if we lost the toss I should come on to bowl at 12.10 and remain at one end until 1 p.m. when the quicker bowlers would return until lunch.' The one solitary day of confusion, said Laker, occurred when Barton forgot to take his wrist-watch on the field and the pavilion clock stopped at 11.45.

The jests and banter, presumably respectfully concealed from him at the time, now elicit a rueful smile. 'Jim, in later years, used to pull my leg by saying that I changed the bowling by the time of the day. It was true in a way. But I had to be aware of the importance of keeping bowlers fresh for six hours in the field, especially when faced by strong batting sides like Middlesex on good batting wickets.' Nonetheless, despite the sallies on time shares, Barton was adroit enough as captain to lead Surrey to their first championship honour since 1914, when in 1950 they shared the title with Lancashire.

Stuart Surridge was not – it now seems inconceivable – an automatic choice as Barton's successor. A product of the Old Emmanuel School at Wandsworth, his appointment was a departure from the norm of Surrey captains arriving via Oxford or Cambridge. The Oval diehards were initially on the look-out for another blue. It is said that W. T. Cook, who captained the second eleven, urged the case for Surridge so persuasively that ultimately the choice was unanimous.

Surridge did have one distinct advantage: his association, while still at school, with the Surrey Young Players. Alongside him were the Bedser twins, Arthur McIntyre, Geoff Whittaker and Bernie Constable. Even then, he was demonstrably 'one of the boys'; and this was given further proof when, as captain, he eliminated the gulf between the amateurs and professionals at The Oval. McIntyre recalled how, in his young days, the ebullient Surridge used to drive them to matches in a decrepit Ford V8 – 'half the team at a time'.

Peter May remembered that Surridge was wholeheartedly committed to his players' welfare. 'He insisted that we all shared railway carriages and stayed at the same hotels, which had not previously been the custom.' May also noted the 'boundless energy' of the engaging pilot. 'With his drive, impatience, often unconventional approach and touch of irascibility, he was regarded with profound respect, trust and indeed affection. His style of captaincy was unusual, but it worked – and we all knew it did.'

Surridge's approach, dynamic in its purpose, was unaccountably barred from expression at other levels. 'Not a single representative honour came Stuart's way, for incredibly there remained at Lord's a hard core who never regarded him as a cricketer nor as a captain,' said Laker, who never wavered in his view that Surridge was the finest captain under whom he had ever played. The evidence for this tribute is incontestable. During his five years as skipper Surrey played 140 matches, won 86, lost 20 and drew 34.

Laker presented a perceptive assessment of the challenge Surridge faced and his galvanising influence on the team.

'From the outset he was a brilliant, fearless fieldsman. Surrey had a bunch of tough, worldly-wise professionals and when Surridge was appointed skipper more than one upper lip curled in disfavour.' There was a scarcely concealed attitude that Surridge, a moderate performer with bat and ball, would not stay the course. 'Yet all the world loves a trier and it soon became obvious to the Surrey professionals that Surridge was an uncommonly determined trier.'

Laker was in an ideal situation as a bowler at The Oval. With another first-class county his responsibilities would have been greater. His task then would have been to make the break-through and take the majority of the wickets. Fortune smiled on him in that he was permitted to bowl in tandem with others of a mettle to match his own skills. As he said, it was his good luck that four Test bowlers should reach their peak at the same time and all play together in the same side. Between them Alec Bedser, Tony Lock, Peter Loader and Jim Laker achieved a yield of 642 wickets in Tests alone. It is difficult to conceive of such a conjunction of talents in one county team ever occurring again.

Alec Bedser, the kindliest of men, was the lionheart who carried the England attack in the post-war years. His was a copybook action and it was superbly co-ordinated in the ease of a run-up over twelve yards. 'Bedser comes in to bowl in small galloping strides until the ball is released by the energy at the shoulders, which swing round from a classical left side pointing to the batsman's position,' wrote Neville Cardus. 'The right hand follows through a nearly full circle. The hint of stiff-ness before the ball goes its stinging, swinging way is proof of the compressed, concentrated power.'

Bedser was generally acknowledged as the finest fast-medium bowler since Maurice Tate and, in the view of many, possibly the equal of the Sussex stalwart. John Woodcock said of Bedser: 'If his labours as a bowler could be collected and piled up around him in some visible shape, he would seem to be standing beside a mountain.' Bedser himself attributed his enduring stamina as a bowler to the countless hours of practice, bowling at first-eleven players and county members for sixpenny tips, in The Oval nets. There was also, he believed, after six years at war, a gain in mature strength before he established his place in the Surrey ranks. Mentally too, he was philosophically attuned as a cricketer. Along with other returning professionals after the war, he had been subjected to far worse pressures in a terrible conflict than would ever beset him in cricket.

The big man was rarely troubled by injuries. He was unflagging even in a heatwave at Adelaide. 'It was 104 degrees in the shade. I had bowled 20 eight-ball overs and, for the first time in my career, I had to leave the field.' Dehydrated, he briefly sought refuge in the dressing-room. 'I lay on the floor in the shower and was as sick as a dog.' He did return to the fray to bowl more overs, to the amazement of his team-mates. 'They said I was as white as a sheet.'

In a career spanning twenty years Bedser took 1,924 wickets, including 236 in 51 Tests at an average of under 25 runs each. Put more succinctly, he played in 485 matches and bowled 106,192 deliveries. Jim Laker paid his own high tribute in describing Bedser as the greatest medium-fast bowler he had ever seen. 'Alec's stock delivery was the inswinger, and his control was such that he could make the ball swing in at the last possible second. He never concerned himself with the outswinger. Instead he quietly developed the leg-cutter to such an extent that on any pitch on which the ball would grip he was virtually unplayable.'

The leg-cutter, manipulated by his huge hands and with which he wrought such havoc, was discovered by chance. It happened in Sydney on his first tour of Australia in 1946–47. Bedser was bowling to Sid Barnes on a perfect batting wicket. Experimentally he had held the ball's seam horizontally. Peter Smith, fielding at mid-off, gasped in disbelief. As much to the bowler's surprise as the batsman's, the ball suddenly shot from leg to off, as it never had before. Barnes said: 'What the hell's going on here?'

John Woodcock relates that some weeks later, in Adelaide,

Bradman came in to bat ten minutes before the close of play. Bedser bowled him for nought. It was one of five consecutive dismissals of the great Australian. Overall he took Bradman's wicket eight times, six of them in Tests. Only Hedley Verity, among English bowlers, exceeded this tally with ten successes. The ball which defeated Bradman at Adelaide was 'spun at speed'. The effect was of a genuine leg-break, and Bedser later said that the discovery was the turning point of his career. In the years to come he was to bring this magnificent ball under almost sure command.

The eventful dismissal of Bradman at Adelaide was missed by his family. His wife and young son, seeking to avoid the traffic, had just left the ground. The roar that greeted the Don's downfall was wrongly construed by John Bradman. He thought that his father had opened his innings with a boundary. 'That'll be Dad hitting a four,' he assured his mother.

Attesting to his keen rivalry with Australia is a record of which Alec Bedser is especially proud. In 21 Tests against the old enemy he took 104 wickets. Only six other Englishmen have matched this century. He is also delighted to be regarded as the best-loved English cricketer in Australia. Enjoying the esteem and friendship of former adversaries, including Don Bradman as a regular host in Adelaide, he makes an annual pilgrimage to Australia. 'The Australians are most hospitable and I have made so many friends out there,' says Bedser.

Fearsomely occupying the twin role in Surrey's opening attack was Peter Loader from Wallington. Loader took 1,326 wickets in first-class cricket, including 39 in 13 Tests. His hat-trick against the West Indies at Headingley in 1957 was the first in post-war cricket. The distinction was matched by Dominic Cork, against the same opponents, at Old Trafford in 1995.

Loader's opportunities at Test level were restricted by the competition of Trueman, Tyson and Statham. Yet he is afforded special esteem by those who played against him. Bob Appleyard, in Yorkshire, believes that Loader provided the extra dimension and conclusively tipped the scales in Surrey's favour in the keenly contested matches between the two counties in the 1950s.

Jim Laker said the wiry and slightly built Loader 'could make the new ball talk . . . He had the uncanny knack of bowling an outswinger from both close to the stumps and also from the very end of the return crease and he could do the same thing with the inswinger. No quick bowler of his era could better his change of pace. He could successively bowl a slow off-spinner and the most vicious of bouncers.' The legality of these two deliveries was questioned in many quarters. Trevor Bailey was plainly disturbed by them. 'Loader's bouncer was quite lethal. I couldn't see it coming.' Bailey was equally unable to detect the Surrey bowler's 'magnificent slower ball'.

Surrey's triumphant march rarely faltered in the 1950s. It was intently followed by the pre-war Surrey amateur captain, Monty Garland-Wells. He was so impressed by Surridge's prediction that Surrey would win five successive titles that he placed an accumulator bet on seven in a row. After four years he accepted a settlement from the bookmaker and, with the proceeds, threw a celebration party for the victorious team.

Surrey were at their most imperious in winning a fourth championship in 1955. They set up a new record for championship points since the system of awarding twelve points for a win and four points for a lead on the first innings was introduced in 1938. Surrey recorded 23 victories out of 28 games to total 284 points. Yorkshire strove hard to overhaul them. They won 21 games and the aggregate of 268 points beat their previous highest total of 260, achieved in 1939.

The ebullience of Surrey's outcricket was the keynote of their successes. They held their catches, 381 in all, and three players – Surridge, Lock and Micky Stewart – shared 150 of them. Stewart, agile and enthusiastic, was a masterly presence close to the wicket. His inspiration was another superb fieldsman, Learie Constantine, whom he had watched and admired as a boy. Stewart still holds the Surrey record of 604 catches; his tally of 77 in 1957, including seven in one match at

Northampton, is the second highest by a non-wicket-keeper, only one short of the record established by Wally Hammond in 1928.

Jim Laker always acknowledged the support of such alert allies and their contributions to his successes. But it was only his accuracy which enabled the helmetless fieldsmen to swoop rapidly to assist him. Laker, in fact, considered that some catches were missed because they were so keen. Surridge said: 'We used to field so close to Jim; it was almost unbelievable, but we rarely got hit.' Micky Stewart, in his position in 'bomb alley', often commented: 'Stewie will get us all killed one day.' Then he would remember that his captain was just as fearless in the same area. Surridge came into a rare category of being worth his place on fielding alone.

Doug Insole said that he could anticipate catches so swiftly that he would often brush others out of his way to take them. Brian Chapman remembered Surridge 'crouching at the bat's tip and, with his mighty hands extended, he was a menace who almost compelled catches.'

Sympathy was usually in short supply if the fortunes of Surrey were on the line. In one match against Leicestershire, Arthur McIntyre was struck a shuddering blow on the head as the ball glanced off the bat of Charles Palmer. Surridge leaned forward to take the catch on the rebound. Palmer was more worried about McIntyre, lying on the ground, but Surridge was preoccupied with the fall of the wicket. 'You're out, Charlie, I've caught it,' he said.

Dennis Cox, placed in a near-suicidal position by his captain, narrowly escaped decapitation in another match at Taunton. 'Arthur Mac and the rest of the boys were laughing because I was too close.' Cox, in some fright, retreated a foot backwards. 'Stewie looked up and indicated an even more advanced position than he had set before.' Maurice Tremlett was the batsman, a powerful striker on the rampage. 'The next ball went past my ear like a rocket and Bernie Constable took the catch at deep cover.' Surridge explained the psychology behind his decision. 'There you are,' he said, 'you got him out.' Cox was scarcely comforted by the compliment. He replied: 'Let's face it, skipper, I'm a coward.'

It was always a test of character to gain acceptance in the Surrey ranks. But when a player had done so, these were exciting times in which to play cricket. One of the great strengths of Surrey was that they had such a good second team. Peter May, in one conversation, told me: 'We often had at least four players on England duty. Those chaps who deputised when we were away were quite happy to play in the seconds. They considered it an honour to represent Surrey.' The batting abilities of one loyalist, Eric Bedser, who regularly opened for Surrey, gave him first-team status as an all-rounder. But his off-spinners were only fully employed when Jim Laker was absent.

Geoffrey Howard, the former Surrey secretary, remembers the assessment of another county stalwart, Bob Gregory, who played from 1925 to 1947. Gregory had no hesitation in advancing the view that Eric Bedser had the potential to become an England bowler. With any other county, Bedser would have been assured of the 'double' (100 wickets and 1,000 runs) each season.

Before Laker's arrival at The Oval, it had seemed certain that Eric Bedser would become Surrey's principal off-spinner. 'Instead he was forced to take a back seat because of my involvement,' said Laker. 'On helpful pitches he held a watching brief, and on good wickets one could easily imagine what went through his mind when he was tossed the ball after the rest of us had toiled in vain. With his enormous hands, Eric could spin the ball like a top.'

John Arlott related how Laker paid a painful physical price for his bowling. 'Like most men who spin the ball really hard, he often wore away the skin from the inside of his index finger. If he bowled on, it would harden, a corn would form and then, as it grew too hard, it would tear away, leaving the raw flesh exposed once more.' Stuart Surridge's boundless respect for Laker was heightened by the Yorkshireman's fortitude. 'Jim's power of spin meant that by halfway through a season he had developed a terrible callus. He would pack it with Friar's Balsam to try to get some relief.'

Ted Dexter also remembered the daily ritual of emergency treatment pursued by off-spinners in that era, which enabled them to surmount their handicaps. In a less spin-conscious age, a modern generation had themselves given evidence of a declining art. Dexter said that he had been told they did not suffer from a 'spinner's finger'. 'Even after bowling fifty overs in a match they do not have a problem. I doubt, though, whether it is a question of luck. The truth is that they grip the ball too low in their fingers and so do not really spin it.'

Laker, in his own appraisal of spin bowling, emphasised the importance of the grip. 'You must force your fingers apart. I know it hurts like hell, but this is a pain which you must ignore.' It was, he said, necessary to press the first finger as far down the seam as possible. Spin was imparted by flicking the first finger upwards and the second finger downwards at the point of delivery. 'My index finger often bleeds when I spin the ball across the seam.'

Peter Loader and Godfrey Evans both believe that there were times when Laker – and Tony Lock, who, as someone dramatically said, 'spun it off the bone' – should not have played. Evans wryly adds that many players, with such disabilities, would simply have collected the insurance money.

John Arlott, as a close friend and later a fellow broadcaster, drew attention to the fact that Laker lacked the long fingers of off-spinners like Tom Goddard, Lance Gibbs, John Clay and Athol Rowan. 'To gain a similar degree of purchase, Laker had to take a grip which stretched his first two fingers to an exceptional and painful extent.' It was estimated that the spread between the fingers was three-quarters of an inch more than on his left hand. Arlott continued: 'After a few years his index finger became so distorted that if he rested while the raw flesh healed, an arthritic condition developed in the top finger joint.'

Confronted with these problems, Laker was not keen to fill the stock-bowling role at The Oval, especially if a match was drifting gently towards a draw. 'Like the voice of Callas,' wrote another off-spinner, Robin Marlar, 'a spin bowler's finger demands judicious use.' Alf Gover remembers that when Laker was apprehensive about the swollen finger he would examine it as a signal that he desired a rest. 'Stewie would urge him on. "C'm on, Jim," he would say, "I'll give you another short-leg." Then Jim would take a wicket and all would be well.'

It was, perhaps, on occasions when the finger was at its worst that other Surrey bowlers would rebel at having to take on spelling duties. Pat McKelvey is aware of allegations that Laker was not always anxious to toil away for hours in what he considered unhelpful circumstances. 'Jim could be courageous, however, and I prefer to assume that on those days when he was thought to be pulling less than his full weight, his intelligence was telling him that these were times when other performers were likely to be more effective.'

McKelvey explains that, unlike Tony Lock, his psychological opposite, Laker absolutely rejected empty heroics. For another observer, Peter Walker, the former Glamorgan and England all-rounder, attempts to downgrade Laker on the count of wayward temperament are unfair. 'You had only to look at his finger to realise that he must have more than fulfilled his quota of stock bowling.'

Micky Stewart, a fervent admirer of Laker's artistry as a bowler, makes another compelling thrust in defence of his former colleague. 'Jim, because of his split finger, was not always able to bowl. This did mean that there was a lot of donkey-work to be done. But for him to have bowled when unfit would have diminished his value and appearances for Surrey.'

Stewart also maintains that Laker, despite the charges of lack of resolution, often bowled brilliantly on good wickets. 'This was when you saw his control of spin, the use of different trajectories, and variations of flight.' Dave Fletcher, as another Surrey close fieldsman, points to the contrast offered by Laker with other slow bowlers of this time. 'You could go down the wicket, assess the length, and get to the pitch of the ball. It was much different with Jim. If you adopted this tactic, you would find that the ball dropped that little bit shorter. He beat you with variations in pace.'

Peter Walker addresses those disapproving voices which seek to present Laker as a bowler who was quick to surrender. 'Any player with an ego which he had would never have *not* tried. If you gave him a wicket to bowl on, and he didn't take five or six wickets, you could sense that he had let himself down, never mind the team. There was no question that luck hadn't gone with him.'

Jim Laker, by common consent, ranks as one of the finest assessors of the game. Wrapped in his contemplative cocoon, he was like a deceiving illusionist in manner. He did not bubble with hilarity; as one friend remarked, he said things that made you smile rather than laugh. Trevor Bailey remembers a 'quiet man who never got enthusiastic about anything.' All was routine, and cricket, as his chosen vocation, was a job to be carried out with the least amount of fuss.

The casual demeanour, an exterior pose which sometimes attracted criticism, was really cultivated as a defensive shell. Doug Insole remembers one fixture between the Gentlemen and Players at Lord's. 'I hit Jim for 20 runs in one over. He walked back, after each boundary, as if the last thing he was interested in was that match.'

The remote attitude which Laker paraded conveyed a misleading effect in cricket circles. Micky Stewart presents a parallel with Bobby Locke, the golfer, who decided that he produced his best results if he planned his rounds at a certain pace. 'That was Jim's way,' says Stewart. 'He kept his emotions under control by adopting a rhythm in his movements. His unhurried approach to cricket gave an impression that he didn't care. But, in fact, he was the most caring of persons.'

8

LAKER AND LOCK

'They were both formidable competitors and induced a kind of fear. There was always the dread of receiving the unplayable ball.'

Peter Walker

It is one of cricket's little ironies that Jim Laker should revere a fellow Yorkshireman, Hedley Verity, a model of probity and discipline, and yet be associated with another slow left-arm bowler, the colourful and controversial Tony Lock.

The menace of Laker, as the senior partner, undoubtedly goaded Lock on to his path of violent conquests. Theirs was a curious and embattled playing relationship. Micky Stewart, as a former Surrey colleague, remembers Laker as a 'shrewd man who could walk into any social environment and be at home'. Lock, 'the country boy' from Limpsfield, was strongly aware that he had to make his impact boisterously on the field. It is the general view that an essentially kind and considerate man probably never quite learned how to cope with his renown as an international cricketer. 'At times, he projected himself very differently from his natural self, which cut across the grain with some people,' says Stewart. 'Lockie did try to cultivate the social niceties, but he just didn't have that ability. Jim, as the more sophisticated type, made him ill at ease. He might have got up Lockie's nose at times.'

Duelling with Lock for England recognition was Verity's successor in Yorkshire, Johnny Wardle. Wardle bitterly resented the fact that his Surrey rival was given what he considered an illegal advantage over him. After his retirement from the first-class game, he wrote: 'Lock used to impart tremendous spin to his jerk and never had to resort to flight to get anyone out.'

Remembering his own disillusionment as a Test cricketer, he said: 'Some people are sympathetic and say that bowlers will be put out of the game. I contend that they should not be in cricket keeping legitimate bowlers out of the game. Others remark that the slow bowler does not do any harm, so why worry about him. My answer is that he gets wickets to which he is not entitled because of his peculiar method of delivering the ball.'

Jim Laker, albeit from a different standpoint, was also sceptical about the dramatic change in Lock's bowling action. Lock had given little evidence of his later supremacy during his apprenticeship years with Surrey. Geoffrey Howard, then Assistant Secretary at The Oval, spent hours batting against Laker and Lock in the nets. 'There was no problem facing Tony; he was just a little roller with the ball. You would never have thought he was going to be an England bowler. Jim was a very different proposition. He was obviously a fine prospect.'

Tom Graveney remembered Lock in his unexciting first phase with some amusement. 'It was in the late 1940s and I played against this soft, gentle little floater. It was a case of "down the wicket and help yourself". I never thought Lockie would amount to very much.' Michael Barton, who captained both Laker and Lock in their early years, endorses these views. 'Lock, at that time, did not spin the ball. He was not then a bowler to take advantage of the conditions. On the other hand, you could throw the ball to Jim – and that was it.'

For two years Lock watched and marvelled at Laker's mounting armoury of skills. He was guided in his attempts to achieve enhanced spin by Laker. They quietly spent some time working on a new grip, very similar to one Laker himself employed. In 1951, Lock was appointed winter coach at Allders Indoor School at Croydon. Over two winters he worked for six days a week giving lessons and improving his own technique.

At the school the beam supporting the roof was low-slung and it caused him to drop his high action when he tossed up the ball. 'Though I was not conscious of it at the time,' said Lock, 'my arm dropped a little in the delivery of the ball. I also found that by "digging" the ball into the wicket, I was able to secure more spin.' Laker said: 'The net at Allders was not sufficiently high for a full extension of the arm at the point of delivery; and for a tall bowler, like Tony, giving the ball even the slightest degree of height was seriously restricted. As a result, Tony increased his delivery stride to almost that of a fast bowler, thus reducing the height at which he released the ball. In order to make doubly sure of no net interference, his left arm was slightly bent at the elbow.'

By 1952 Lock was a new bowler. The high action had disappeared during the school practices. The unfortunate legacy was a sinister kink in his bowling arm. John Arlott commented: 'He was now the ultimate destroyer as a spin bowler. He could wrest turn from the deadest of wickets: on anything approaching a spinner's pitch his break was staggering. His quicker balls came through at a wicked pace.'

Laker remembered Lock's faster ball, which some people thought conservatively accounted for 25 per cent of his wickets. 'It would burst through a batsman's defence before he could pick up his bat from the blockhole.' Another Yorkshireman, Ted Lester, recalled the amazement of his colleague, Vic Wilson, in one confrontation with Lock at The Oval. 'It was like Tyson at his fastest. Vic hadn't got a very high back-lift. He hadn't got his bat up before the middle stump was ripped out of the ground.'

There was no warning of these alarms in the preceding years. Laker's advance before his name was coupled with Lock was an object lesson, almost curtly expressed for the benefit of his future partner. On a worn or rain-affected wicket he was often unplayable. One of the mysteries of this period, between 1949 and 1951, is that Laker played in only four Tests in home series against New Zealand, West Indies and South Africa.

The brimming measure of his authority only once stirred the selectors' interest in 1950. He represented England in the victory over the West Indies at Old Trafford. On a spinner's pitch he bowled tidily, if without substantial rewards, and was third top-scorer, with 40, in England's second innings. Roy Tattersall, the Lancashire off-spinner, in his finest year, took 193 wickets to head the national averages and gain favour over the Yorkshireman. Yet Laker, with 166 wickets that summer, did not allow his rival to dominate the championship headlines.

A bowling marathon of 77 overs yielded 12 wickets for 86 runs against Gloucestershire at Bristol. His first-innings figures of 8 for 45 included a spell of 6 for 16 in 11 overs. Against Nottinghamshire at Trent Bridge he mixed, with Alec Bedser, a deadly cocktail of spin and pace. They each took four wickets in the Notts first innings to support the contention of Alf Gover that this pace and spin combination disrupts the batting tempo of opponents. 'Alec was so accurate,' said Gover, 'and he and Jim were a fine combination.' There were another seven wickets for Laker against Somerset at Wells where, on a bleak day in May, the batsmen wore overcoats while waiting to go in.

Laker was involved in testing rivalry with fellow Bradfordian Bob Appleyard in the race to become the first bowler to obtain 100 wickets in 1951. He reached this goal on 12 July. Appleyard had seemed likely to beat him, having taken 99 wickets by 28 June. But he was taken ill with pleurisy on the second day of Yorkshire's match against the South Africans and missed the following two games. Ironically, at almost the same time as Laker gained his hundredth wicket Hutton inadvertently prevented parity when he failed to take a sharp catch off Appleyard in a match against Sussex at Hull.

Laker's feat won pleasing recognition from the Surrey officialdom. In his postbag was a note from H. D. G. Leveson-Gower: 'Dear Laker, this is just a line to congratulate you on getting your 100th wicket. A very fine performance of which Surrey County Cricket club are very proud.'

Lord's was always a happy hunting ground for Laker. In two matches in one week in May at the headquarters in 1951, he took 17 wickets. For Surrey against the MCC he returned match figures of 10 wickets for 34 runs. The MCC, whose ranks included four county captains – Bill Edrich, Doug Insole, Charles Palmer and Guy Willatt – were dismissed for 62 and 70. In their second innings Laker bowled unchanged to take six wickets for 19 runs in 18.1 overs. In the following match at Lord's, this time representing the MCC against Essex, Laker once again routed his opponents. His figures were only slightly dented by two sixes struck by Ray Smith. Laker completed a merry week with seven wickets for 36 runs.

During the month of May he had brought his tally to sixty wickets. The achievement was noted in the 'Sportsmen's Diary' in the London *Evening Standard*. The writer commented that this bowling feat should rank equally with 1,000 runs in a month. Five other bowlers had matched Laker's achievement. They were Hedley Verity and Alf Gover, with 67 and 60 wickets respectively in 1936; 'Tich' Freeman and Charlie Parker, with 65 wickets in 1931; and Tom Richardson, another great Surrey bowler, with 63 in 1896.

There was more to excite Surrey followers in the dramatic change in the fortunes of the match against Worcestershire at The Oval. Worcestershire, set a target of 256 in three and a half hours, reached 78 without loss by lunch. Their openers, Kenyon and Outschoorn, were in stern occupation of the crease. Eighty minutes later the innings was over and Surrey had won by 114 runs. Laker, with twelve wickets in the match, took his last five wickets for four runs.

In his two appearances for England against South Africa in this season, Laker reinforced his claims for permanent status at this level. At Manchester in July he was Tattersall's spinning partner. It could fairly be said that England's victory by nine wickets was largely orchestrated by Laker and his Surrey colleague, Alec Bedser. They shared an eighth-wicket partnership of 53 runs, the margin of the first-innings lead. Bedser, in the South African second innings, took five wickets for 11 runs in 32 deliveries and achieved a match analysis of 12 for 112. The Surrey pair shared 16 of the wickets. Laker's four victims were McLean, Eric Rowan, van Ryneveld and Fullerton, all batsmen of quality.

Laker was again in masterful mood in the final Test at The Oval. He returned match figures of ten wickets for 119 runs. England, in a keenly contested match which decided the series, won by four wickets. 'Unafraid to pitch the ball well up to the batsmen, Laker attacked them persistently,' reported *Wisden*. 'Bowling round the wicket, he gave the ball plenty of air and his finger spin whipped the ball off the pitch and across the bat towards his leg trap of Hutton, Brown and Tattersall.'

Jim Swanton watched the Yorkshireman as he held sway on the first day. South Africa, at one stage 106 for 1, lost another six wickets for the addition of 40 runs. 'Laker began the afternoon from the pavilion end and there he stayed right until tea. Throughout his long spell Laker bowled with a tautness and control, which demanded eloquently: "Who says I am not an England bowler?" '

Vivian Jenkins, writing in the *News of the World*, dwelt on the merits of Laker and his rival off-spinner, Athol Rowan. 'Both are skilled exponents of the off-break. They had all their opponents paying them deserved respect in the conditions. At the same time, they separated the sheep from the goats among the batsmen, and it was here that England – and Laker – came out on top.'

Trevor Bailey said that the transformation of Tony Lock from just another slow left-arm bowler into a lethal destroyer was remarkable in many ways. 'It could never have occurred if the umpires and authorities of those days had been as bent-arm-conscious as they are today.' Bailey remembered standing in the slips with David Sheppard as Lock swept his way through a powerful West Indian batting line-up at The Oval. He posed a question to Sheppard. 'How do you play a left-hand medium-paced bowler who keeps pitching leg stump and fizzing the top of the off stump?' Neither of them could provide an answer; nor could the hapless West Indians as they attempted to combat the unnerving deliveries.

Lock did rise to eminence during a regime of lenient stew-
ardship. Bailey and Peter May both recalled a diminished
sensitivity in this situation. Those brave umpires who did call
offending bowlers were looked upon as publicity seekers.
'Lock obviously alarmed certain umpires with his quicker ball,
which was doubtful at times,' said May. 'But the tendency at
the time was to sweep such unpleasantness under the carpet.'

In 1952, Lock was called three times for throwing in the
match between Surrey and the Indians at The Oval. The
umpire, at square-leg, was Fred Price, the former Middlesex
and England wicket-keeper. Peter May, who had just come
down from Cambridge, was deputising as captain. He asked
Price for an explanation of his decision. 'We were all amazed.
Fred was in no doubt that Tony had thrown his faster ball.' It
was the first time that Lock's action had been officially
regarded as questionable. 'Why,' said Lock, 'should one
umpire no-ball me when all the other umpires have allowed
me to go on bowling as I please?' He considered that Price
should have had the courtesy to give him a prior warning.

After Lock had been no-balled again on the tour of the West
Indies in 1953–54, Alex Bannister commented that both the
Surrey committee and the player himself should have heeded
the warning lights. 'On this important issue they should not
have been content to allow matters to slide. It was not something that could be conveniently ignored, but a question to be
tackled straightforwardly in the triple interests of England,
Surrey and Tony Lock. To be no-balled on a "foreign field" was
a severe shock for Lock and his team.'

Laker was not convinced that his partner was a persistent
offender. 'Lockie was never an out-and-out thrower but there
were many occasions when he contravened the laws. His arm
was certainly bent and generally remained bent through the
delivery, which was acceptable. It was when he straightened it
to jerk the ball out with greater pace that he broke the law.'
There were, though, severe doubts even in the Surrey dressing-
room about the legitimacy of Lock's faster ball. Laker
continued: 'Apart from leg-pulling about how well he could

throw the javelin, we did not discourage Tony in his new enthusiastic approach to the game. We did not want to undermine his confidence. So many bowlers over the years had got away with throwing or jerking the ball that we decided that we were not going to act as the jury. It was up to the umpires to decide.'

Trevor Bailey, as a neutral observer, believes that Laker was privately less indulgent about Lock's bowling. 'Each of them, of course, were looking to their own laurels. But Jim was slightly cynical about Tony. He was the *bowler* and the bloke at the other end was not a legitimate bowler.' David Sheppard remembers one conversation with Laker shortly after Lock had changed his action. 'Lockie is throwing this year,' said Laker. 'If I can turn the ball two inches, he is turning it twice as much.'

Len Hutton neither deplored nor condoned Lock's transgressions. Along with other leading cricketers of the time, he believed that Lock was no more culpable than other bowlers, many of them respected names in cricket, who had escaped censure. In 1952, soon after succeeding to the England captaincy, Hutton was diplomatic about the young Surrey bowler. He was at his most circumspect when asked about Lock's remodelled action. The question was put to him: 'Isn't Tony's action a little strange?' Hutton's face flickered with the satisfaction of a man who knew that he had found a match-winner. 'It is,' he warily replied, 'but I think I will beat the Aussies next year with him.'

At The Oval, crowning the Coronation summer of 1953, Hutton's prophecy was fulfilled. The expressions of joy on the Palace balcony in June were replicated by the waves of acclaim which greeted the triumphant cricketers on another balcony at Kennington in August. Laker and Lock paraded their dominance as partners for the first time to cast a blight on the Australian batsmen. In a tumultuous finale, England won by eight wickets to achieve their first Ashes victory since the 'bodyline' series in Australia twenty years earlier.

Denzil Batchelor, writing in *Picture Post* before The Oval Test, summarised the events of a fluctuating series and the earlier four drawn games in typically extravagant style. 'We brace ourselves for the last act reflecting on the somersaults and double somersaults – each an adagio act of a game performed. Bedser, terrible as an army with banners, swept the Australians off the field for a meagre score at Nottingham. We had our chance of a kill and collapsed like a bevy of maiden aunts deprived of their *sal volatile*. Later in the game we rallied and deserved to win.'

Batchelor continued his invigorating recital: 'At Lord's, having batted dismally, we fought back and deserved not to lose, an even prouder boast. At Manchester, we grew accustomed to reading, day after day, the headline: "Only rain can save England" – to discover in the end that only rain saved Australia. At Leeds, we allowed the Australians to treat us as silent film used to be treated: we were gagged, bound, tied to the rails in the path of an oncoming express with a phial of poison gas on one side and a time bomb on the other. Then, the fuse went out in a rain storm, a change of wind blew the poison gas the other way, and the express train inexplicably went into reverse.'

The excitement aroused by the thrilling pageant at The Oval in August led to a swift rearrangement of television schedules. Ronnie Aird, the secretary of the MCC, issued a statement in which he said that because of the 'enormous public interest' the MCC had decided to allow the BBC to transmit the whole of the final day's play. The decision was forced by the aggravations of the previous day when the state of the game had played havoc with other television programmes. Aird said it was hoped that the MCC response would not curtail attendances at county games. For those loyal followers there would be the opportunity to watch a tele-recording of the final scenes of the match.

England had wrested a slender lead of 31 runs on the first innings. Spin was clearly the key to victory, but the narrow gain meant that the expense of it had to be carefully budgeted. 'Hutton had to hoard his resources with infinite care,' wrote Jim Kilburn in his account of the third day's play in the *Yorkshire Post*. 'He could not afford any relaxation in his pressure, or one mistake in policy. The hazards were as enormous

110

as the prize.' *The Times* reported on an 'afternoon of upheaval
. . . All that followed was no dream. It was hard reality, an age
of exploration and discovery, as the vast crowd sat agog,
enthralled by the quick current of new life.'

Australia surrendered to spin on a dusty wicket. Laker
began the downfall. Hutton's winning ploy, ten minutes into
the innings, was to introduce him at the Vauxhall end. Laker
rubbed the shine off the new ball; and, with the last ball of his
first over, he beat Hassett's back stroke with a vicious off-break
to obtain an lbw verdict. It was, in the words of Jim Swanton,
the start of a 'breathtaking procession'. In the next fourteen
minutes the heart was torn out of the innings. Hole, Harvey,
Miller and Morris all fell to Laker and Lock. The four wickets
were taken in the course of sixteen balls for just two runs.

There was, at the last, a stirring counter-attack by Australia's
youth, headed by Ron Archer, the 19-year-old from
Queensland. Archer hit a six and seven fours in a valiant 49. He
and Davidson added 50 in thirty-eight minutes. *The Times*
reported: 'Archer held the tattered standard high from the
moment he arrived on the scene. He led the answering challenge with brilliant forcing stroke-play.'

Australia went in to tea with their score at 131 for six. On the
resumption Lock swiftly brought the innings to a close. In four
overs, he dismissed Davidson, Archer and Langley for two runs.
Lindwall hooked him for six, and was then missed at slip before
launching into a massive strike off Laker. Compton, pressed
hard against the pavilion rails, held on to a towering catch.

Laker and Lock shared nine wickets in the innings. Lock, in
fact, had been a doubtful starter for this crucial match. He had
been handicapped by a split spinning finger during the season
and was only selected after an examination on the first morning. *Wisden* commented: 'England owed much to Lock. The
pitch gave him little help, yet such was his finger spin allied to
flighting and change of pace that he took five wickets for 45
runs. Laker, too, played a valuable part. He accounted for the
dangerous right-handed hitters, Hassett, Miller, Hole and
Lindwall.'

111

England's famous victory was one to stay in the hearts and minds of those who witnessed it. One contemporary expressed his feelings with a moving phrase. He said: 'We are given memories so we can have roses in December.'

The revels of Laker and Lock on Test days at The Oval were greeted with patriotic fervour. There were differing reactions from Surrey's county opponents. Insistent claims were made that the wicket was expressly tailored for the home bowlers. Certainly, it did frequently present problems unknown in the pre-war groundsmanship of 'Bosser' Martin when the wickets were as unyielding as concrete. Laker and Lock did not have to suffer the frustrations of the toilers of those days. They revelled in the boon of a transformed Oval. It was reshaped by Bert Lock after it had been prepared as a wartime prisoner-of-war camp.

Arthur McIntyre pertinently stresses that the Oval wicket aided both teams. 'We had to bat on it as well as the opposition.' Micky Stewart was one of the home batsmen confronted with its perils.'The Oval wasn't the easiest pitch to bat on in the 1950s. It used to break up either before noon on the first day or before tea on the second day. I fielded for Surrey for three years before we faced a total of 300.' If The Oval could be a preposterous terrain, then there is statistical evidence to deny its overriding value in Surrey's successes.

Jim Laker was always very protective of his bowling figures. He sternly resisted those critics who said that his reputation was based on the aid given to him at The Oval. The wickets, uncovered in the 1950s, varied in the degree of preparation, not just at Kennington but throughout the country. Of Laker's 1,944 wickets, only 687, at just over 17 runs apiece, were taken on the ground where he played a third of his cricket. Over eleven years at Lord's against the great Middlesex teams of the period his figures were fractionally better than at The Oval. His record in the West Country also served to demonstrate that his skills were undiminished away from home.

Trevor Bailey does, though, remember that The Oval wicket

rey's championship staff in 1954.

ieged by autograph hunters (right).

in pugnacious mood as a batsman.

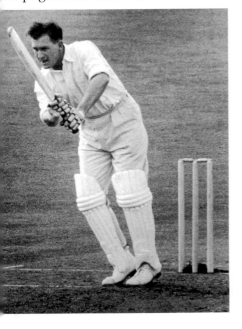

Surrey County Cricket Club

KENNINGTON OVAL

SURREY v. WORCESTERSHIRE
Wednesday, August 25th, 1954 (3 Day Match)

3D.

WORCESTERSHIRE

		First Innings		Second Innings	
1	Kenyon, D.	c Surridge, b Bedser	8	c Stewart, b Lock	0
2	P. E. Richardson	c May, b Bedser	0	c McIntyre, b Laker	9
3	Outschoorn, L.	b Laker	9	c Lock, b Laker	3
4	Broadbent, R.	c Laker, b Lock	3	c McIntyre, b Laker	1
5	Hughes, N.	run out	0	hit wkt b Bedser	2
6	Devereux, L. N.	not out	2	retired hurt	1
7	Jenkins, R.	c Stewart, b Lock	1	c Laker, b Bedser	1
‡8	Yarnold, H.	c Barrington, b Lock	1	not out	14
*9	Perks, R. T. D.	c Barrington, b Laker	0	b Bedser	2
10	Flavell, J.	c Constable, b Lock	0	c Clark, b Laker	3
11	Ashman, J.	c & b Lock	0	c Bedser, b Loader	2
		B , l-b	, w , n-b	1	B , l-b , w , n-b	2
		Total	25	Total	40

FALL OF THE WICKETS

| 1—1 | 2—16 | 3—20 | 4—20 | 5—21 | 6—23 | 7—25 | 8—25 | 9—25 | 10—25 |
| 1—0 | 2—5 | 3—13 | 4—16 | 5—16 | 6—18 | 7—23 | 8—26 | 9—40 | 10— |

BOWLING ANALYSIS

	First Innings							Second Innings					
	O.	M.	R.	W.	Wd.	N.b.		O.	M.	R.	W.	Wd.	N.b.
													1
Bedser (A.V.)	9	4	12	2				6	3	7	3		
Loader	6	3	5	2				2.4	1	3	1		
Laker	8	3	5	2				17	9	25	4		
Lock	5.3	4	2	5				10	7	3	1		

Deciding game which made

Surrey County Champions 1954

SURREY

		First Innings		Second Innings
1	Clark, T. H.	c Richardson, b Perks	10	
2	Stewart, M. J.	c Flavell, b Perks	11	
3	P. B. H. May	not out	31	
4	Constable, B.	c & b Ashman	29	
5	Barrington, K.	not out	10	
‡6	McIntyre, A. J.			
7	Laker, J. C.			
*8	W. S. Surridge			
9	Bedser, A. V.			
10	Lock, G. A. R.			
11	Loader, P. J.			
		B , l-b , wl , n-b	1	B , l-b , w , n-b
		Innings dec.		
		Total (3 wkts)	92	Total

FALL OF THE WICKETS

| 1—12 | 2—31 | 3—77 | 4— | 5— | 6— | 7— | 8— | 9— | 10— |
| 1— | 2— | 3— | 4— | 5— | 6— | 7— | 8— | 9— | 10— |

BOWLING ANALYSIS

	First Innings							Second Innings					
	O.	M.	R.	W.	Wd.	N.b.		O.	M.	R.	W.	Wd.	N.b.
Perks	12	1	43	2									
Flavell	3	1	17	0									
Ashman	8	3	29	1		1							
Devereux	1	0	2	0									

*Captain   ‡Wkt.-keeper

Toss won by—SURREY

RESULT—Surrey won by an innings and 27 runs

Umpires—F. S. Lee & E. Cooke   3rd Day 11.0—5.0 or 5.30   Lunch 1.30 All Days

HOURS OF PLAY—1st & 2nd Days 11.30—6.30

Printed on the ground by the Surrey County Cricket Club Printing Department

Reaping the rewards of audacity in a match which lasted just over five hours and was concluded before lunch on the second day.

This card does not necessarily include the fall of the last wicket

Surrey County Cricket Club

KENNINGTON OVAL

SURREY v. AUSTRALIANS
Wednesday, May 16th, 1956 (3 Day Match)

3D.

AUSTRALIANS

			First Innings		Second Innings	
1	J. W. Burke	New South Wales	lbw b Laker	28	c & b Lock	20
2	C. C. McDonald	Victoria	c Swetman, b Laker	89	c Laker, b Lock	45
3	K. Mackay	Queensland	c Surridge, b Laker	4	lbw b Laker	4
4	R. N. Harvey	Victoria	c Constable, b Laker	13	c May, b Lock	10
5	K. R. Miller	New South Wales	not out	57	c Swetman, b Lock	2
‡6	L. Maddocks	Victoria	b Laker	12	c Laker, b Lock	0
8	R. R. Lindwall	Queensland	b Laker	0	c Constable, b Lock	4
*9	I. W. Johnson	Victoria	c Swetman, b Laker	0	run out	5
7	A. K. Davidson	New South Wales	c May, b Laker	21	c May, b Laker	7
10	P. Crawford	New South Wales	b Laker	16	not out	5
11	J. Wilson	South Australia	c Swetman. b Laker	4	st Swetman, b Lock	1
			B4 , l-b8 , w , n-b3	15	B , l-b4 , w , n-b	4
			Total	**259**	**Total**	**107**

FALL OF THE WICKETS

1—62	2—93	3—125	4—151	5—173	6—173	7—175	8—199	9—217	10—259
1—56	2—73	3—83	4—85	5—85	6—89	7—92	8—101	9—104	10—107

BOWLING ANALYSIS

	First Innings						Second Innings					
	O.	M.	R.	W.	Wd.	N.b.	O.	M.	R.	W.	Wd.	N.b.
Loader	15	4	30	0		2	2	2	0	0		
Surridge	8	2	8	0			1	1	0	0		
Laker	46	18	88	10			25	10	42	2		
Lock	33	12	100	0			31.1	9	49	7		
Cox	5	0	18	0		1						
Clark							8	4	12	0		

J. C. Laker's Bowling Record
1st innings
10 wickets for 88 runs

SURREY

		First Innings		Second Innings	
1	Fletcher, D. G. W.	c Maddocks, b Johnson	29	not out	9
2	Clark, T. H.	c Maddocks, b Burke	58	not out	8
3	Constable, B.	c & b Johnson	109		
4	P. B. H. May	st Maddocks, b Johnson	27		
5	Barrington, K.	c Miller, b Johnson	4		
‡7	Swetman, R.	st Maddocks, b Davidson	0		
11	Cox, D. F.	b Davidson	13		
6	Laker, J. C.	c McDonald, b Johnson	43		
*8	W. S. Surridge	c Harvey, b Johnson	38		
9	Lock, G. A. R.	b Davidson	0		
10	Loader, P. J.	not out	12		
		B10, l-b3 , w1 , n-b	14	B1 , l-b1 , w , n-b1	3
		Total	**347**	**Total (0 wkt.)**	**20**

FALL OF THE WICKETS

1—53	2—112	3—147	4—192	5—195	6—221	7—278	8—302	9—313	10—347
1—	2—	3—	4—	5—	6—	7—	8—	9—	10—

BOWLING ANALYSIS

	First Innings						Second Innings					
	O.	M.	R.	W.	Wd.	N.b.	O.	M.	R.	W.	Wd.	N.b.
Lindwall	2	1	10	0			8	4	4	0		
Crawford	1	0	4	0			7	3	9	0		1
Johnson	60.3	12	168	6								
Davidson	44	14	101	3								
Wilson	19	9	34	0		1						
Burke	7	2	16	1								

*Captain   ‡Wkt.-keeper

Umpires—McCanlis & Gray

HOURS OF PLAY—1st & 2nd Days 11.30—

Printed on the ground by the S

The first of Laker's triumphs against the Australians is acknowledged by the congratulations of Sir Pelham Warner.

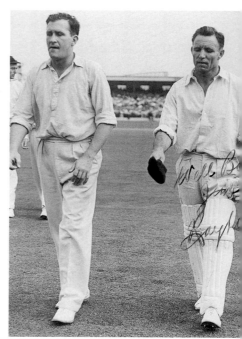

Masters of spin: Jim and Tony Lock.

Ray Lindwall, undefeated in the Austra
first innings, returns with the conqueror

A dusty welcome for the Australians at Old Trafford in 1956.

an Johnson, the Australian skipper, shakes the hand of the master.

The Australian team group, including those who perished against spin at The Oval
and Old Trafford. Back row: Burke, Mackay, Craig, Burge, Benaud, Crawford, Archer,
Rutherford, Wilson. Front row: Maddocks, McDonald, Miller, Johnson, Lindwall,
Langley, Harvey, Davidson.

A victory toast with his captain, Peter May.

The presentation of a silver salver inscribed with the record-breaking details by the MCC President, Earl Alexander of Tunis, at The Oval.

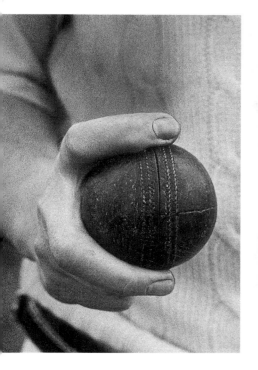

Spinning grips:
The off-break and the leg-cutter (above left and right), together with the occupational phenomenon of the extended right forefinger (below left), the legacy of bowling marathons.

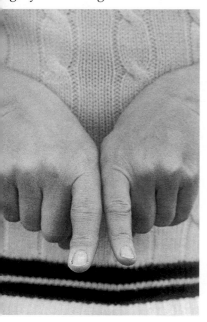

Jim, as the expert television commentator, reports on England's victory by 25 runs in the third Test against Pakistan at Headingley in July 1971.

Jim with Brian Johnston, household names in broadcasting.

Jim with the family dog, Toffee.

The valiant gentleman.

presented such terrors as to bring forth a wail from opponents, who voiced the refrain: 'Ashes to ashes, dust to dust. If Laker doesn't get me, Lockie must.' The threat of a formidable pair was as menacing as any posed by a fast-bowling combination. Peter Walker, the Glamorgan all-rounder, says that their presence induced a kind of fear. 'There was always the dread of receiving the unplayable ball.'

The character of their unswerving command was perhaps best summed up by Freddie Stocks, the Nottinghamshire batsman. In one match at Trent Bridge, after Surrey had built up a substantial total, the home side were twice dismissed in a forlorn reply. 'It seems like a different wicket when thoust bowling,' said Stocks when he returned to the pavilion.

Ronnie Burnet, the former Yorkshire captain, recalled one occasion when he was confronted by the prodigious spin of Lock. 'This particular wicket at The Oval was like straw. Yorkshire lost five wickets for 60 before lunch on the first morning. Lockie was bowling round the wicket and his first ball to me pitched on the leg stump. I watched it carefully, didn't get a bat on it. The ball just "exploded" as it pitched. It was caught by second slip!'

Tony Lock's indomitable spirit typified the aggressive approach of Surrey in their championship years. The big man, with his bald pate glinting in the sunshine and his sleeves buttoned down as he bowled, was endowed with a boundless fury. He seemed impervious to injury. Gordon Ross recalled: 'I have seen him strapping up a swollen knee in the dressing-room which, if Surridge had seen it, would have kept him out of the side.' Laker watched his partner bowl a spell of thirty overs with his knees and ankles sheathed with bandages. 'There was not a word of complaint. How I wish some of our modern cricketers could have seen him take the field. Many of them would not even have attempted to walk down the pavilion steps.'

Lock won admiration even among his fiercest rivals in Yorkshire. One of them paid him a handsome compliment. 'Lockie would be the man you want alongside you in the trenches.' His full-throated appeals as a bowler contrasted with Laker's gentle, almost apologetic enquiries. One wag remarked: 'When Lockie appeals at The Oval, someone else is given out at Lord's.'

Lock's fielding, off his own or another's bowling, bordered on the miraculous. Neville Cardus recalled Lock holding 'quite sinful catches, catches which were not there until his rapid, hungry eyesight created them.' Micky Stewart considered that the spectacular catches, brought about by sudden, full-length dives, were the easiest taken by Lock. 'His best were when he took the rockets, close in, without anyone noticing.'

Fred Trueman cites one example of Lock's aggression against Yorkshire. Brian Close, not easily outwitted, was the surprised batsman. Close had driven strongly on the onside and set off for a run. 'Tony moved across, picked up the ball in his left hand and, in one sweeping movement, hit the stumps.' Close sprawled full-length in a vain attempt to regain his crease. 'As Brian was picking himself up covered in dirt, he saw the smiling face of Roy Swetman, the wicket-keeper, looking down at him. Swetman roguishly remarked: "Even that one pitches leg and hits the middle and off." '

The fervour of a hyperactive cricketer contrasted sharply with Jim Laker's earliest memory of his partner in 1947. He remembered the 'tall, slim and enthusiastic youngster, with a head full of ginger hair, and a quiff falling down over his eyes.' Laker and Lock were paired together in a second-eleven game at Bristol. On the sandy pitch the ball spun at right angles. 'Monty Cranfield tore through us with nine cheap wickets which seemed to suggest that I was due for a hatful.' In Gloucestershire's reply, Laker pursed his lips in annoyance as four straightforward catches slipped through the hands of his short-leg fieldsman. The culprit was Lock. 'I looked at the crestfallen Tony and said to our skipper, the Hon. R. R. Blades: "Do the kid a favour and stick him on the boundary. He will never be a short leg as long as he plays the game." '

Laker's judgement, forgivably expressed in the circumstances, was to prove the most wayward of assessments. It was a comment which Lock never forgot and he relished reminding his senior of the gaffe in the years ahead. By the end of his career Lock had taken 830 catches, a total only exceeded by Frank Woolley and W. G. Grace.

Both Jim Swanton and Ted Dexter have described the events leading to Lock's decision to change his action on the 1958–59 tour of Australia and New Zealand. Swanton recalls that Harry Cave, the New Zealand bowler, had filmed highlights of his country's tour of England in the previous summer. The film included the exploits of Lock, who had enjoyed sweeping success against New Zealand, taking 34 wickets in the series at 7.47 runs each. Lock attended a screening of the film when the MCC party travelled on to New Zealand in 1959. 'Lock was horrified when he saw himself on film,' said Swanton. 'He came back home determined to correct his action.'

Ted Dexter, one of England's young recruits on the tour, also remembered Lock's embarrassment. 'The lights were dimmed and suddenly we saw the old 8mm film of the match at Lord's. Lock was running in to bowl in very slow motion. From the first ball there was a pronounced bending and straightening of the arm. When the lights went up, there was Lock white-faced and silent. The next day, he came to the nets and bowled very slowly, with no sign of the quicker ball.'

The revelation on film preceded an intensive period of reappraisal by Lock. At the age of 30, he was faced with a challenge amounting to a command. He had to re-order his cricket and produce a different delivery which would suppress criticism and satisfy an extra-vigilant jury. Arthur McIntyre remembered the work Lock put in at The Oval nets. 'He tried all sorts of styles until he hit on the right one. I don't think I've seen a greater trier than Lockie. Sometimes blood would be pouring from his fingers as he slogged away to get it right.' The process of rehabilitation took many months but it led to unreserved praise. Dexter, Lock's captain on the 1961–62 tour of India, said: 'Lockie bowled superbly for me on that tour. There was all the flight and variations you could wish for.'

The rekindling of Lock's talents and the adjustment to a

slower style brought him a late harvest of wickets. He emigrated to Australia in 1963 and led Western Australia to a Sheffield Shield triumph, their first for twenty years, in 1967–68. In the previous season he became the first post-war bowler to take over 50 wickets in Shield cricket. During this time he also spent three seasons with Leicestershire. At Grace Road his bowling and enthusiastic leadership laid the foundations for an imposing era of success. Within two years he took Leicestershire to second place in the county championship, the best position in the county's history.

'They loved him in Australia and accepted him as one of their own,' recalled Laker. Lock had much to do with the development of future Australian Test players, including Dennis Lillee and Rodney Marsh. His inspirational qualities brought belated distinction to West Australian cricket and helped to bring about the introduction of Perth as a Test centre. On his retirement at the age of 41 in 1971, he could look on a remarkable swan song in his adopted land. In nine seasons in Australia he had collected 316 wickets in 74 games.

The mellowness of age brings understanding. The gulf between two great bowlers was bridged in their twilight years, when they found an ease in each other's company. Jim Laker, in one of his last books, reflected on other outstanding left-arm bowlers of his time. He placed Johnny Wardle in the topmost rank of Test bowlers. Derek Underwood gained his approbation as a marvellous performer. Neither of them, he insisted, would have been exchanged for Tony Lock. Together Laker and Lock had captured 4,788 wickets in first-class cricket, 367 of them in 95 Test matches.

'I would take a lot of convincing,' said Laker, 'that, as a spinning combination, we ever had any serious rivals.' Certainly this would not be disputed at The Oval. A poll of Surrey members and supporters in 1995 placed Laker and Lock joint second in the list of the top 20 of an illustrious assembly of great cricketers who have represented the club.

Gallantry, as represented by Tony Lock, will assure him of a distinguished place in the annals of the game. As the years lengthened and the memory of his meagre reward receded, he was able to accept one chastening experience. He was the angry onlooker during the astonishing and unparalleled triumph of Jim Laker at Old Trafford in 1956. In a signal of regret, Lock said he was sorry that he had taken one wicket to disturb the balance of a memorable feat.

9

LAKERING THE AUSTRALIANS

'The ball, just like a hovering hawk
Tossed from a falconer's hand,
Swooped in hunger for the kill
When the hunter did command.'
Colin Wilkie, folk singer and lyricist

For Jim Laker this year was a watershed; in cricketing terms, it was a crisis to be linked with the last despairing shout of colonialism on the banks of the Suez Canal. His sporting expedition prospered, unlike the fiasco of a shaming military manoeuvre.

At 34, Laker had represented England in only 24 Tests, less than half those played in this period. His triumphs over the Australians in his benefit year of 1956 were especially cherished because they dispersed the disappointment of a beginner in an unhappy trial against them eight years earlier at Headingley. Laker was now the mature bowling artist and intent on resolving his status. The intermittent appearances for England had baffled his admirers, who were stunned by the injustice of his exclusion.

Laker's passage to glory began in an ominous dress rehearsal for the forthcoming Test series. The first instalment of wickets was collected for Surrey against the Australians in May. They were gained on a sweltering day and on an unhelpful pitch. He had actually declared himself unfit after a sleepless night helping to nurse his sick daughter, three-year-old Fiona. Stuart Surridge, the Surrey captain, persuaded him to play and he was equally determined to cajole further exertions after tea on the first day. Laker had then taken four wickets and Surridge brushed aside the protestations of the tired bowler. 'No, Jim,' he said, 'there are more Australian wickets for you in this innings.' Three of them, those of Maddocks, Lindwall and Johnson, were taken without cost in two overs on the resumption. As one observer said, 'Laker cut through them like a grocer's wire through Cheddar cheese.'

The *Times* correspondent projected a compelling picture of Laker's laconic style and test of endurance at The Oval. 'He came on to bowl, broad of beam and red-faced, and he continued to the end, completely unemotional, his shoulders hunched. Always he hitched up his trousers, always he licked his fingers. His run-up never varied, his legs hardly bending at the knees, his strides short.'

Laker bowled unchanged from just before half-past twelve for four hours and 20 minutes. In a spell of 46 overs from the pavilion end, broken only by the lunch and tea intervals, he took 10 wickets for 88 runs. Not since 1878, when left-arm bowler Edward Barratt, another Surrey man, did so for the Players, had ten wickets in an innings been achieved against the Australians. Barratt conceded only 43 runs in 29 overs out of a total of 77 and his feat was acknowledged by a bonus of £5. Laker's reward was the match ball and a cheque for £50 from the Surrey committee.

Bill O'Reilly, as the Australian spokesman, commented: 'Laker smothered the Australian batsmen with his science. His perfectly pitched off-spinners took just enough turn to encourage doubt and flat-footed loitering. This was the day when the thoroughbred came thundering out of the ruck.' The memory of Laker's stamina was but just one element in a performance which excited the admiration of Denys Rowbotham in the *Manchester Guardian*. Rowbotham enthused about the 'ball's lovely curve through the air, its deceptiveness confounding judgement'. There was, he added, 'the insistent, nagging accuracy of length, the bite of spin, and those disarming deliveries

119

that did not spin of which people will talk when they look back on the match'. Laker himself conceded that five of his wickets were taken with straight balls, the batsmen playing for the turn when the ball came on through.

Laker's command was such that, apart from two brief assaults by Davidson and Crawford, no Australian mastered him. He did, though, have two slices of luck. Lock, with sharply contrasting figures of 0 for 100 in 33 overs, should have had one wicket to reward his toils from the less favourable Vauxhall end. Miller skied an unaccepted catch to Dennis Cox at deep extra cover. According to Pat McKelvey, Cox always claimed that he thought about the nuances of the situation as the ball plummeted towards him. Cox decided to muff the catch on purpose and make the attempt look as realistic as possible. So Laker's return ought to have been limited to nine wickets, or even eight since the catch which Swetman took to dismiss the last man, Wilson, was dubious. Laker, referring to Cox's chivalrous gesture, said: 'I was so tired I just wanted the innings to end. I would certainly have held the catch if it had been mine.'

Laker's conquest was given increased significance when compared with another bowling marathon by Ian Johnson, the Australian captain and off-spinner, who sought to challenge their Surrey oppressor. He looked for similar dividends but his faith in spin, negligible in Australian hands, was misguided. It was a much criticised policy: he gave his fast bowlers only three overs. Johnson pursued economy when greater thrust was needed. He took six wickets but conceded 168 runs in 60.3 overs.

Ranged against him – and Alan Davidson – in Surrey's reply was Laker again, complementing his wickets with furious runs, 43 in all. Bernie Constable, with a century, and Laker added 57 for the seventh wicket in 39 minutes. Jim Swanton reported on the pattern of the partnership. 'A greater contrast in styles could not be imagined. There was Constable, sweeping, gliding and stepping away to cut, while Laker drove at almost everything, long hops included, with that grandiloquent back-lift and flourish of the follow-through.' Laker's batting, on this and other occasions, paraded a freedom quite at variance with the constraints of his bowling. His bat sang sweetly in one over from Johnson which yielded 16 runs.

Surrey gained a lead of 88 runs on the first innings. For a time, it seemed that Lock, now switched to the pavilion end, might emulate his partner in also taking ten wickets. An amazing coincidence did not occur although he did take the first six wickets before Laker intervened with a decision against Mackay. 'As soon as Lock began to bowl straighter and to a fuller length,' wrote Jim Swanton, 'he had the Australians in continual distress. There was venomous spin, a stark Spofforthian hostility and threatening fielding to his own bowling.' Lock's figures for the innings were seven wickets for 49 runs; but in fact all his wickets were obtained in one spell of 23.1 overs costing 36 runs.

Denys Rowbotham considered that the change in Lock's fortunes might have been partly due to Laker suffering a reaction to his efforts in the first innings. 'Lock's blood was up as soon as he saw his first ball rear angrily at Burke. Thereafter all the colour drained from the Australians' cheeks; they wore the haggard look of a cornered foe.' From a position of safety at 56 without loss, the Australians collapsed in the next ninety-five minutes to 107 all out. Surrey won by ten wickets to become the first county to beat an Australian touring side for forty-four years.

It must have appeared to Tony Lock, in a perplexing season, that the fates were conspiring against him. The Brylcreem manufacturers had provided an award of a silver cup and £100 for the best bowling performance of the season. Laker's haul for Surrey headed the list until Ken Smales, another Yorkshire off-spinner, took all 10 wickets for 66 for Nottinghamshire against Gloucestershire at Stroud. For the connoisseurs of statistics this was an unusual duo in one season.

Early in July, with Laker absent through injury, Lock must have thought that the prize was safe in his keeping. Against

Kent on a wet wicket at Blackheath he took 16 wickets in the match. He lowered the run count to 54 in obtaining his 10 wickets in the second innings. The unkindest cut of all was the further reduction of one run in Laker's analysis in the extra-ordinary Test at Old Trafford. It was the last straw for the crestfallen Lock, not only outwitted as a bowler but forced to surrender riches, which in this, and most other seasons, he would have well and truly earned.

Australia never recovered from their eclipse by spin at the hands of Surrey at The Oval. Their indecision had psychological roots. Preying on their minds was the stranglehold of Laker and Lock and the loss of the Ashes on the same ground in 1953. In their technical dilemmas they became nervous and too often impetuous. Time and time again they were betrayed by the vulnerability of their young batsmen against the sharply turn-ing ball. They were cruelly exposed like blank-faced dunces in the classroom.

'The Australian', wrote Norman Preston in *Wisden*, 'is mainly a Saturday afternoon cricketer, brought up on hard, true pitches, blazing sunshine and in clear light.' Trevor Bailey confirmed the disparity between the two opposing forces. He emphasised the advantage enjoyed by England players in regularly playing on bad wickets. The supreme accolade, as paid to Len Hutton, was that he was a master in such condi-tions. 'We have always tended to play better on turning wickets. The Australians didn't play on many and we did.'

The winning salvo by Australia in the second Test at Lord's was a false dawn, soon to be darkened at Leeds and Manchester. In mitigation, the Australians were rendered help-less on spinners' wickets and in one of the wettest summers in recent memory. But even more pertinently, they lacked the menace and craftsmanship of Laker and Lock. In the final Test, at The Oval, where they were spared further humiliation by rain, this deficiency was underlined when England had to bat on a treacherous pitch. They were unable to capitalise on the opportunity. The four tosses which Peter May won in the series would not have affected the outcome had the coin dropped the other way. Had Australia batted first on the heavily criticised wickets, the two matches in which England pronounced their superiority with innings victories would conceivably have finished earlier.

The question of the ideal cricketing wicket, or those which so disturbed the impotent tourists in 1956, was developed by Jim Swanton in the *Daily Telegraph*. Swanton said that only twice in England and never abroad could he recall Tests in which the surface had so disintegrated. One had been the Lord's Test of 1935 – the 'leather-jacket' year – when the square was ravaged by this pestilential insect. A South African leg-spinner by the fabulous name of Xenophon Balaskas spun England to defeat. The other was the rough-cast track of a wicket at Old Trafford in 1950 upon which the West Indies were summarily dispatched. 'Both of these wickets', said Swanton, 'were worse than those at Headingley and Old Trafford.'

Swanton did, however, argue that the conduct of any first-class match required a proper wicket, irrespective of the bowling at either side's disposal. The aggrieved Australians endorsed this sentiment as they observed the cascading dust on the first morning of the third Test at Headingley. This match was the turning point of the summer; but the opening sequence of events pointed to Australia consolidating their lead in the series.

Ron Archer, deputising for Miller with the new ball, took three wickets for 3 runs in nine overs. He dismissed Cowdrey, Oakman and Richardson; and one of the England selectors, Les Ames, arriving late, nearly offered his resignation when he looked at the scoreboard. England were reeling, like a capsized ship, at 17 for three. The rallying partners were Peter May and the 41-year-old Cyril Washbrook, who had been recalled to the England team after an absence of five years.

The selection of Washbrook, himself a selector, was heavily criticised; but the Lancashire veteran confounded the sceptics in an epic swan song. The seeds of England's ensuing triumph were sown by Washbrook and May. They added 187 for the fourth wicket before Laker and Lock, with 18 wickets between them, zestfully flourished on a wearing pitch. 'Who would have thought,' said one incredulous supporter, 'when we sat here on Thursday morning, with England 17 for three, that we should be here today, cheering victory by an innings?'

The Headingley wicket, related one correspondent, was already opening its arms to spin on the afternoon of the second day. In one hour after tea, Australia tumbled from 38 for 1 to 69 for 6. The misery of Mackay epitomised their misfortunes. *The Times* described one teasing over from Laker: 'Mackay was trying rather pathetically to unravel the mysteries. His contortions were most strange!' Mackay and Burge were two of Laker's victims in the innings.

Burge's dismissal was an instance of how Laker baited his traps. 'Laker bowled one ball that erred a fraction short of a perfect length,' explained one correspondent. 'He then delivered his top-spinner right on the spot. It skidded through to find Burge's pad plumb in front and his bat in the air.' Miller and Benaud, in defiant company, offered Australia tentative hopes of a lifeline. Their seventh-wicket stand of 73 was a vain attempt to avert the follow-on. There was an intermission of rain, which poured continuously for thirty-six hours, before the final act of submission on the Monday.

The grim duel on the last day was played against a bleak backcloth. Smoke rose in ghostly spirals from the red-bricked houses at the Kirkstall Lane end and the flags hung lifelessly from the white masts on the pavilion roof. 'We were told that rain was falling all round Leeds,' wrote Don Bradman in the *Daily Mail*. 'Watching play in the hazy gloom, a patriotic Australian could not be blamed for believing that it would fall here any minute.' Peter May, the England captain, was also on tenterhooks, fearful that the torrents might engulf his team's hopes. 'The real menace was rain,' he said. 'It chilled me to hear that rumble of thunder down Kirkstall way, half an hour before lunch.'

Beneath the canopy of grey skies and in deteriorating light Laker and Lock were again paired in a concentrated and relentless attack. Miller, this time in tandem with Harvey, fought the rearguard action. 'As the struggle continued, one could not help but note that the Ashes were now right on the dividing line,' ventured one Australian correspondent, R. S. Whitington. Denys Rowbotham, in the *Manchester Guardian*, described the hazards facing the batsmen, repeatedly confounded by quick spin and changing pace. 'Miller was three times rapped on the pads. Finally, with the temper of some caged and wounded animal, he was goaded into a huge pull. The spin beat him and his flailing bat merely rent the air. Then Harvey was all but beaten by Laker's quicker ball. During this time Laker and Lock bowled six maiden overs in succession and there was nothing the two batsmen could do about it.' Miller's defiance ended when he played half-back to Laker. 'The off-spin popped and Trueman swooped to take the catch at short-leg as the ball slithered down from Miller's glove.'

The prized wicket of Harvey was all Lock's work. Harvey's 69, out of a total of 140, was a courageous accomplishment spread over four and a half hours. Don Bradman thought that for determination, concentration and self-discipline it ranked as possibly the finest innings of Harvey's career. The valiance of the little master ended when Lock, sprawling down the wicket, acrobatically took a return catch.

Australia lost their last eight wickets for 32 runs. The impeccable accuracy of Laker and Lock was reflected in their figures on the last day. Laker, firmly in charge at the pavilion end, took four wickets for 24 runs in 19 overs. He conceded only one run in his first eight overs. Lock was just as miserly with a return of two wickets for 16 runs in 15.5. overs.

'Both were a good deal more than just accurate,' insisted Denys Rowbotham. 'The naggingly strict length and consistent straightness of their bowling reduced to a minimum the number of balls that need not be played. They added subtle variations of flight which disguised the changing length, now drew the batsmen agonisingly forward, next forced them hurriedly back and then, at crucial moments, confounded their judgement and made the batsmen move fatally the wrong way.'

It was a shared achievement but the major plaudits belonged to Laker, with eleven wickets in the match. He headed the procession of players as they ran the gauntlet of congratulatory hands. It was an occasion to savour. The Yorkshire exile, on this homecoming, had led England to their first victory – by an innings and 42 runs – over Australia at Headingley. Laker received a cheque for £50 to mark his feat, presented to him by William Harrison, a Yorkshire businessman. Harrison had told Laker that the prize was his if he took three wickets before lunch. 'It was a pleasure to pay out,' exclaimed the delighted benefactor.

More than forty years on, Bert Flack, at 86, provided his testimony in relating the intriguing prelude to a performance which still induces a sense of wonder. He was newly installed as groundsman at Old Trafford when Jim Laker wreaked unparalleled havoc. During practice on the day before the Test Flack was completing his preparations for the match. Gubby Allen, the chairman of the England selectors, accompanied by Tommy Burrows, the Lancashire cricket chairman, walked out to examine his work.

'They looked at each other and spoke together without turning to me,' remembered Flack. Allen then approached the groundsman and asked him if the wicket he had just inspected was to be used for the Test. Flack expressed surprise when Allen announced his displeasure. 'I'm not satisfied,' he said. There was a further conversation between Allen and Burrows. 'The chairman wants more grass off,' was the message communicated to the astonished Flack. 'Take a little more off, Bert, and that'll please him,' said Burrows. Flack was highly indignant. 'That's stupid. The match won't last three days. The surface is not all that well-knit.'

Flack pondered on his dilemma for some minutes. 'Finally, I got my cutter out and went up and down the wicket a couple of times. Then, I thought: "Well, why not, if the chairman wants a three-day match, he shall have it." ' The blades were adjusted and he began his cutting again. 'And that did take the grass all off, believe you me.' Flack then replaced the covers so as to hide the wicket from the inquisitive press corps. The England players, who had seen the wicket before the shaving, had now concluded their practice. They walked over to ask the groundsman why the pitch had been covered so promptly. It was a bright afternoon and their curiosity was not lessened by Flack's reply. 'We're expecting rain,' he said before hurrying away to avoid further questioning.

Geoffrey Howard, then the Lancashire secretary, described the surface of the wicket as 'fragile' and it was slow and lifeless before the subsequent rains transformed its character. He maintained, at variance with Flack's account, that the wicket had been prepared in exactly the same way as in the previous year at Old Trafford. The Test between England and South Africa in 1955 yielded over 1,300 runs. South Africa won an exhilarating match, the best of the series, by three wickets, with just three minutes to spare.

Howard had no reason at the outset of the 1956 match to believe that the proceedings would take on a different aspect. He does diplomatically aver that there were influences which should not have been exerted on Bert Flack. 'There was nothing malicious to excite offence but the words of members of the selection committee should not have been expressed in the presence of the groundsman.'

The Test series stood poised at one all. The selectors, following the success of Cyril Washbrook at Leeds, made another significant choice in bringing back David Sheppard. After going into the ministry, Sheppard had almost completely severed his connection with first-class cricket; he had played only four innings for Sussex before the Test at Old Trafford. One of the curiosities of a famous match was that the first five England batsmen – Richardson, Cowdrey, Sheppard, May and Bailey – were all amateurs. The last time this had happened against Australia was in 1899 when Fry, MacLaren, Ranjitsinhji, C. L. Townsend and Jackson comprised the top order.

There was the fanfare of an opening stand of 174 between Richardson and Cowdrey. It was England's best start against

Australia since 1938, when Hutton and Barnett began with 219 at Trent Bridge. The brisk runs paved the way for a resplendent century by Sheppard. Before the end of the first day there were tell-tale signs of a crumbling wicket. Accusations were made that the pitch had been specially prepared for England's spin bowlers. These were naturally and swiftly rejected by the Lancashire authorities, but no acceptance of blame could have diminished one of the historic bowling performances in Test cricket.

The maligned wicket had been quite accommodating for England's batsmen on the second morning. The speed of their scoring – 152 runs in two hours and ten minutes – was an expression of urgency but did not signal the terrors ahead. England, with some ease, totalled 459. Jim Laker always reminded the critics of this score in the lingering post mortems on the match.

Before Australia's innings their captain, Ian Johnson, had looked on with distrust at the dusty wicket. He requested just a light rolling. Bert Flack made a swift exit to other duties after watching the first ball of the innings. He knew with certainty what was happening from that moment. 'I saw a puff of dust rise on a perfectly good length. Brian Statham was bowling at the Stretford end. The ball lifted over the head of Godfrey Evans behind the wicket and went for four, nearly six, byes.'

Australia, at one stage 48 for 0, were bowled out for 84. It was their lowest score in England since their 65 at The Oval in 1912. Their previous lowest total was 58 after a ferocious storm at Brisbane in the 1936–37 series. The debacle at Old Trafford began with Lock's dismissal of Burke, caught by Cowdrey off a half-hearted pull. It was to prove his only wicket in the match. Overshadowing all else was Laker in his meanest mood. He took nine wickets for 37 runs. In 22 balls he claimed 7 wickets for 8 runs.

Jim Kilburn, in the *Yorkshire Post*, said that the ground at the Queensland capital, Brisbane, notoriously difficult after the city's tropical storms, never created a more dramatic collapse. 'Half the Australian batsmen never came within speaking distance of their conqueror, and they certainly had nothing to say with the bat. The pitch helped Laker, as did the batting; but most of all he helped himself, whirling to triumph on the crest of success as irresistible as a Pacific breaker tumbling upon one of Sydney's golden beaches.'

Don Bradman less rhapsodically pointed to a magnificent display on a dry, dusty pitch. 'The Aussies seemed powerless to cope with him. They did not bat well and I am sure in their minds they exaggerated the difficulties facing them.' Geoffrey Howard singled out Colin McDonald as the one Australian to show technical awareness; the others, he said, played as though gremlins had invaded the wicket.

Bill O'Reilly was more vigorous in his condemnation of the problems of his besieged compatriots. 'Let's have it straight. This pitch is a complete disgrace. What does lie in store for Test cricket if groundsmen are allowed to play the fool like this?' The procession of the Australian batsmen began when Peter May switched his spinners round to allow Laker to bowl with the gentle breeze drifting from the Stretford end. O'Reilly said that Lock demonstrated that you can bowl *too well* to get wickets. 'Time and time again he got his orthodox leg-breaks to jump and turn away so quickly that no batsman except Jim Burke was quick enough to get bat to ball.'

Bert Flack recalled that Lock, from the Warwick Road end, was turning the ball so much that it was veering into the hands of first or second slip rather than the wicket-keeper. Geoffrey Howard said Lock did not use his brains and forgot his business. As the match wore on and Laker's wickets multiplied, Lock grew increasingly cross with himself. Over by over, he gestured in disbelief, placing one agonised arm across his chest and then the other on top of it.

Jim Laker was convinced that the ball with which he dismissed Neil Harvey in Australia's first innings was the crucial breakthrough. It ensured that England would go on to retain the Ashes. 'Neil was the finest left-hander I ever bowled against and in our many challenging duels in the past the honours had gone very much his way. But, as luck would have it this time, I managed to bowl him a beauty first ball. From around the wicket, I held it back sufficiently for the ball to drift in and pitch around the leg and middle stumps. It turned just enough to clip his off-stump.'

Of all his wickets at Old Trafford, this was the one he treasured most. Bill O'Reilly, in his account of a 'spectacular comedy', agreed with Laker on the merits of the ball which overthrew Harvey. 'It beat the little left-hander so conclusively that the dismissal prepared everyone for the dismal execution that followed.'

Lilly Laker, back home in London, had been so preoccupied with organising baby-sitters for her young children that she was unaware of the events at Old Trafford. There had been no time to listen to the radio or read a newspaper. She travelled north to meet her husband on the Friday evening. At Warrington station she was amazed to discover a legion of reporters and photographers escorting the man of the hour to the platform. 'Good Lord!' she said, 'What on earth have you been up to? Why are all these people here?' Jim had to clarify the situation before they embraced in a very public hug amid the waiting cameras. There were to be more displays of affection, embarrassingly flaunted in the pictures on the front pages, before the curtain fell on this extraordinary Test match.

Lilly's arrival coincided with a dramatic change in the weather. She saw just forty-five minutes' play on the Saturday afternoon, and just one of Jim's wickets – the fall of Burke, caught by Lock, in the second innings. By early evening on Sunday she was en route for home. Laker said: 'If we had known what was going to happen during the next two days, she would certainly have stayed on to share in the greatest moment of my career. It is something we have both regretted.'

Australia, seething at their first-innings failure, followed on 375 runs behind. The extent of their fury is revealed by Bert Flack. It was his unenviable task to ask Ian Johnson which roller he wanted for the second innings. As he walked towards the Australian dressing-room he was in danger of being lynched. On the balcony the players were in a threatening mood, clutching their throats as if to indicate that he would be manhandled if he approached much nearer. Johnson lifted his head in disdain at Flack's enquiry. 'Please your effing self,' he said.

A torrential storm had struck Old Trafford on the Friday night. Before that occurred, McDonald had retired with a knee injury; and Harvey, tossing his bat high in the air in disgust, was out without scoring for the second time in the match, tamely hoisting Laker's gentle full toss into the hands of Cowdrey. It was a sorry dismissal off by far the worst ball Laker delivered in the match.

Bert Flack, only allowed to cover the ends of the wicket, had to sit and watch the descending rains. 'There was this little island of importance to the rest of the match. The rain shuttered down on the rolled surface, which was dusty but still impervious to moisture at the time. It stood on the top because of the convex shape of the square, flooded to the extent of half an inch of rain.' At the last, said Flack, the Australians were beset by one of the stickiest marled wickets he had ever seen. Never before had he watched a ball pop and jump so much; it seemed as if magic was summoned by Laker's fingers.

Laker recalled the appalling weather which intervened on the Saturday and Monday of the match. It was as dark and wet as November. Gale-force winds sprung up to handicap batsmen and bowlers in the brief spells of play. Ordinary bails were useless and were replaced by stronger ones made of a heavier lignum. 'In fact, they were never disturbed in the sessions lasting an hour on the Monday. The wet pitch was quite dead and Craig and the gallant McDonald, who had returned to the crease, were untroubled as the score moved on to 84 for two.'

The weather relented on the last day, but the prospect of an England victory was remote at lunch. Australia, at 112 for two, looked likely to save the match. Laker did not join his teammates for lunch. He relaxed with a beer and a sandwich in the dressing-room. 'As I gazed out towards the Derbyshire hills, the clouds began to disappear and the sun broke through.' It shone brightly throughout the afternoon to render conditions which glow just as serenely in the dreams of spin bowlers.

Jim Swanton said that Laker's first-innings performance was phenomenal enough, but its merit was clouded by the deficiencies of the Australian batting, as also by the palaver over the state of the wicket. 'There was no room whatever for argument regarding his bowling in the second innings. He bowled 36 overs, practically non-stop, except for the taking of the new ball, all the time attacking the stumps and compelling the batsmen to play. He never wilted or fell short in terms of length or direction.'

Neville Cardus, watching Laker's triumph, said that the Australians, though overwhelmed by him, should also have been grateful for the education he gave in a science they had recently neglected. Colin McDonald held England at bay for over five and a half hours. His 89, flawless in its execution, was considered one of the best innings ever played by an Australian batsman on a turning wicket in England.

Cardus said of it: 'It was proof of a quickness to learn and of flexible and adaptable talents. Here was an innings organised technically, the finest played this year by an Australian for the purposes of a lengthy tenure on an English wicket in a Test match.'

At Old Trafford, Jim Laker was the supreme inquisitor who was finally released from the shackles of criticism. 'Ten Little Aussie Boys Lakered in a Row' was the joyous headline in the *Daily Express* next day. Laker wove a spinning plot as cunning as any devised by Agatha Christie. England won the match by an innings and 170 runs to retain the Ashes. Laker's figures will surely never be eclipsed. He took 10 wickets for 53 runs, and a match total of 19 for 90 in 68 overs.

Les Ames recalled: 'The Australians were not good players against off-spin. They did rather give up the ghost. The top of the wicket went after the first day. Jim, with his marvellous control, turned the ball at right angles.' Laker became the first bowler to take 19 wickets in any first-class match, surpassing Sydney Barnes's 17 for 159 on the Johannesburg mat in 1913. In seven games against Australia in 1956 Laker took 63 wickets, including 46 at a cost of 9.60 each in the Tests. Only Barnes, with 49 wickets in four Tests against South Africa in 1913–14, has exceeded this figure.

Robin Marlar, in his tribute written thirty years later in *Wisden*, said that there was still an air of wondrous disbelief that Laker could have taken 19 wickets. 'Lock, the most avaricious of bowlers, was at the other end. Nor should it pass notice that Statham and Bailey, both unquestioned occupants of the hall of fame, sent down 46 overs between them without a strike. Even if you accept that the 1956 Australians were not one of the best sides from that country, there were still great cricketers in the team: Harvey, Miller, Lindwall and Benaud. In truth, even though it happened, we can describe Laker's feat only as incredible.'

Tom Graveney, originally selected for the Manchester Test, always banteringly told Laker that had injury not prevented him from playing he would have failed to take the crucial catches which produced the record. Graveney's deputy, the Sussex all-rounder Alan Oakman, was an influential ally with five catches at Old Trafford. It was a fitting, if unexpected, finale to his two-match Test career. Hasty consultations in Manchester on the day before the match led to a telephone call by Gubby Allen, the chairman of the selectors, to Hastings police station. He asked: 'Do you know where Alan Oakman lives?' Back came the reply: 'We do and if he is in town we will pick him up in five minutes.' Four minutes later there was a loud rap on Oakman's front door. A policeman, leaning on his cycle, told him that he had to report to Old Trafford on the following morning.

Oakman's selection was confirmed by Peter May on his arrival at the ground. His credentials as a short-leg fieldsman were proudly acknowledged in Sussex; he enjoyed a key partnership with another off-spinner, Robin Marlar. At one point in the Australian first innings Oakman was stationed in the unaccustomed position of mid-on. The profitable switch occurred when David Sheppard, fielding in the bat-pad position for Laker, suggested a change to the English captain. Sheppard had not played regularly in first-class cricket for some time. There was an awareness that his reflexes were not as sharp as they had been. Sheppard asked: 'Could I go to mid-on or mid-off where I'll have more time to see the ball?'

May accepted the advice of his former Cambridge colleague and Oakman was deputed to bring his vigilance to the leg trap. Oakman recalled: 'Having the greatest confidence in Jim's accuracy, I stood nearer than usual. I can remember Keith Miller coming in, taking guard and looking round the field, particularly out to deep square leg and mid-wicket.' Miller told him: 'That's a dangerous position, Oakie. If I middle one, they will have to carry you off.' Three balls later he pushed forward to Laker and Oakman stooped to take the first of his catches, low down around his ankles. Later that year, Oakman attended a dinner with the record-breaker. He was introduced as the man who had helped Laker by holding five catches against Australia. There was a wry smile on Laker's face. 'Alan,' he whispered, 'you're not still living on that?'

There was an amusing postscript to Laker's feat. After the match Don Bradman and Alex Bannister saw Sydney Barnes in the car park at Old Trafford. 'Well, what do you think of that?' they asked. Barnes, the legendary bowling maestro and Laker's illustrious predecessor at Saltaire, gruffly replied: 'No bugger ever got all 10 when I was at t'other end.'

Barnes's response did, in fact, accentuate one of the mysteries of the match, the inability of Tony Lock to capitalise on the conditions. His match return was one wicket for 106 runs in 69 overs. John Arlott wrote that never was the difference between Lock – in the days of his 'old' action – and Laker more clearly demonstrated than at Old Trafford. 'Lock took his wickets by the size and speed of his break in which no one in the world was his superior. But, when the ball would come through only slowly, he lacked the power – and the patience – to defeat top-class batsmen who concentrated on defence.' Arlott added that Laker was a constant testimony to the adage propounded by Jack Hobbs, who said that good batsmen were not dismissed by swing, break or speed so often as by the mistake of playing back when they should play forward, or forward when they should play back.

*

Laker, besieged by the media and well-wishers, did not begin his journey home until nearly eight o'clock after an unforgettable day in Manchester. He had been driving for about two hours when he decided to pull into a pub at Lichfield. He recalled: 'Inside the crowded bar, a tiny black-and-white television set was showing highlights of the day's play in the Test match.' It can be safely said that he would not have been allowed to remain anonymous in the glare of publicity directed on sporting stars today. Yet not a single patron then recognised the tired celebrity seated behind them. He drank his beer and ate a sandwich, all the while listening to the excited gossip of the other customers.

There was no chance of remaining unrecognised in London. When he arrived home at between two and three in the morning, there was a massive reception party awaiting him.

"Hello, There! Fancy Seeing You Again. Step Right In...Even The Worms Are Turning On Our Beautiful Wicket!"

Camped outside his flat was a small army of photographers. None of the Laker household was exempt from attention that night. It was not long before his two little girls, Fiona and Angela, much bewildered by the fuss, were roused from their slumbers to face the cameras. 'At the most I managed a couple of hours' sleep before checking in, bleary-eyed, next morning at The Oval for another game for Surrey,' said Laker. 'But the gods were still with me. It poured with rain all morning and play was abandoned for the day.'

The bewitching skills at Old Trafford brought congratulations for Laker throughout the country, his modest acceptance of an unequalled performance thought especially pleasing. He was named by the BBC as the Sportsman of the Year. Thousands of readers responded to an invitation by one national newspaper to compose a telegram commemorating the achievement. From a rowing club came this tribute: 'Reserving a seat for you in our boat next year. In-out; out-in; in-out.' A reader in Hampstead wrote: 'Congratulations! Home James, you don't spare the Aussies.' Another telegram from Wembley conveyed wit and delight. 'Thanks for making us feel 19 and the Australians 90.'

A Canadian correspondent and baseball enthusiast described Laker as the outstanding 'curve-dispenser' in modern times. Of the sensational 'pitching performance' he said it was somewhat akin to a no-hit, no-run game. 'It is quite a thing to do, more than a baseball pitcher turning in a perfect game. The pitcher is on his own. But the cricket bowler has a partner at the other end, who is likely to botch up your chances of dismissing all ten by putting out some himself.'

In modern times Laker's triumph would undoubtedly have ensured financial security for the rest of his life. In 1956 his Test match fee was £75. He estimated that he earned an extra £1,000 through various company donations and articles in national newspapers. 'Just to show how commercially naive we were in those days I signed 1,000 copies of the final scorecard printed at Old Trafford. They sold like hot cakes for my benefit – at two shillings each.'

The major influence in Laker's decision to turn down a business appointment in Australia was the magnificent response to his benefit. It was, of course, reinforced by the fact that he was the lauded cricketer of the year. The proceeds of his benefit totalled £11,000 and the contributions which he found most touching were those of pensioners, dipping into their meagre funds, to send him postal orders for half-a-crown.

The Australian business offer, made by Rothmans, the cigarette manufacturers, was a three-year contract worth more than £3,000 a year. Laker was invited to take up an appointment as chief press and public relations officer based in Sydney. The inducements were first-class travel expenses, a car, and accommodation for himself and his family. Laker had been selected for the 1956–57 tour of South Africa. So his first response was to send a cable to Rothmans in Australia: 'Thanks for your excellent offer. Rather heavily engaged with the Australians at present and must deal with the South Africans. Hope to join you later.' The news of his impending appointment provoked much press discussion, both adverse and sympathetic. One leader writer neatly encapsulated the dilemma: 'Laker has the problem of every sporting hero. What do I do when I am *yesterday's* hero?'

Three weeks later Laker declined what must have been a highly tempting opportunity. 'The lure of England and The Oval has proved too strong. Cricket has meant everything to me in the past, and it offers a future. At 34, I've got some years left in the game, and I aim to make the most of them.' Rothmans, commented Laker, had been most considerate and generous in their attempts to meet every possible difficulty. They had emphasised that their intention was to provide him with a job for life. It was not, they insisted, just a question of capitalising on his success that summer. Rothmans were prepared to extend the terms of the proposed contract to include an entitlement to leave in England every few years.

As can be imagined, there were urgent pleas from Laker's supporters to stay at home. In the end, these were the voices which prevailed. 'The roar of the crowd really does mean something to me and I would miss it a lot,' he said. He stressed that he had received no counter-offer to help him change his mind, nor had the Surrey club intervened. 'Cricket on its own has triumphed,' he concluded.

At The Oval, in August, Laker knew that he had made the right decision. A rousing swell of applause welcomed him home. During the tea interval, between the innings in the Test, he was presented with a silver salver by the MCC President, Earl Alexander of Tunis. It was engraved with the full scores of the match at Old Trafford in which he had set up so many bowling records.

The historic figures at Old Trafford still produce a surge of pride at the accomplishment of a diffident hero. As Jim Laker pursued his nonchalant way to glory, he did not for a moment suggest that he was writing cricket history. He carried on as if nothing out of the ordinary had happened. While he remained seemingly unruffled, there were others perched on the edge of their seats in a state of high excitement.

Perhaps the most vivid example of single-minded devotion to a champion cricketer was presented halfway across the world in tropical Fiji. Throughout that July night in 1956 one expatriate diehard kept himself informed of the news by wireless. His armchair vigil did not end until the last Australian wicket was taken.

The inimitable voice of John Arlott, describing the events unfolding at Old Trafford, rippled over the airwaves. The commentary transported the listener to industrial England where the sweatered cricketers were at play in conditions more like the Arctic than midsummer. As the night progressed, Jim Laker pursued his record-breaking course. Whoops of delight punctuated the fall of each Australian wicket.

Finally, as the palest shade of grey tinged the sky, a weary but happy Englishman swept into the bedroom to announce to his wife. 'We've kept the Ashes. Laker has broken every bowling record.'

'That's wonderful,' the wife replied sleepily. 'Now what about getting us some tea?'

10

THE INTELLIGENT INQUISITOR

'For the possessor of cricket brains the resources are endless
and a successful enjoyment of the game unbounded.'

Hedley Verity

In an illuminating monograph John Arlott found substance,
despite its immodesty, in the boast of William Lillywhite, the
first master of round-arm bowling. Lillywhite said: 'I s'pose if
I wuz to think every ball, they'd never get a run off me.'

The astute stratagems of Jim Laker were also distinguished
by thought. 'There have been off-spinners – though few – who
spun the ball as much as Laker; some of them had comparable
control,' wrote Arlott. 'But no one has ever matched him in
those departments and had, also, such a quality of intelligence.
From this stemmed other assets: it produced observation,
judgement and flexibility which enabled him to assess changing circumstances and adapt his method to suit them.'

All the great exponents of spin fashioned their craft with the
care and devotion of a great musician. Their apprenticeships
were as exacting, in their different ways, as those of Menuhin
or Tortelier. The masterclass of another great Yorkshireman
was one of the many studied by Jim Laker in his salad days.
Hedley Verity, noted the aspiring youth, never pressed as a
slow left-arm bowler. He was immaculate in his control of
length and direction whether the wicket was helpful or not.
The fact that he scarcely bowled a bad ball just increased his
venom on a sticky wicket.

Laker remembered inspecting a wet wicket at Bradford after

Verity had quietly ushered one set of opponents to their doom. 'There were just two "spots" on the turf – and you could have covered each of them with a soup-plate.' He calculated that Verity had bowled fifteen overs in this final demoralising spell. 'But there was not a mark on the pitch outside these two areas, where his normal-length ball and the slightly quicker one just short of a length had made their impressions.'

Hedley Verity was a model tutor, bequeathing the paramount standards of accuracy. His lessons were the ideal bowling primer. The ABC of bowling was presented by Verity in the following words: 'Good length is the shortest length at which a batsman *should* play forward.' Verity cited the example of his predecessor, Wilfred Rhodes, in the allurements of flight. The deception of Rhodes was to make batsmen believe that the ball was pitching further up than was actually the case.

Clarrie Grimmett, the Australian leg-spinner, said perfect flight should be just above eye level. 'If you stand on a bridge and watch a car approaching, you can judge with certainty its speed. Yet if you stand at eye level or just below eye level it is particularly hard to tell how fast it is coming.' It was, in practice, the same for the spin bowler, said Grimmett. A ball of low trajectory was easy to pick up in pace and to decide where it would land on the pitch. On the other hand, a ball delivered above the level of the eyes made it difficult for a batsman to judge with certainty the spot where it would land.

Hedley Verity's thoughts on a singular and perplexing art drew attention to the fact that to gain maximum turn the slow ball should have all the bowler's energy behind the spin. 'Energy used for the development of speed in a fast bowler is converted – in this respect – by grip and action instead of pace.' In his treatise on the principles of bowling, Verity demonstrated an intelligence which became a byword in a career sadly curtailed by his death in action in the Second World War. Jim Laker was a diligent pupil who profited from the example, earning, in time, accolades for his own tactical acumen.

David Sheppard, as the Cambridge University captain in 1952, remembered the proud words of a craftsman. They were delivered with serious intent but masked, in Yorkshire fashion, as a waggish ad-lib. There was no boastfulness; it was simply a matter of record. Sheppard had invited Laker to bowl and coach in the nets at Fenner's. Laker told him: 'I had a bad season last year. I bowled two long hops.' Later on, when Sheppard stood in close at backward short-leg for England to Laker's bowling, he was able to verify the truth of this claim of accuracy.

John Arlott stressed that Laker was never mechanical. 'He achieved his results on turning wickets at the lowest possible cost, while on batsmen's wickets he set problems of length and flight. His variations were subtle, designed to deceive a batsman a pitch-length away, therefore rarely visible to spectators. But to watch a great batsman play an over of apparently identical deliveries in six different ways indicated the profundity and range of his resources.'

Trevor Bailey, another fervent admirer, recalled the perfect balance and rhythm of Laker's action. 'He was so grooved that he could have run in to bowl blindfolded.' The West Indians called Laker the 'praying man'. There was a succession of short steps, the pivot, and then the sharply stretched left hand, palm upwards, before the ball was delivered side-on at the strictly regulated '12 o'clock' position. Micky Stewart, an observant fielding ally with Surrey, referred to the signal application of a bowling artist. 'One of Jim's major assets was that he controlled a cricket ball in all conditions.'

Bailey presented a compelling cameo of Laker in his book *The Greatest of My Time*. First, he related, 'there was that slightly disdainful hitch of the trousers before he commenced his measured approach to the wicket. When he was hit to the boundary, he would instinctively give his magic and very enlarged spinning finger a contemplative inspection and a little gentle massage.

'No bowler enjoys having a catch put down. Some curse, some rave, some cry, some gesticulate. But these actions were too melodramatic for Jim. He merely stood there and waited for the return of the ball, quietly tapping his foot. He lifted his eyes upwards as if asking justice for bowlers and perhaps suggesting that it would not be amiss if a thunderbolt should strike the offending fieldsman.'

All the contemporary evaluations would suggest that Laker should have enjoyed automatic status as an England player in the 1950s; and nothing in his career was more remarkable than his relatively small number of Test appearances. For a decade, in the opinion of all but a minority, he was the best off-spinner in the world. Yet between his first and last Tests, England played 99 matches and he took part in only 46 of them. They still earned him a yield of 193 wickets. In that time, only three other England bowlers, Trueman, Statham and Bedser, exceeded his aggregate.

Laker's achievements at Old Trafford in 1956 did bring about a late reappraisal of his gifts. In Trevor Bailey's view, it was not a moment too soon: 'He is and has been for at least five years a magnificent off-spin bowler.'

Don Bradman, just as questioningly, bearing in mind Laker's omission from two Australian tours, thought it implausible that he should suddenly emerge as a bowling force. He had watched Laker bowl at Old Trafford. 'The spinning pitch did help him enormously, but is this the whole explanation of Laker's tremendous success?' Bradman maintained that figures over a long period were a reliable guide. He said that Laker's form in 1956 was not so far removed from normal as his Test performances in that year would appear to suggest. Laker's figures over four seasons had remained fairly constant. His wickets had been obtained at an average rate of approximately eight overs each. 'Yet, against an international team this year, Laker's bowling average is virtually halved, and he has obtained a wicket every six overs.'

On paper, commented Bradman, it was Tony Lock, rather than Laker, who had made a noticeable improvement over his review period. Despite this apparent advance, Lock, in 1956, had had to inspect a bowling average nearly doubled. Instead of a wicket every seven overs, he had toiled for sixteen overs for each one. Taking the four Tests in which both Surrey spinners played, their respective figures were: Laker, 43 wickets (at 8.79), Lock, 15 (at 22.47).

Bradman said of Laker: 'He delivers the ball from about as high a trajectory as one can achieve, consistent with maximum spin, using splendid body and shoulder movement. Indispensable to his success is the watertight field to which he bowls. He has two leg slips, another man (very short and about square), mid-on, square leg on the fence, and a deep mid-wicket, sometimes on the boundary, sometimes halfway out. The close men take care of pure defence by the batsmen and the outer ring look after the swishes. But the inner ring is the real menace. While these men are allowed to remain in position, they will snap up those chances which are inevitable on a turning pitch when the batsmen play back to balls not short of a length, or when they play forward without smothering the spin.'

The allegations that Jim Laker was a liability on hard overseas wickets had been proved manifestly false on his second tour of the West Indies in 1953–54. As a spinning tyro, he had shown his mettle against the emerging 'three W's' (Worrell, Weekes and Walcott) in the Caribbean six years earlier. Now he had to contend with this majestic trio in their ruthless maturity on wickets glistening to aid sprightly strokeplay. Walcott, a massive hitter who struck the ball at finger-splitting speed, headed the West Indies averages in the series, in ten innings scoring 698 runs at an average of 87.25.

Fortunately for England, Walcott was matched in batting temper by Len Hutton, whose assured mastery rallied his team after defeat in the first two Tests. Hutton stood loftily alone on his pinnacle; overall he averaged 96.71, and his runs, including a double century, in the last three Tests gave him an average of just under 150.

Laker's bowling marathons yielded the prize of Walcott's wicket four times in this series. His overall record against the great West Indian is testimony to the way he measured up to an imposing challenge. He took Walcott's wicket thirteen times

143

in their meetings. Only Bill Edrich and Arthur Milton headed Walcott in the list of batsmen most frequently dismissed by Laker. Tom Graveney, who went on his first tour in 1953–54, recalled: 'Jim bowled beautifully in the West Indies. Walcott was a feared striker, particularly strong off the back foot. He often looked to square-cut Jim and would hole out at short third man.'

Everton Weekes was another West Indian with a gargantuan appetite for runs. Laker was especially intrigued by his unusual Christian name. In one conversation with Weekes, he asked him why he had been given this name. It transpired that Weekes's father was a devout supporter of English soccer and that Everton was his favourite team. Laker could not help observing that it was fortunate that his father had not supported West Bromwich Albion.

Trevor Bailey, another member of the MCC party in the West Indies, also enthused about the quality of Laker's bowling in unfavourable conditions. He selected, as an example, the Yorkshireman's return of four wickets for 71 runs in 50 overs in the second innings of the fifth Test at Kingston, Jamaica. Bailey, who had himself taken seven wickets in the West Indies first innings, considered this to be one of the greatest feats of slow bowling he had witnessed abroad. It was a vital contribution in England's victory by nine wickets, which levelled the series.

Alex Bannister recalled a barrage of bouncers at Sabina Park. Frank King, the Barbadian fast bowler, and Fred Trueman countered each other in this forbidding tussle. King, in fact, was the culprit when Laker was struck a fierce blow in the eye in the previous Test in Trinidad. He was partnered there by Trueman when the West Indies took the new ball for the third time in a high-scoring match. King was the major threat and in a lively mood. At the other end was Frank Worrell, a more amenable proposition at gentle medium-pace.

Laker described a mid-wicket conference briskly conducted by Trueman. 'I have assessed the situation, Jim lad – thee take King and I'll look after Worrell,' he cheerfully announced. 'Blindly and dumbly I agreed,' said Laker. 'Minutes later, in attempting something quite out of my province, namely a hook shot from a King bouncer, I was zig-zagging my way to the pavilion with my eye pouring blood and requiring more stitches than I can remember.' Cheering him sheepishly on his way to hospital was an appalled Trueman. His parting words were: 'That's the shrewdest assessment I've made for some time.'

Laker's injury, fearsome to contemplate, did naturally enough make him apprehensive about resuming his duties in the Test at Kingston. Moreover, he had strong doubts whether he could properly fulfil his bowling role because his vision had undoubtedly been impaired. Hutton knew that Laker, even at less than full fitness, was a key link in his armoury. He persuaded him that England would be disadvantaged if he did not play.

So a valiant bowler entered the fray in the tiny cockpit, crammed with boisterous spectators, at Kingston. Framing the scene of his triumph were the superb outlines of the mountains, ridge upon ridge, in their ever changing tints of green. 'Only those who knew the story appreciated the great work Laker did for England,' reported the *Sunday Express*. 'Because of his long bowl earlier in the West Indies innings, Laker's spinning finger had become swollen to nearly twice its normal size. His attempts to spin had rubbed away the skin, leaving the flesh raw and bleeding. Hutton could only afford to use him in short spells but, as soon as Laker said he was ready again, on he went.'

Wardle and Lock, in left-handed tandem, were the supporting bowlers, tight in their economy, as Laker took his rests at Kingston. Courage to defeat accusations of a faintheart was paraded on this day. 'His was a first-class exhibition of spin bowling founded upon subtle variations of pace and flight,' reported one witness. The *Times* correspondent forecast more happy days for Laker. 'He has never been a certain starter for England. But in conditions a long way from helpful, he was the best of the English slow bowlers. Unless his form deserts him, he should be first choice among the off-spin bowlers for the next tour of Australia.'

Alex Bannister, in his summary of the events in the Caribbean, considered that Laker, in the early stages of the tour, was too often prematurely withdrawn from the attack. 'All slow bowlers', he wrote, 'must be given some time to work out their theories, especially when pitting their wits against some of the world's best batsmen on good wickets.'

Hutton had, as we have seen, been given evidence of Laker's skills in adversity at Kingston. What was insupportable was to cast a slur on his fellow Yorkshireman. There were two instances of a strange opposition in Hutton's tour report submitted to the MCC and published in *The Cricketer* in 1996. Of Laker he said: 'He is an extremely fine bowler. But he has a tendency to be afraid of certain batsmen instead of adopting the attitude: "I am a better bowler than you are a batsman." When a good batsman is at the wicket he is inclined . . . to indicate his unwillingness to bowl.'

The report also included a contention that 'Laker should be considered in committee before future selection for overseas tours.' In British Guiana, shortly before the end of the West Indies tour, Laker was given his first clue that he would be excluded from the following series in Australia. The story has been related by Laker and Tom Graveney. Hutton, Laker, Graveney and Brian Statham were sitting in the hotel lounge, sipping cold drinks. The subject of Australia was broached by the England captain. 'Now, Brian, how would you like to go to Australia?' Statham replied: 'Not 'arf, skipper, I want to go again.' Turning to Graveney, Hutton said: 'And what about you, Tom?' 'I'd love it. There's nothing I'd like better than an Aussie trip,' said Graveney. A noticeable pause followed before Hutton looked in Laker's direction and enquired: 'Like another drink, Jim?'

The gulf which divided Len Hutton and Jim Laker probably stemmed from differing temperaments. How much it was caused by Hutton's deference, as England's first professional captain, to the amateur hierarchy is a matter for conjecture. The first supposition is that their paths would almost certainly lead to a fruitful and pleasing rendezvous. Hutton's close friendship with Hedley Verity, one of his encouraging mentors as a Yorkshire junior, would have borne out the benefits of match-winning spin. Laker's own reverence for Verity would also appear to have contributed to a meeting of cricket minds. In addition, there was the knowledge of the tussles between Yorkshire and Surrey when Laker at times disturbed the serenity of Hutton's batting.

Yet, as Laker recorded, the question of speed or spin was one Hutton always found difficult to resolve. The obsession with fast bowling overseas, and particularly in Australia, was based on two factors. One was an historic precedent and the other the legacy of his heroic stand as the lynchpin of the English batting against Lindwall and Miller in the post-war years.

Bill Bowes delighted in relating one conversation with his former Yorkshire colleague during the Test at Sydney in the 1946–47 series in Australia. 'You know what they're saying, Len? They reckon you're freetened of fast bowling.' Hutton did not respond to the allegation; but his swift and luminous smile signalled his acknowledgement. Bowes was well aware that Hutton would not allow this notion to linger in the minds of the Australians. The Yorkshireman was goaded into furious action. Neville Cardus said one of the tragedies of the match was the way an enchanting innings by Hutton came to an end. 'It is not reckless to assume that a century of grandeur was nipped in the bud, a rare page blotted in the book of cricket's history.'

The exuberance of Hutton's strokeplay reflected the indignation of an affronted man. 'He survived an appeal for lbw off the first ball; and then, in a most easeful sequence, he rippled the sunlit field by stylish drives, quick and wonderfully late,' wrote Cardus. In less than half an hour Hutton struck six boundaries. 'In the last over before lunch,' added Cardus, 'the cruellest bolt of mischief brought Hutton down to prosaic earth.' He attempted another forcing backstroke off Miller and, after hitting the ball, lost the grip of his bat with one hand and the uncontrolled swing of it broke his wicket. Hutton's 37 runs took him only twenty-four minutes. It was a classic cameo of an innings and, reported the *Sydney Morning Herald*, even the most ardent partisan would have welcomed another hour of Hutton's majestic strokeplay.

Eight years later, as the victorious captain in Australia, Hutton had at his disposal bowlers to avenge his earlier fortitude. The arrival of Trueman, Tyson, Statham and Loader in the 1950s gave him the ammunition to wage a counter-attack. It was then demonstrably a case of 'the buggers have given it to me; let them have some of it back'. Hutton was able to replicate, in a less hostile manner, the annihilation of Australia by the pace of Harold Larwood under the austere direction of Douglas Jardine in the 1932–33 series.

Hedley Verity on that latter tour, like Bob Appleyard in Hutton's party, was the spelling bowler, employed to control proceedings while the fast bowlers rested. Appleyard regarded his selection ahead of Laker as one of the biggest compliments of his career. 'But I did have an additional string as a seamer. I wasn't just relying on spin.'

There were a number of mysterious selections on Hutton's tour. The most contentious was the choice of Jim McConnon, the Glamorgan off-spinner. It was reputedly influenced by his bowling against Surrey at The Oval in July 1954. Glamorgan won by 110 runs as Surrey were bowled out for 76 in their second innings. McConnon was said to have posed greater problems than Laker and Lock on a pitch affected each day by overnight rain. He returned figures of seven wickets for 23 runs in 11.5 overs. However, the evidence is inconclusive: the Surrey spinners shared fifteen wickets in the match.

Peter Walker, a later Glamorgan and England player, maintained that the theory that McConnon had 'more in the air' than Laker was only propounded by those who had not played against the Yorkshireman. 'Jim had everything. He spun the ball acutely, possessed great control, and could bowl it at any speed, depending on the wicket.' Within the game, said Walker, there was incredulity that Laker's name did not appear in selection lists directly after that of the captain. He believes that the decision to exclude Laker was taken because of the fallacy that he could not bowl on hard, fast wickets. 'Every time he was put to that test he bowled beautifully.'

Frank Tyson is one dissenting voice amid the general praise. 'Jim was indeed one out of the bag as I remember him. He once caught Northamptonshire on a wet wicket at Wantage Road – and it was just a waste of time going out to bat. His control, spin and speed through the air did not give batsmen a hope.' Tyson does, however, believe that Laker did not always do justice to his skills on overseas wickets. 'He did have a reputation, particularly among the Australians, of not having a big heart. Jim failed to take the wickets he should have done on occasions because he did not stick at it.'

The inference that Laker wilted under punishment is disputed by others. Micky Stewart, observing that no bowler relishes being attacked, contends that the situation, in Laker's case, was not as severe as has been alleged. Doug Insole, the MCC vice-captain on the tour of South Africa in 1956–57, remembered that Laker always *expected* to get wickets and was not content until he had gained his first scalp. 'Jim did dislike unorthodoxy by batsmen, as did Lock. They both thought it an indignity.' In South Africa, recalled Insole, Laker bowled in a much more measured way than anywhere else. 'This was a very happy tour and Jim and Johnny Wardle, mesmeric with his wrist spin, were a successful duo. Jim, as a finger spinner, wisely perceived that he would not achieve much turn on these wickets. He concentrated on line, length and flight and did this beautifully.'

Arthur McIntyre, a key witness as the Surrey wicket-keeper in this period, presents another view of Laker bowling on good wickets. 'Where Jim was so great in these conditions was when he would get a ball to turn and create doubt in the batsmen's minds. On a really bad wicket he was capable of undercutting the ball to make it go straight on without any change of action.'

There is also the testimony of Richie Benaud to reject the supposed frailties in temperament. The strength of Laker as a bowler, said Benaud, was vested in his ability to turn the ball even on the best of pitches and in his control of both spin and swerve. 'He was close to the perfect off-spinner with his controlled and balanced run to the crease. He was a real thinker on bowling and on the game.'

Len Hutton, in his autobiography published in 1984, distanced himself from the preference for McConnon on the Australian tour in 1954–55. He said the omission of Laker left him very unhappy, but it seemed there were too many long memories of his early failure against Australia. 'At the time it was standard English thinking that off-spinners were wrong for Australia.'

Hutton's own position as captain on the tour was not clear-cut; he missed two Tests against Pakistan through illness in 1954, and his appointment was not ratified until mid-July. So it is probably fair to say that his own authority was diminished and other influences prevailed to land McConnon in his ranks. Hutton did concede that McConnon was a good bowler but much less deserving than the bowler left at home. 'In my opinion,' he added, 'there was no justification for his selection, certainly not in front of Laker.'

Geoffrey Howard, the MCC manager on the 1954–55 tour, remembers a selection committee meeting on the train en route for the third Test at Melbourne. The panel of selectors comprised Hutton, Edrich, Evans, George Duckworth and Howard. All of them, apart from Howard, wanted to play McConnon. Howard expressed his dissent, telling his fellow selectors: 'If you put up a team sheet and McConnon is in, these will be the reactions: "He will wonder how he can refuse whereas Bob Appleyard would be absolutely furious." ' Discretion prevailed and Appleyard was selected at Melbourne. McConnon was spared the ordeal of Test exposure. A groin injury first put him in hospital and then, after he had broken a finger at Hobart, he returned home.

The reasoning against off-spinners, expressed before the dramatic change in Australian conditions in the late 1950s, was that they were a luxury. Alec Bedser said that before and after the Second World War finger spinners were employed as stock bowlers. On his first tour of Australia in 1946–47 the wickets in country matches as well as Tests had been devoid of turn. The transformation in the nature of the wicket at Melbourne occurred when the ground was bulldozed to flatten out the slope of around five feet for the Olympic Games in 1956.

Amid the selection debates in 1954, one of the ironies of the year was that, after being passed over for the tour, Laker and Lock suddenly found rampant form. In their last ten championship games they took 103 wickets between them, Laker securing 59 and Lock 44, both for an average of less than nine runs apiece. They led a remarkable revival as Surrey won their third successive championship. Micky Stewart, in his recent managerial capacities, has produced the figures of his former Surrey colleagues to astonish current England players. Presented with this information, they have expressed their disbelief at the omission of Laker and Lock.

The flowering of Jim Laker in his country's colours was checked because his captain was an apostle of speed. 'Len always gave me the impression that he regarded spinners as the last resort,' declared a disappointed bowler. 'Whenever I bowled under his captaincy, I felt I had to get a wicket quickly, otherwise I would soon be off. Short spells are all very well for the quickies, but not much use to spinners, who should always be prepared to bide their time, provided the skipper is understanding.'

Roy Tattersall, as a fellow off-spinner, reinforced Laker's complaint about Hutton's sparing use of spin. 'Len was a fine captain, but a little awkward to play under. He took you off too soon, often after only four or five overs when you felt you were getting the better of your opponent.' Tattersall afforded a glimpse of Hutton at his most enigmatic. It occurred during one swiftly concluded spell in which he had failed to take a wicket. He was summoned by Hutton at the end of one over and asked: 'What's the matter. Are you tired?' It was often difficult to know whether Hutton was in earnest or in impish mood. Tattersall resolved to match one jest with another. 'I thought I would play him at his own mocking game. "I think you're right, Len; I do feel buggered." ' Hutton offered a shy, perplexed smile at the response, perhaps a little abashed by his own severity. The two players were all square in this bout of repartee.

The recognition of Laker as England's premier spinner was not quickly determined. Gubby Allen, the chairman of the selectors, was almost grudging, even after Laker's triumphant hours at Old Trafford in 1956. The acclaimed bowler might then have expected an unqualified tribute. Instead, Allen's commendation merely welcomed Laker as a candidate. 'Laker obviously now moves right up to the top of the Test possibles,' he said. 'I hope the old unfair fetish, "save him for The Oval", will be hit on the head. But who of half-a-dozen good 'uns do we leave out?'

There was no denying the considerable number of challengers jostling for attention in what is now regarded as the age of the off-spinner. Nearly every county club had one and several – including Surrey, Yorkshire and Sussex – played two, while for a time Gloucestershire fielded three. Laker, Appleyard and Fred Titmus, whose qualities as an all-rounder won him many devotees, would qualify as great bowlers in any era. Other international-class exponents, either then in harness or soon to appear on the scene, included Ray Illingworth, Roy Tattersall, John Mortimore and David Allen. One unlucky bowler was the Welshman Don Shepherd, who took over 2,000 wickets at just over 20 runs each but was never picked for England or went on a major tour.

Tattersall and then Appleyard, over whom Laker leapfrogged in 1956, briefly held sway to counter Laker's England ambitions. Bill Bowes, one of cricket's most astute observers, placed Appleyard as one of the top three bowlers – the others being Bill O'Reilly and Sydney Barnes – in his fifty years as a player and reporter. Neither Appleyard nor Tattersall could properly be categorised as orthodox as Laker. Tattersall switched from seam bowling on the advice of his Lancashire coach, Harry Makepeace. He held his long forefinger alongside the seam and pushed his off-spinner in a manner that helped to disguise his away-swinger. He was, like others in his trade, respected for his accuracy. He never forgot the warning of Makepeace: 'Always remember that the lives of your close fieldsmen are in your hands.'

Appleyard, at 27 and comparatively unknown, won acclaim when he took 200 wickets at a cost of 14.14 runs each in 1951. His achievement was regarded, in Yorkshire circles at least, as the most sensational performance by a debutant since Wilfred Rhodes. In his short career, cruelly curtailed by illness, he dovetailed swing and spin at a lively pace. Jim Swanton recalled: 'Appleyard had a distinctly individual talent. I cannot think of a close parallel to him as a bowler. He had a deadly accuracy and the ball was sharply spun and cut.'

Johnny Wardle, Appleyard's Yorkshire bowling partner, said: 'Bob sometimes bowled like Alec Bedser and sometimes like Jim Laker and you scarcely realised the difference until you were out.' Tattersall, in his assessment of the perils of Appleyard, considered that even when the Yorkshireman was deploying his spin he could get his seamers to operate. 'Bob was so quick; you couldn't go down the wicket to him; he had you penned in your crease.'

It is the belief of Trevor Bailey that only Appleyard, among English bowlers, even approached the calibre of Jim Laker. Overseas, the South African, Hugh Tayfield, and the West Indian, Lance Gibbs, were his equals as an off-spinner. Both these bowlers, said Bailey, had learned their art on less responsive pitches and were relatively never so effective as Laker from round the wicket. Bailey referred to Laker's model bowling action: sideways on, close to the stumps, looking over his left arm, and coming down hard on a braced left leg. 'There was nothing dainty about his body action. He swivelled so sharply that he would even dig a pit in the soft turf. It was the perfection of his basic action that was largely responsible for his control.'

Brian Statham, another England colleague, confirmed the power of Laker's spin and his wicked designs as a bowling destroyer. 'On the right kind of wicket big Jim spun the ball more viciously than anyone else in the world. In fact, standing at the bowler's end, you could sometimes *hear* the ball spinning as it left his fingers. And you didn't always get the same ball to play at. Sometimes it would float away from the bat. His pace was varied; sometimes you got a shorter one to tempt you to give a catch.'

David Allen, the Gloucestershire off-spinner whose career overlapped with Laker's, recalled that to see Jim bowl on a spinning wicket was to watch a craftsman at work. 'His control of the ball through his delivery stride was exact and you felt that he could pitch the ball on a sixpence.' In one match at Gloucester in 1959 the decision was misguidedly taken by the home authority to shear some grass off the wicket. The disconcerting result was a 'raging turner' for Laker and Lock, who took 19 wickets between them. One lower-order batsman, David Smith, had the temerity to attempt to slog Laker. Jim sensed the inclination and then released his quicker ball on the leg stump; the would-be aggressor was comprehensively yorked.

Allen, along with Ray Illingworth, followed Laker as the England off-spinners in the West Indies in 1959–60. Allen was the least experienced member of the MCC party, but he played a key role in England's first series victory in the Caribbean. After the conclusive win by 256 runs in the second Test in Trinidad, he received a telegram from Laker. 'Congratulations on your performances in the West Indies. If you can bowl there, you can bowl anywhere in the world.' Considering that they were almost strangers, this was a wonderful boost to Allen's confidence as an emerging Test cricketer. The message is still cherished by him. Afterwards, he told his tour colleague, Ken Barrington, about Laker's kind gesture. 'That was typical of Jim,' replied Barrington.

The priorities of bowling restricted Laker's spurts of enterprise as a batsman. He was not lacking in resolution, as he showed in 1948, his best season. His tally of 828 runs in that year included 63, the highest score of the England innings, in his first Test against Australia at Nottingham. Alf Gover, a veteran member of the Surrey team when Laker arrived at The Oval, recalled the beginner's enjoyment of batting. Gover once challenged Laker on the extravagance of his back-lift, which veered in the direction of gully. 'I might start out there,' said Laker unashamedly. 'But I'm always behind the ball.' Trevor Bailey referred to one of Laker's shots: 'a very handsome off-drive, played very well at times. Jim also got a lot of runs off the outside edge, down towards third man.'

Laker's aggregate of 7,304 runs, included two centuries, one of which – his highest score of 113 – was obtained in an eighth-wicket stand of 198 with Ken Barrington against Gloucestershire at The Oval in 1954. He was also run out on 99 – the guilt of the dismissal is unrecorded – against Kent in 1948. In all, he was associated in nine century partnerships in county and other matches.

One of his most significant innings was constructed in a Test crisis against Australia at Leeds in 1953. Trevor Bailey was once more battling to stem the tide running against England on the last morning. He and Laker shared a stand of 57 for the seventh wicket. Bailey recalled: 'It was a beautiful day and Jim was a little surprised when I told him to appeal against the light.' The Australians looked up at the bright skies before realising that the delaying tactic was intended to hasten the impending adjournment for lunch. 'By the time we'd made our appeal there wasn't time for another over,' added Bailey.

England led by only 83 runs when Laker came in, ahead of the injured Compton. E. M. Wellings reported: 'Bailey and Laker hit back magnificently in a black hour for England. They were superb, Bailey confidently exact in defence, and Laker aggressively defiant during the partnership lasting just under two hours.'

Neville Cardus enthused about a 'truly gallant stand. Some of Laker's hits had an assurance and style which might well have been envied by the young Australians who chased the ball as it sped through the offside. Bailey defended on principle, half-volleys or good ones; he patted the pitch violently several times in each over. Laker, who made nearly all the runs, hardly patted it at all.'

Australia introduced the new ball before lunch and Lindwall and Miller sought desperately to put an end to the resistance. Six of their overs made no impression on England's champions. In a hundred minutes Bailey and Laker added 53, of which Laker had scored 45. His innings included six boundaries, executed, as Cardus related, with a 'calm, classic forward poise, almost comical considering the circumstances'. Arthur Mailey, in his lunchtime reflections, said that Laker showed no apprehension about the state of the game and just kept on hitting boundaries. 'Bailey, whose every move illustrated concern, pain, suspicion and horror, scarcely scored a run.'

Time was of more account than runs and Bailey admirably fulfilled his brief. He was last out with a score of 38 after a batting marathon lasting four hours and 22 minutes. It was followed by another rescue act with the ball. Australia were finally set 177 to win in five minutes under two hours after tea. They failed by only 30 runs after scoring 111 in 70 minutes. Harvey and Hole at one point scored 24 in two overs.

Victory was a near certainty until Bailey brought a halt to the run chase. Moving off a long run, his sorely needed defensive strategy at last shackled the Australian batsmen. He bowled probingly outside the leg stump, with six fieldsmen on guard to the onside. In six overs only nine runs were conceded and the tension in the England ranks abated. Bailey had won a reprieve in the nick of time.

The stamina which Jim Laker displayed in his bowling marathons gave the lie to the claim of one famous athlete who said that English cricketers were unfit. In the modern regime this would rightly be regarded as an affront. It does, however, remain a truism that cricket requires a different level of fitness from other sports. John Arlott strengthened this view. 'It may well be true that few cricketers could sprint a quarter-mile under pressure in any considerable time. But we may wonder how many fully-trained runners, encumbered by flannels and cricket boots, could open the bowling, flat out, at half-past eleven in the morning.'

Arlott expressed the extent of the continuing labours of a bowler compared with those of the athlete. He added: 'Then, at intervals of fielding for six hours, could they come back after lunch, in mid-afternoon and at the end of the day, and, each time, bowl five or six accurate, high-speed overs; or, as Laker often did, bowl for two or three hours in the heat of a tropical afternoon with such undeviating steadiness as to pin down the finest attacking batsmen in the world?'

It is a tale of perseverance with little respite and often without reward. Away from the bowling crease, Laker looked on fielding as a stately occupation. He was a safe and alert catcher in the gully. But the frenzy of fielding akin to a sliding tackle in soccer was an expenditure of energy he disdained.

Doug Insole recalled Laker's puzzled reaction following one breakneck chase by two South African fieldsmen at Cape Town during the 1956–57 series. On one side of the ground there was a wooden stand with a hollow beneath the seats in the first row. Tayfield pursued one fierce drive, with his colleague, Endean, in close attendance. Tayfield dived in front and over the ball and flicked it back from the boundary before disappearing, head and shoulders foremost, under the stand. He was a bedraggled figure, blinking in clouds of dust, when he pulled himself clear. Watching these heroics was Laker. 'If I had to do that to save runs, I would give up the game,' he said.

John Arlott propounded a fascinating argument, disputed by other successful and experienced bowlers, that Jim Laker could actually control the width of his break. 'Laker achieved this by quite a number of methods – by changing the point of his grip so that his spinning finger slipped on the smooth surface of the ball instead of gripping on the seam; more fallibly, by trying to pitch the ball on the smooth surface so that it slid on; by varying the point of release; and by checking his follow-through.'

One example of Laker's adroit variations occurred in a Cavaliers' match on a Sunday afternoon. An undergraduate batsman was opposed to Laker for the first time. The first ball pitched on a length and turned, quite mildly, to be met by a watchful half-cock stroke. The next ball was treated in the same way. The young man relaxed, having decided that Laker was merely another off-spinner. 'The third ball', related Arlott, 'looked the same as the two before and the batsman moved unhurriedly across to play it, only for it to bite, turn, hurry through and hit his stumps while his bat was only half-way down.'

In his twilight years as a cricketer, Laker could exercise charity as a bowler, especially in his encouragement of young players. This was demonstrated in another match for the Cavaliers against a North Middlesex eleven in 1964. His opponent was a batsman then under consideration by Middlesex. Laker had been asked to make a judgement. He bowled his first ball and trapped the aspirant in front of the wicket. He did not appeal. The boy was clearly dismissed in the same way to each of the next three balls. Laker still refused to ask for a verdict. Gaining in confidence, the young recruit then dispatched a loose ball, temptingly delivered, for four. The umpire, having been appraised of the necessary preferential treatment, now turned down a quiet appeal, equally deserving, by Laker for lbw off the last ball of the over.

It was time for decisive action. The novice had had his chance to make his mark. The first ball of the next over swept through his defences to bowl him. Jim considered the shattered stumps and said: 'I think he was a bit unlucky.'

11

THE WILDERNESS YEARS

'Jim did have a good memory for snobs. I doubt that people would have got far with him had they tried to pull either rank or title in a high-handed manner.'

Richie Benaud

The censure of a resentful man occurred in an age of fettered professionals. It was a *cause célèbre* which stunned admirers of an acclaimed cricketer. Jim Laker, on his retirement, was judged a renegade after the publication of a controversial book bearing his name. The withdrawal of the newly conferred honorary membership of the MCC and his Surrey pass in 1960 carried an unmistakable message: as a good servant he was expected to be seen and not heard.

The catalogue of grievances aired in *Over to Me* testified primarily to his abiding dislike of the social chasm then existing in first-class cricket. If a man's character can be told by their star sign, this would emphasise Laker's commitment to a changed order. He was born, like another forthright Yorkshireman, Fred Trueman, under the sign of Aquarius, which credibly represents him as not being in awe of authority. Laker's upbringing by a rebellious parent, at war with injustice, had also fostered a disdain for those in higher office. It fuelled an honest quest for truth.

Micky Stewart described his Surrey partner as an intelligent fellow who did not suffer fools gladly. 'Jim was at odds with the game run under the traditional Oxbridge axis. If people of this status were equipped to play, or administer the game, then he had no objections. But if they were there just because of their background, he would not hold back in his views.'

Laker, as another former county colleague, Peter Loader, recalls, had made at least one overture of complaint to the Surrey secretary. 'We accepted the situation as the way things were, but Jim thought it was all wrong. From time to time, some of the boys would say: "Jim's having a bleat again." ' Laker expressed his feelings in a civil manner in one meeting with Brian Castor. He submitted that it was disgraceful that the dedicated professionals at The Oval should be accorded inferior status. As Loader remarks, the appeal did not do Laker any good; if he was not actually rebuked for his impertinence, the entreaty fell on deaf ears.

Laker always maintained that his reputation for being 'difficult' was unfairly based. In one early brush with authority, in 1948, he thought he had right on his side. 'I was invited to go up and play in the Scarborough Festival, which was run by H. D. G. ("Shrimp") Leveson Gower as his own private party. He had his favourites but he was our president at Surrey and I felt that I had been given the presidential blessing.' Unfortunately, he incurred the displeasure of the autocratic Leveson Gower. 'There were eight amateurs in the side in which I played and when lunchtime arrived on the first day they put on their blazers and set off for the president's marquee.' Laker, Bill Edrich and Tom Pritchard decided it was in order to join them for lunch. 'We were told in no uncertain terms by Shrimp that we were not welcome with the nobs.' As Laker put it, he may have made a few critical comments on the rejection. He was never invited to play in the Scarborough Festival again.

Two curt announcements by Surrey and the MCC in the spring and early summer of 1960 had the impact of a prosecution which allowed no defence. An MCC statement on 30 June read: 'After full consideration, the committee resolved that certain passages in the book constitute a serious disservice to cricket and decided to terminate forthwith Mr Laker's honorary cricket membership with the club.'

In May, Surrey had withdrawn Laker's pass to The Oval. This granted him entry to the ground, pavilion and dressing-rooms. The letter from Commander Bob Babb, who had succeeded Castor as county secretary, especially deplored the criticism of team-mates and others who had worked so hard to ensure the success of Laker's benefit in 1956. 'There have been other books recently which lovers of cricket have regarded as harmful and in bad taste, but, in the opinion of the committee, yours has done greater disservice to cricket than any of them,' added Babb.

Laker was deeply hurt by the unexpected repercussions – and the loss of coveted privileges – following his book, which John Arlott, among other friends, felt should not have been written. Arlott, in defence of Laker, said he was convinced that the book was not intended to be sensational but only to state a case in which he felt entitled to a hearing. 'In punishment', said Arlott, 'he was beaten with an official stick which had been prepared for cricketers who wrote – or lent their names – to books of a deliberately sensational character.'

Laker himself was later to offer an apology for the insensitivity of some of his comments. But his immediate response was a lack of regret at his inflammatory words. 'I had a story to tell and I wrote what I believed and still believe. Whatever the committee says, I feel the public was entitled to have my opinion. I had a lot of criticism in my playing days and was unable to reply at the time. It would be interesting to discover just how many people, who are shouting so loudly, have actually read the book.'

Over to Me was serialised in the *Empire News*. Laker rejected other accusations in an interview with the paper's correspondent, L. N. Bailey. 'I have been accused of attacking cricket and cricketers in writing my book. I don't like the word. All I have done is to offer criticism of what I think was wrong, which I have every right to do. I hate going out of cricket under the cloud of having my free Oval pass withdrawn. I have been accused of attacking the Surrey club which employed me. Is it wrong for me to say that I don't think Surrey treat their professional cricketers as they ought? They regard them as mere employees.'

Laker said that it must be difficult for the public to comprehend why no Surrey professional was allowed to be a member of his own club. They must also have been perplexed by a situation where professionals are herded into one room while the amateurs are segregated in another. 'A professional player is expected to go quietly to the ground, hang up his hat and coat, bowl all day, and then go peacefully away.'

He then produced a set of facts to explain the benefit criticism. 'The gate receipts from my benefit game were £800; the match expenses were £1,200. If I had not insured myself against rain, I would have had to pay Surrey £400 out of my own pocket. Eighty per cent of the money for my benefit came from outside the club – from the general public; and it is for the general public that I have written my book. They are entitled to know what goes on. Maybe my book will start a lot of people thinking about improvements which can be made.'

The furore over the book also engaged the attention of Harold Hobson, the drama critic of the *Sunday Times*. Hobson, in his column 'One Man's World', declared himself unimpressed by the indignation of his cricketing friends. This trenchant and influential observer, who was later knighted for his services to the theatre, was coincidentally a Yorkshireman. He was born of mining stock in Rotherham.

Hobson exclaimed: 'Do we believe in free speech, or don't we? Or do we believe in freedom of speech for politicians, generals, critics and actors, but not for professional cricketers?' He presented the comparative reaction of a well-known actor manager which had greeted one of his unfavourable theatre reviews. The letter began: 'If you enjoy having incurred the hatred and contempt of 25 hard-working men and women, you should be a happy man this morning.' A few days later the episode was forgotten; their friendship was restored over lunch and drinks at a West End club.

So, in Hobson's view, should the argy-bargy over Laker's book, and the over-reaction of its critics, have been tempered with good sense. He applauded the book's style, while not agreeing with all of its sentiments. 'I cannot see why those who know most about cricket should not be allowed to say what they know; and if in doing so they reveal, like Laker, a vigorous and pugnacious character, so much the better. It is a gain for literature. The impression so widely propagated that *Over to Me* is all vitriol is just not true.'

Michael Green, in *The Times*, also conveyed his sympathy. He offered the wry thought that it was possible that the MCC were actually in league with Laker. 'If they wanted to secure a wider circulation for his book, they could not have achieved more. The chief effect of their action will be that twice as many will read the book that "creates a disservice to cricket".' Green said publicity was a modern weapon but there was nothing modern about the Laker affair. 'He has stepped out of line and must go back to the servants' hall. One hopes this condition does not apply to all honorary members. After all, the forthright Duke of Edinburgh is one. And, like Laker, he bowls off-breaks.'

Ghosts, of the opportunist literary variety, also haunted Jim Laker. It was extremely questionable what had been his personal contribution to the book. Within the family, it is believed that he initially consulted his brother-in-law, an eminent editor and researcher. Laker, later a *Daily Express* writer and a proud member of the National Union of Journalists, was perfectly at ease with words. It is a mystery that passages of a book, which voiced such deeply held convictions, should apparently have been entrusted to an aspiring sports writer with Hayter's Agency in London. Laker had had discussions with one Hayter's man, R. A. (Ron) Roberts, a young journalist from Taunton, on the tour of South Africa in 1956–57. But according to Frank Keating, in an article published in 1997, the book's 'ghost' was Christopher Ford, who also worked for the *Guardian* and *The Times*. Attempts to trace him and elicit his comments on the ill-starred venture have been in vain.

Unaccountable actions are not just the preserve of fools; they can, when emotions rule the head, cast a blot on men of finer intelligence. Laker's own version of the events leading to the discord were recounted in the introduction to his book on the Australian tour of 1961. This contained observations on ghost writing. *Over to Me*, he said, was started with all the goodwill in the world, to be written by his own hand. 'I had before long to summon outside help. I had spent many long hours in consultation with my ghost, but then made the cardinal error, due to pressure of time, of not correcting the final proofs and the damage was too late to be repaired.'

Doug Insole, who roomed with Laker on the tour of South Africa in 1956–57, did inspect some proof pages. He was appalled by one allegation of extreme gamesmanship by the South African off-spinner, Hugh Tayfield. Having read the comments, he remarked: 'You can't say this, Jim.' Laker replied: 'What's he said?' Insole was clearly baffled by the uncharacteristic carelessness. 'Jim was laying himself wide open to be disciplined without apparently wanting to defend himself.'

In his own recital, Laker fully accepted the blame for the opinions expressed which, he said, were largely a reflection of his honest thoughts. 'There were some I regret being published and many I would like to have offered in rather gentler terms. If I had been satisfied to spend more time and expressed my arguments and criticisms in my own way, I would have gone down as an off-spinner who wrote a book.' The rueful coda to the statement was invested with anxiety over the unforeseen expulsion. 'Now, I fear, I shall be known as an outrageous author who also bowled off-breaks.'

An editorial in *Playfair Cricket Monthly* in June 1960 considered it a tragedy that Laker, possibly the greatest off-spinner of all time, should have gone into print as he had done. It was a dire and unhappy time. Trevor Bailey referred to a tactless tilt at authority which happened in the days before player power, when the game's administrators ruled supreme and nobody dared challenge decisions in court. Amid all his cricket achievements, reflected John Arlott in his *Wisden* review of the book, Laker had seemingly found little happiness in it all. Jim Swanton thought it was a symptom of the frustrations at the neglect by the England selectors. 'The fact that he allowed these to spill over into a ghosted autobiography, which alienated him from the cricket world, was something he soon came greatly to regret.'

Laker always rejected imputations that the revelations in his book were simply made to harvest a cash windfall. As he said in an interview in the *Daily Mirror*, he had offered a gift of about £500 (the approximate profit after the ghost's fee on the book) to the MCC. He had asked that this should be donated to the cause of 'the furtherance of cricket in any part of the world'. It was the act of a contrite man. The MCC dismissed the offer as impracticable. 'The only reply I got was to say that I had been struck off the list of honorary members.'

Jim Swanton, while conceding that Laker was not perhaps the easiest bowler to lead, said that there were times when he might have received more sympathetic guidance. 'It rankled with Laker that not until his 37th year, his fingers arthritic and calloused from taking 1,700 wickets, was he put to the acid test of Australian wickets.'

Laker's first and only tour of Australia in 1958–59 was sadly preceded by a quarrel with his England and Surrey captain, Peter May. It was a disquieting confrontation between two hitherto close cricket – and family – friends. As young players at The Oval, and before Laker owned a car, May had been pleased to act as chauffeur with lifts to home matches. Laker, along with others both at Surrey and elsewhere, had watched the growing maturity of May. He was proud then and later to be linked with a player who is now regarded as England's finest post-war batsman.

In a eulogy in his book *Spinning Round the World*, published in 1957, Laker extolled May as the 'Number One skipper of my time'. He praised the resolution and great strength of character of his young amateur colleague. Equally impressive had been

165

the ability to sum up a position with speed and accuracy which might have been obscured by an outwardly shy demeanour. 'Yet to the keen eye,' wrote Laker, 'Peter already had these attributes as obvious qualifications for future captaincy. His greatest asset is his knack of making his players feel confident in themselves.'

After such high praise, it difficult to conceive why, scarcely a year later, a gulf should divide Laker and his Surrey captain of whom he had said the sky was the limit. There was now an aloofness; Laker later sorrowfully said it was impossibly hard to really know May as a person. The quarrel was made all the more implausible by the serenity of another triumphant summer. Surrey were once again invincible, despite illness, injuries and heavy representative calls, and won their seventh successive championship.

On the Test scene, New Zealand were outclassed at Edgbaston, Lord's, Headingley and Old Trafford and only rain saved them at The Oval. Laker and Lock were in rampant form and able to please themselves against the hapless tourists. They shared 51 wickets in the series; and Lock's 34, at a miserly average of only 7.47 runs each, illustrated their menace in propitious circumstances and the wettest summer in memory.

The seeds of the feud between May and Laker in 1958 were sown after the match between Surrey and Kent at Blackheath in July. This was always a keenly contested derby fixture. Kent were the winners by 29 runs. Surrey had been set a target of 252, at 88 an hour. They needed 104 in the last hour and Lock, in whirlwind style, hit 57 in 37 minutes. Arthur McIntyre, who struck six boundaries in a quarter of an hour, believed that one cause of the row was Laker's batting in the vain onslaught. 'Jim holed out when Surrey needed only a few more runs to win.'

May, in his disappointment at the loss of important championship points, vented his anger on Laker. His reported allegation that Laker had 'not been trying' was in the nature of a red rag to a bull, a distressing indictment of a senior player. In eight consecutive days Laker had bowled 175 overs. His always fallible spinning finger was beginning to show distinct signs of wear and tear. Laker bowled 54 overs at Blackheath, 38 of them (two wickets for 64 runs) in the Kent first innings. This had been preceded by 63 overs and a match return of five wickets in Surrey's victory over Glamorgan at Swansea.

Peter Loader is adamant that any charges of inadequacy against Laker at this or any other time 'were completely out of line'; while Micky Stewart attributes the dissension to the fact that 'Jim was sulking because he was knackered'. Stewart conceded that Laker might have been out of order, but still believed that the episode was blown up out of all proportion. Godfrey Evans, as one England colleague, believes that friction between May and Laker was sooner or later inevitable because the Yorkshireman was ill-supported by his captain and they differed over cricket strategies.

There had been, as Arthur McIntyre explained, angry words between the two men on other occasions. Cricketers, like most men in competition, can be short on sympathy. It is possible that Laker 'cried wolf' too often; and that the wounds of his spinning finger were treated with unwarranted ridicule by his team-mates. 'Jim used to miss matches because of the injury whereas Lockie would still play when his finger was bleeding,' said McIntyre.

Raman Subba Row, another former Surrey and England associate, contends that the rift was a consequence of May's style of management. It strongly contrasted with the policy adopted by his predecessor, Stuart Surridge. 'Stuart was more earthy and recognised the difference in people. There was not the same kind of fraternity with Peter. He had a more structured approach to captaincy.'

Both Micky Stewart and John Dewes assess the conflict as being between two proud and stubborn people. 'You would not want to get on the wrong side of Peter,' says Stewart. For Dewes, one of May's colleagues at Cambridge, it was a more diffuse argument. He disagrees with those who portray May as an unforgiving man. 'Peter, because he was the outstanding batsman of his generation, had the England captaincy thrust upon him. It was not his natural bent. He developed a hardness which was a shell; he was not like that inside. With someone like Jim, who was also a great player, and hard, too, he would be tight in manner.'

In this focus on a needless spat between two cricket champions, it should also be said that the dour exterior presented by Laker concealed a highly emotional man. He preferred, where possible, to avoid disputes, not just in cricket but in family crises as well. He was not easily roused in temper, but those who abused his friendship were swiftly cold-shouldered. It is a Yorkshire trait to exercise a strict evaluation of people. Right or wrong, the estrangement was a direct consequence of an old friend betraying his trust. There was, equally, a brusque side to May's nature; in a sense, they ultimately proved incompatible because they mirrored each other's defects.

The ensuing events were to find May and Laker locked in a situation from which there was no easy retreat. Laker, by his own admission, acted impulsively in at first withdrawing from the impending tour of Australia. The prized opportunity was initially spurned because he felt that he did not enjoy the full confidence of his captain.

Laker's explanation of their quarrel in *Over to Me* now carries the voice of a melancholy aria. The impression gained is of two men doggedly determined not to lose face in the argument. What was needed was a quick intervention to reduce the tension and bang good sense into two weary heads. Such a man was Gubby Allen, the chairman of the selectors. Unhappily, he was not available when the call from Commander Babb to Lord's passed on Laker's decision to pull out of the Australian tour.

As he recorded, Laker soon realised that he had acted without sufficient thought. Harsher and coarser words had been said in the heat of a cricket match. But he added that, apart from the slur on his integrity as a professional cricketer, the dispute held a special significance. It was in relation to the Australian tour that the allegation of not trying became so important. 'Much as I looked forward to another chance to bother the Australians – and on their own wickets – the thought uppermost in my mind was that I could not play under a captain who had the opinion of my attitude to cricket that May had shown.'

The impasse between May and Laker was resolved following a timely mediation by Denis Compton. Compton instigated a meeting between the two players at Lord's which was rapidly followed by two more at The Oval. 'To his credit, Peter solved the situation,' wrote Laker. 'He told me that he had been thinking deeply about the whole affair . . . he suggested that I should forget he had ever said anything. There were, if I'm not mistaken, sighs of relief all round. I was glad that the unpleasantness and uncertainty were over.' Laker was restored as a member of the MCC party, although another Yorkshireman, Ray Illingworth, surmises that he may have been May's preferred replacement.

Honours were thus satisfied, but it would be futile to pretend that Laker and May ever again achieved the rapport of their youth. The situation was not helped by the presence in Australia of Freddie Brown as manager of the side. Geoffrey Howard has referred to the fact that Brown and Laker were 'mutually antagonistic . . . Neither of them suffered fools gladly and Freddie wasn't all that sensible himself. He could be very prejudiced against individuals.' Fred Trueman, also making his first tour of Australia, fell into this category. Brown considered that Trueman was a potential trouble-maker on the tour. On board ship during the voyage out there was a brisk command from the MCC manager. 'One spot of bother from you and you're on the next boat home,' the Yorkshireman was told.

Back in England before the departure there had been another unseemly wrangle in Yorkshire involving Johnny Wardle, which spilled over on to the pages of the national press. Wardle was then at the height of his bowling supremacy and acknowledged, after his conquests in South Africa in 1956–57, as the master dual-purpose spinner. As with Laker, Wardle had also expressed his discontent with imperious cricket rulers. 'If I had created a few ripples with my pebbles on the placid surface of the lake,' wrote Laker, 'there were some who thought that

Wardle had done the job properly by heaving in a ruddy great brick.'

The prejudice exercised by Freddie Brown against Laker had been shown in 1950–51, when Brown, as captain, had dismissively ruled against the Yorkshireman's selection for that Australian tour. There were to be other instances of irrational behaviour in 1958–59.

As in all his jousts with authority, the key element was how well Laker was handled as a player. His withdrawal from the fourth Test at Adelaide, cited by some of the tourists as an act of betrayal, was enforced by the worrying state of his spinning finger. There had been many nights when he had been kept awake by the pain. In the previous Test at Sydney, from which England emerged with an honourable draw, Laker took five wickets in a marathon spell of 46 overs, at one stage conceding only 49 runs in 19 overs.

The legacy was that the condition of his finger had deteriorated to a point where he could bend it to no more than thirty degrees from the straight. After a net in Adelaide, Laker voiced his doubts about playing in the match. Peter May, hoping for an improvement, suggested that a decision should be delayed until the following day. The MCC management drew up twelve names for the Test. The understanding was that Frank Tyson would play if Laker was unfit.

On the following morning Laker confirmed that he would be unable to play. The late announcement, perfunctorily delivered by Freddie Brown, produced hostile press criticism. It led to claims that Laker should have played despite the injury because this was a vital Test. It was his duty to play, it was said, no matter what happened to the finger afterwards. Laker responded: 'If there had been any logic in these arguments I would have done my damnedest to play. If I had thought I could do anything to help England win the match, no thought of the future would have stopped me. But I knew the truth; had I played I would have been letting down England who most likely would have been landed with a useless passenger.'

Laker did play in the final Test at Melbourne. Serving as a

complete riposte to those who said he was a slacker was the fact that he played despite suffering from tonsillitis and with a temperature of 103. Medical opinion was firmly against his decision. Freddie Brown overruled and contradicted the doctor. He told the press: 'Laker has a bit of chill, but the doctor says he is fit to play.' Laker fought against his illness, when it was most grim, to take four wickets for 93 runs in 30.5 overs in Australia's first innings. But on each night of the match he was back in bed soon after six o'clock. 'They at least had the decency to send me in to bat at number 11' was his wry comment on a depressing experience.

There was more trouble in store for the embattled cricketer. His last conflict with Freddie Brown occurred after he had requested his omission from the New Zealand leg of the tour. Brown accused Laker of an intention to break his contract. Communication with Lord's produced the response that a medical certificate was required to confirm that the condition of his finger prevented his further participation in the tour.

An appointment was arranged with a leading specialist early on the following morning in Melbourne before play in the Test. Laker was accompanied by Brown to the surgery. The MCC manager led the way into the consulting room. He presented his version of the story to the doctor. After a few moments, the puzzled physician said: 'Don't you think it would be better if Mr Laker tells me about his own finger?'

Laker presented the important details and his finger was then thoroughly examined. 'I sincerely hope you haven't been playing cricket for three or four weeks', was the first comment of the doctor. He continued: 'If you play for another two months you will run the risk of doing yourself serious and permanent damage.' Freddie Brown, faced with this irrefutable conclusion, had to concede defeat. 'Soon, and without regret,' related Laker, 'I was out of his uncomfortable jurisdiction, and on my way home.'

Laker, against the odds, won new laurels on his first and only tour of Australia. His deeds were accomplished in a dismal

171

context. The scene was one of mounting friction; it was a series which brought to an end a triumphant chapter in English cricket. Under the leadership of Len Hutton and Peter May England had remained unbeaten for seven years, winning series against India, Australia (twice), South Africa and New Zealand.

Richie Benaud, newly installed as Australian captain, wryly remembered the pre-tour publicity which sounded victory fanfares for England. 'At a time when some of the players were on the way down rather than on the way up, Peter May was ill-served by the publicity. Our rivals were listed as the greatest-ever team to leave English shores. They had an enormous amount to live up to and sometimes that kind of adulation can be worse than the fiercest criticism.' By the end of the Australian series, the optimism was shown to be unfounded. England were beaten resoundingly, 4–0, in the worst tour of Australia for thirty-seven years.

Peter May, on his last and ill-fated tour of Australia, was beset by unnerving aggression. The bombardment of the throwers carried unpredictable menace. It almost led to a breach in Anglo-Australian relations on the scale of the body-line controversy of 1932–33. The crisis was only averted by careful diplomacy. May insisted that the tour, rather than being his greatest failure as England captain, was probably one of his greatest successes. 'At the end of it England and Australia were still speaking to each other.'

Amid the rigours of the tour, May was personally subjected to intense criticism. Friends and contemporaries believe that he did not subsequently have the same appetite for cricket. Colin Cowdrey believes that the scars of the tour never properly healed. 'Having been peerless as both batsman and captain, Peter was quite taken aback by the hostility of the criticism and badly hurt.' A writer in *Playfair Cricket Monthly* commented: 'May has had some stinging press criticism to suffer. He must think back sometimes to his carefree days at Charterhouse and Cambridge where cricket was a game to be enjoyed without the continued scrutiny and constant grumbling of the world at large.'

172

For Jim Laker, too, this coveted tour carried mixed blessings. He went out to Australia in the full knowledge that his rivals were waiting to bury the memory of their humiliation at his hands in England in 1956. 'The Australians grudged, or at least qualified credit for this bowling,' declared John Arlott. 'But they could not withhold it when, with the conditions completely against him, he shone against opponents in a dominating position.' Richie Benaud was one Australian intent on a fierce reception for Laker. 'We were quite determined to get after Jim and were quite sure we could do that, but he bowled really well again.'

Laker was handicapped throughout the tour by an arthritic finger, which contributed to his retirement from first-class cricket at the end of the 1959 season. Yet he bowled the most overs, 127.6, in the series, took the most wickets – 15 out of 54 – and headed the England Test averages. Only two other bowlers, Trueman and Lock, exceeded his tally of 38 wickets (average: 17.23) in all matches on the tour.

Only one Australian batsman, Neil Harvey, found the answer to Laker's enduring craft. Harvey's magnificent 167 (out of a total of 305), and less worthily the 'bowling' of Ian Meckiff, brought victory for Australia in the second Test at Melbourne. England were dismissed for 87 in their second innings; and Meckiff explosively took six wickets for 38 runs in the rout. Jim Swanton reported: 'I never saw anything so blatant as Meckiff's action as, with the swell of the crowd in his ears, he came up that afternoon full pelt from the bottom end towards the pavilion.'

Swanton, though, enthused about the majesty of Harvey's innings. 'A crowd of 71,000, on a working day, turned up to acclaim his 100 with the echoing roar that is peculiar to the vast Melbourne arena.' Tom Graveney also recalled the grandeur of Harvey. 'He was the only batsman who sorted Jim out. Jim didn't know where to bowl to Neil. This was the only time I've ever seen him in trouble once he became a great bowler.'

Graveney was Laker's fielding accomplice at long-on in the state match against South Australia at Adelaide. Laker had match figures of ten for 101 in 41 overs, including five for 31 in the first innings, as MCC won by nine wickets. 'They were all probably under orders to slog him,' remembers Graveney. 'Jim just waited for them and dragged the ball a little wider. All I had to do was to stand out there and say "Thank you very much" as I caught 'em.' *Wisden* prosaically noted: 'Graveney's fielding in the deep was a feature of the MCC outcricket.'

Brian Chapman, in the *Daily Mirror*, said of the exploits at Adelaide that Laker had to destroy a legend. 'He had to overcome one of the most cherished doctrines in Australian cricket faith. This was that a conventional off-spinner is a "no-hoper" over here. He was regarded as a meek sacrifice to batting slaughter.' Chapman went on: 'If any slaughter was done today, Laker was the executioner and the state batsmen were the unwilling victims.'

Bill O'Reilly also commented on Laker's splendid bowling which, he said, would end the wishful thinking that Australian wickets would cripple his enthusiasm and reduce to insignificance his value as a Test bowler. 'Laker is a master of length and direction. He can adapt his pace cleverly to make attacking batsmen pay miserable dividends.'

Keith Miller, in the *Daily Express*, also acknowledged the temptations of the wily master. 'He bowled 139 balls [in the South Australian first innings] and only one was loose. The batsmen found it suicidal to attack him. He made good use of the unusually long straight boundaries of the Adelaide Oval. Big hits here are often catches instead of sixes.' Miller praised the tight control, variations in flight and genuine finger-spin. 'Laker did not pitch his off-spinners any more accurately at Old Trafford in 1956 than he did today.'

Jim Laker was not destined, amid the subsequent discords in Australia, to reap the rewards of victory in a series which had so long eluded him. But he did prove, to his own satisfaction and in the opinion of other discerning judges, that he was still a bowler of champion mettle. Peter Loader, a fellow tourist, said: 'The Australians had thought they were going to belt him. But Jim was not disposed to let them get after him.'

*

Too many bridges were burned in the doleful aftermath of Laker's Australian tour. Four years were to elapse before Surrey relented to restore his privileges at The Oval. The reconciliation at Lord's began in the same year, 1964, when Laker represented the Old England XI against the Lord's Taverners in a match to raise funds for the National Playing Fields Association. Donald Carr, then MCC Assistant Secretary, recalled that Laker was first included in the Taverners' eleven. 'My boss, Billy Griffith [the MCC Secretary], changed the order of players; he and the committee felt they would much prefer him on the other side.'

This decision was, in effect, an olive branch to the banned Yorkshireman. Laker was reunited with his old Surrey captain, Stuart Surridge, whose merry half-century for the Taverners included five sixes. Reg Simpson, the former Nottinghamshire captain, spreadeagled the field with elegant strokes to hit a century. Laker himself, moving in off measured strides, took four wickets, three of them – Insole, Carr and Eric Bedser – producing a shrug of content; and the other, that of his old county mentor, Alf Gover, eliciting an apologetic smile.

The ice had been broken and the path was finally cleared for Laker's reinstatement as an honorary member of the MCC in 1967. He greeted his pardon and return to favour with becoming gratitude. 'I have written today expressing my happiness. When the membership was given to me I regarded it as the greatest honour in cricket. I still do. In a way, I feel as though I've been released from a seven years' sentence.' Laker celebrated the occasion with friends at a small party at the Cricketers' Club in London.

Donald Carr, an influential administrator at Lord's, was one of the peacemakers in a happy release. 'Jim was a rather contentious figure as a player; but afterwards he became a genuine supporter of the establishment. He became a respected man, friendly and knowledgeable. It was nice to think of him like that.' Godfrey Evans agreed with this verdict.

175

'Once Jim had ripped the chips off his shoulders, everybody wanted to talk to him and shake him by the hand. It was a great tribute to a thoroughly nice man.'

The crusade of Jim Laker had been pursued with his clear conviction that the professional cricketer was unjustly denied his true deserts. The cries of outrage were, as many people said, a burden which sullied his personality. It was not calculated to make him the easiest of travelling companions. His attempts to remedy injustice were also, however unconsciously, a bid to establish his own identity. The pattern of his childhood put him on a vigilant guard; he was thrust into the world armed as a rebel. All of which goes some way towards explaining his rejection of the status quo.

The abolition of the distinction between the 'gentlemen' and the 'players' in 1962–63 – and the subsequent abandonment of matches between them, one of the oldest fixtures in the cricket calendar – struck an especially pleasing chord. 'It remains the best thing that has happened in the game in my lifetime,' maintained Laker in later years. He had always thought that class distinctions were a ridiculous concept. 'One respects a person for what he does rather than who he is. I would rather doff my cap to a professional like Len Hutton than an undeserving amateur.'

In a neatly ironic postscript to his career Laker moved to Essex, the county which, at Peter Smith's dictation and but for a cancelled trial, he might have joined fifteen years earlier. Prompting the recruitment was Trevor Bailey, who had been a fellow speaker at a sporting dinner in Manchester. Bailey and Laker travelled back to London by train. Over breakfast Bailey casually mentioned that Essex were short of a spin bowler. It was, as he related, a 'masterpiece of understatement'; but he had been encouraged to make the request when Laker said he would like to play a little more cricket. 'To my surprise and delight, Jim agreed to play a few games for Essex as an amateur.'

Laker's own version of the recruitment was that it was mooted, but not agreed, in a conversation with Bailey very early one morning in Manchester. He said it was a fine instance of promotion for Essex. On the following day he picked up a copy of the *Daily Express*, and was somewhat surprised to learn that he had agreed to play for the county as an amateur. 'The news came as a surprise to most of my business associates as well, since my views about amateurs were well known.' By this time, however, he wanted to erase his controversial image. 'If Essex really did want me to play for them, then I would simply go and play.'

Laker had not then been reprieved by the MCC and there were voices of dissent among the Essex committee at his special registration to represent the county. 'They were not all that enthusiastic despite the fact that Jim was prepared to play as an amateur for just his expenses,' said Bailey. He was astonished by the reaction. 'I found this hard to comprehend because I had acquired a great cricketer and personality for nothing. It was like signing George Best at the end of his career and persuading him to turn out without wages. In contrast, the Essex players were, without exception, proud to have the opportunity of playing alongside a master craftsman.'

Laker did, as Bailey and his Essex colleague Doug Insole remembered, experience confusion in his new surroundings. There was, for example, the story of his bewilderment at Romford. Before the start of one game there on a typically well-grassed wicket Laker was invited to report on its condition. He spent some minutes, his brows furrowed, in the inspection. Finally, he strolled back to the pavilion to give his verdict. 'I'm sorry, Trevor,' he said, 'I couldn't find it!'

Doug Insole also related one amusing conversation between Laker and Brian Edmeades at Ilford. 'Brian was a real Cockney lad, with extravagant sideburns, who invariably sported winkle-picker shoes.' Edmeades arrived that morning and asked Laker to examine his newly acquired watch, a bargain, he thought, at a fiver. 'It looks like a perfectly good Swiss watch and worth far more than that,' replied Jim. 'But you will have to accept that it fell off a lorry!' Their talk took another turn when Edmeades congratulated Laker on his own timepiece, one of the championship gifts at The Oval. 'That's a nice watch; how much did it cost you?' Jim said: 'Well actually, Brian, it was *free*.' 'Three nicker,' exclaimed Edmeades. 'You've got a bargain there.'

Laker played in thirty matches for Essex, twice heading the county's bowling averages, and is remembered as a 'father figure' to a host of aspiring youngsters. In his forties he was still a fine bowler. In 1963 he produced a match return of ten wickets for 106 runs in the innings victory over Northamptonshire at Romford. On another pleasurable occasion he reminded the Yorkshire holiday-makers in Clacton of his exact control. The enticing fingers conjured a haul of seven wickets in the match. *Wisden* reported: 'Laker, in 10 matches, demonstrated once more that he was second to none as an off-break exponent.'

Trevor Bailey recalled that Laker's first match for Essex was against Derbyshire at Valentines Park, Ilford. 'There were some people, including members of the media, who doubted whether he would still be effective, as it was several years since he had last played county cricket, and he was never over-enthusiastic about practice.'

The expectant crowd did not have to wait long to discover that class will prevail. 'Jim made his usual deceptively casual approach, over went his arm, the ball dropped on precisely the right spot, and turned sufficiently to take the inside edge,' said Bailey. The catch was dropped by Gordon Barker, another Yorkshire exile, fielding at short leg. 'I must say, in Gordon's defence,' added Bailey, 'that he had never fielded in that position to a bowler of that calibre before. His only complaint, apart from fury at missing the chance, was that it earned him bigger headlines than when he scored a century!'

Jim Laker never gave less than value, even as a veteran before the curtain fell on a distinguished career. With his unwavering command, he still asked formidable questions as a bowler. The interrogation of a novice left-hander at Leicester is etched in Trevor Bailey's memory. 'It was one of the few times that I've actually appealed for lbw from cover. I knew the boy was out and I knew it was going to happen.'

The dismissal was the bowling equivalent of the three-card trick. The young batsman played the first three of Laker's deliveries with immaculate forward defence. The fourth ball was tossed a little higher, straightening slightly from round the wicket. It was played with equal certainty. Laker's fifth ball was appreciably shorter, quicker, and went on with the arm into the batsman. He instinctively moved back and was lbw even before he realised that he was the victim of an adroit manoeuvre. He had been reeled in like a fish on the hook of an expert angler.

'It was dreamtime bowling,' said Bailey. 'Only a great bowler, with perfect control, could have accomplished such a bowling confidence trick. It was an education for any aspiring off-spinner.'

12

A NATURAL IN VISION

'Jim brought clarity of recall to his commentaries. He
knew what true cricket quality was; he had seen it and
remembered it.'

Tony Lewis

In the sepulchral gloom at Old Trafford on a famous July day
the excitement on the field was matched by endurance in the
commentary box. Keeping a vigil in the dusk was Jim Laker.
He was engaged in a monumental feat of sustained description. The winning runs at last brought release from his task and
the crowds raced on to the ground to acclaim their heroes.

Nick Hunter, as Laker's television producer, recalls the
unparalleled events of the Gillette Cup semi-final between
Lancashire and Gloucestershire in 1971. Rain at lunchtime had
put the BBC transmission ninety minutes behind schedule. It
was assumed, in the rapidly deteriorating light, that play
would be suspended until the following day. 'Jim was alone in
the box and I was alone in the scanner.' At 6.30 the lights were
being switched on in the pavilion and the figures on the scoreboard shone brightly like ghostly beacons. The cameras,
focused on the action, gave an unreal lustre to the declining
day. 'We didn't think for a moment that we were going to be
there for another two and a half hours,' says Hunter.

At seven o'clock the umpires conferred and Laker, with a
gesture of thankfulness, surmised that a closure was imminent.
It was a false interpretation; another hour passed, and then
another, before the bleary eyes of the commentator looked on

the scene for the last time. A cascade of boundaries by David Hughes, 24 runs coming off one over from John Mortimore, swept Lancashire to victory by three wickets. The elation of the cricketers did not exceed the relief of the man watching them. The uninterrupted commentary had allowed no diversion to attend to the calls of nature. At the end both Laker and Hunter leapt from their seats and joined each other in a breakneck dash to the lavatory.

Nick Hunter had earlier responded with amusement, bordering on ridicule, to a telephone call from Paul Cox, the BBC Controller, in London. He had been informed of the plan, in the event of continued play at Manchester, for the 'Points of View' programme at ten to nine to be cancelled. It proved to be a perceptive decision. 'We went on air live on BBC 1, as arranged, and overran the 9 o'clock News by five minutes,' recalls Hunter. The dramatic cricket finale for once gained precedence over other headlines. Laker's commentary remit now had the attention of a nationwide audience.

It was past ten o'clock before the pandemonium abated and the lingering remnants of a vast crowd of over 23,000 finally made their way home. Afterwards Laker was asked: 'How did you keep so cool?' He replied: 'Well, it could have been worse. I could have been out there bowling.' It was a typical shaft of deadpan humour; but it was also an expression of sympathy for a fellow off-spinner, John Mortimore, who had been bludgeoned in the gloaming.

The march of time veils the prestige of broadcasters with first-class cricket lineage. Their renown may be restricted to a medium in which they have gained a new prominence. A modern generation is denied the nostalgia of their elders; for them, past achievements are just shadows in cricket folklore. Richie Benaud, Laker's television soulmate, related the story of a group of boys collecting autographs outside the Channel Nine commentary box one December evening in Sydney in 1982. One angelic little lad of about 12 displayed an admirable spirit of enquiry. After his book had been signed, he looked up and asked: 'Did you ever play cricket for Australia, Mr Benaud?' Benaud replied that he represented his country until 1963, which was obviously well before the boy was born. 'Oh,' said the impressed youngster, 'that's great. I thought you were just a television commentator on cricket.'

Jim Laker would not, similarly, have been affronted by a lack of recognition of his former cricketing status. The invitation to join the BBC – an association which was to last for nearly twenty years – was a complete surprise. One business associate remembers that when the proposition was first put to Laker, he responded: 'With my voice, I'd put everyone to sleep.' Laker himself recalled that his prospective employers were seeking to recruit someone with cricketing knowledge gained from playing at the highest level. He was soon to be elevated into a company of experienced professional broadcasters, including such influential and encouraging mentors as John Arlott, Brian Johnston and Peter West.

His debut assignment on BBC 2, as deputy for Learie Constantine, was at Fenners in April 1968. The Sunday afternoon match featured the International Cavaliers' XI, which was soon to be superseded by counties in the John Player League. The presenter was Frank Bough and the novice broadcaster was reassured by the avuncular presence of John Arlott, his fellow commentator. The butterflies quivered but Arlott quelled Laker's anxiety. He turned to the newcomer and whispered: 'You'll be fine. Just imagine we are sitting in the saloon bar of a pub; be natural and say whatever you think is right.'

Laker had also sought the advice of his old cricket tutor, Alf Gover, who was widely experienced as a broadcaster and journalist. Gover had exhorted him not to disguise his Yorkshire accent. He endorsed Arlott's instruction to present himself in a natural manner. Laker profited from these consultations to earn the commendation of the BBC. Nick Hunter recalls those early broadcasting days. 'Jim might have been doing it for years. He just settled into commentary. I don't remember any growing pains with him.'

The rewards of a new career happily coincided with the

restoration of Laker's honorary life membership of the MCC. All was forgiven at The Oval, too, when at Alf Gover's instigation he was invited to become an ex officio member of Surrey's public relations committee. The sound judgement he brought to this sphere undoubtedly enhanced the prestige and led to the rehabilitation of a once spurned cricketer. The pleasures grew when he received the accolade of honorary life membership at The Oval. There was also, as Laker recorded, a feeling that if he was going to make a significant contribution to Surrey's cause he should transfer to the club's cricket committee.

Raman Subba Row, seeking to shed some of his administrative duties, recommended Laker's appointment as his successor as chairman of this committee. It heralded the start of a fruitful relationship with Micky Stewart in his role as cricket manager. Stewart provides evidence of Laker as a caring man during his term of office. 'If any Surrey youngster did particularly well, there would invariably be a few lines of congratulations penned by Jim, who probably didn't know the boy very well.'

Subba Row also notes the attention paid by Laker to grass-roots cricket in the county. There were regular visits to speak to local schoolchildren and at club dinners. 'Jim never charged a penny for these activities. He derived great pleasure from putting in that effort in the service of Surrey and cricket generally.' Subba Row adds that Laker was loath to bore his listeners with his own reminiscences, however much they might have been welcomed. Laker's excellence as a speaker, which made him a magnet on the cricket lecture circuit, was shown on one occasion at Croydon. 'Jim spoke for about twenty-five minutes,' recalled Subba Row. 'You could have heard a pin drop.'

Alf Gover was right to urge Laker to parade his Yorkshireness on television. The inimitable silent g's (battin', bowlin' and fieldin') did at first produce crusty letters from those viewers who said Laker should learn to speak properly. Nick Hunter was dismissive about this criticism. 'That's you, Jim,' he said. 'Don't worry.' Laker soon mastered the intricacies of talking to pictures on the screen. In his new medium, as he had done as a player, he took his cricket very seriously. He was keen to learn, always prepared to listen to advice, because he wished to establish his broadcasting credentials as soon as possible. Peter West, 'the totally dependable professional' and affable anchor man, was Laker's guide during the apprentice days. 'Westie protected Jim in vision in the beginning; he didn't throw any bouncers at him,' says Hunter.

The former BBC executive producer makes plain the terrors of television and the traps that lie in wait to snare broadcasters. 'It can be quite frightening and produce shell shock for someone who is inexperienced, or hasn't commentated before.' Hunter refers to the stern requirements of concentration and energy. 'With cricket, you can be sitting comfortably in the box one moment; and then, in a trice, be summoned to carry out an interview when bad light intervenes, or when a declaration has been made.'

The commentator, in the words of one Australian television executive, has also to listen to his producer with an ear as keen as a ferret's. Equally, he said, the producer 'will listen avidly to your commentary, thus ensuring the magic phrases are pertinent to the viewer's picture'. Hunter asks viewers to imagine the swift reaction required to follow the instructions of the producer during a commentary. These are conveyed to the broadcaster on his headphones via the 'lazy talkback mike' used for comments off the air. 'It can distort or mangle what the commentator is trying to say. At times, it can account for seemingly extraordinary pieces of commentary.'

The differing levels of appreciation of cricket among viewers poses other daunting problems for the commentator. The boredom of repetition, which Laker always studiously avoided, cannot be condoned. The juggling of information does, however, require an awareness which permits neither condescension or understatement. Bridging the gap between the viewer watching a cricket telecast for the first time and the club cricketer who knows a deal about the game and only needs minimum explanation is like walking a tightrope. Richie Benaud observes that resolving the complexities of television commentary can only be done by striking a balance of conversation with the person to whom you are talking through the lens.

It often stretches credulity to learn about the letters of puzzled viewers, which might have been designed to cause amusement. There was one occasion when Jim Laker was said to have been bowling with one short-leg. Hearing this, one woman wrote in to rebuke the commentator for being so personal. There was merriment in the box at the receipt of another letter. Brian Johnston reported that Peter May, having reached his century, was lucky because he was dropped when two. It elicited a response lamenting the carelessness of mothers with young children.

Nick Hunter had been captivated as a boy in the 1950s by the exploits of Surrey, which gave a special significance to his work with Jim Laker in television. His hero-worship had not receded; it was a privileged task. 'There was an aura about him although he never played the VIP,' he recalls. 'Anyone who has taken 19 wickets against Australia can walk on water. I was certainly keen to make sure we got things right for him. We treated Jim, as was his due, with considerable respect.'

Peter Walker, as both a Glamorgan cricketer and later a broadcaster, had ample cause to view Laker with trepidation. His first impression was of extreme dislike. At Swansea, Walker completed his maiden century against Surrey with an inside-edged shot off Laker's bowling. It was a treasured moment for a young player, then in his early twenties. Laker did not deign to congratulate Walker on his achievement; he just shook his head sadly and returned to his bowling mark. Cricket can be cruel; the wounding slight might have been a sign that he had given an unaccepted chance during the course of the century. But the lack of acknowledgement did rankle with Walker. He thought: 'What an awful bastard.'

Their paths crossed again when Walker succeeded Frank Bough as the presenter on the Sunday League programme on BBC 2. By then Laker had mellowed considerably but he was still sceptical of those who failed to measure up to the highest standards as cricketers. 'If he did not rate you as a player, you were always talking from a defensive crouch to him,' says Walker. There was an austerity in Laker's bearing and the apparent cynicism projected the attitude of a wary man. Fortunately for Walker, Laker was an admirer of his former cricket rival as a superb close fieldsman. Laker told him: 'I wish I'd had you fielding to me at short-leg.' For someone who, like most Yorkshiremen, was sparing in his compliments this was a tribute to be savoured. 'I felt as though I'd been given a knighthood,' remembers Walker.

Wariness possibly described Walker's state of mind when he was paired with Laker in a cricket broadcast from Tewkesbury. Their producer at this historic venue invited Walker to set the scene in a five-minute introduction to the programme. The famous abbey was the chosen topic. It was a far too short dissertation on the merits of the church. 'After two and a half minutes I ran out of things to say. So, in great desperation, I set off talking about the two teams in the match.'

On happier ground in this recital, he developed the theme at great length. He forgot, in his enthusiasm, that his words were normally the prerogative of the opening commentator. He cheerily concluded his summary; and then, as the first ball was about to be bowled, he announced: 'Here is Jim Laker.'

There was a pregnant pause before Laker responded. 'Thank you, Peter,' he said, 'there's not much really to say now.' Nothing was said for over two overs. Their producer, Bill Taylor, a quiet Scot, grew increasingly anxious during the protracted silence. He pleaded with Laker: 'Please say something.' Laker was finally prevailed upon to begin his commentary but it was a tense interlude. Walker adds: 'This was the biggest put-down I ever had in my broadcasting life. But it was an invaluable lesson not to pre-empt what was to come. After Tewkesbury I never again tried to upstage Jim.'

Misdeeds, intended or otherwise, can produce greater understanding. The legacy of this broadcasting altercation was a deep friendship between Walker and Laker. 'I came to realise that Jim was a big man in every sense.' Walker's celebrity interviews in the Sunday cricket tea intervals, afterwards published in book form, were hailed as informative and entertaining digressions. 'Jim was very astute and helpful with his observations on my subjects. He was also immensely kind with his praise when I had to hold the ship together, virtually on my own, on rain-affected days.'

Another of Laker's producers was Bob Duncan, a boxing promoter with a voluble presence. Peter Walker recalls: 'You never needed a talkback in your ear with him. You could hear his instructions from the other side of the ground.' Duncan was the foil for Laker's wicked sense of humour. 'Jim used to wind up Bob endlessly. Bob was bright enough to realise what he was watching himself. But he was totally dependent on Jim's cricketing judgement on matches to be covered in the future.'

Jim Laker, Richie Benaud and Ray Illingworth, who joined the BBC commentary team as an analyst in the early 1980s, were regarded as an unbeatable triumvirate. The alliance of an Australian and two Yorkshiremen carried more than a trace of their origins. They did not get fussed over things or ever go foolishly over the top. All was tight and under control. Illingworth earns high praise from both Peter West and Nick Hunter. 'Ray was able to narrow down tactics, or the way someone was playing, with tremendous clarity and fairness,' says Hunter.

Benaud, alone among the trio, had trained as a journalist. He had begun his career on the *Sydney Sun* in 1956, developing his precision as a news reporter in the police rounds department. He joined the BBC at first on radio before transferring to television in 1963. Peter West has commented on Benaud's calm, versatility and unquestioned impartiality as a broadcaster. 'He seems able, at one and the same time, to give his attention to the game in hand, a study of the *Sporting Life*, press articles for home and overseas consumption, broadcast scripts for Australia and any golf or racing that happens to be visible on a spare screen.'

The energy of Benaud also aroused the admiration of Brian Johnston. 'After a full day's commentary, Richie will appear in front of the cameras after the close of play and, without notes, give a slick and accurate summary. He also has to cue in the various film inserts to illustrate what has happened.'

As with Laker, one of Benaud's early BBC teachers was the late David Kenning, a magnificent director of television operations. 'David', said Benaud, 'was always keen to emphasise to commentators that our job was to identify, illustrate and add to the picture for the benefit of viewers.' Benaud recalled one Test match at Lord's when there was an ugly crowd disturbance. He was sufficiently diverted to forget that they were a camera short. 'Torn between keeping one eye on the monitor and describing what was occurring there, and keeping one eye on what was happening away to my right, I committed the cardinal error of describing the latter before the cameras arrived.' In his left ear came the gentle admonition of his producer. 'How *very* interesting, Richie,' said Kenning. 'And how nice it would have been to show the millions sitting in front of their television sets the pictures you were describing so beautifully.'

Ted Dexter, another broadcaster of that time, said it was entirely apposite that the evolving ball-by-ball commentary should become the preserve of a former Australian captain and leg-spinner, and Laker, arguably the most successful orthodox finger-spinner ever to represent England. 'It cannot be mere coincidence', he wrote, 'that two voices that convey cricket in all its complexity should have the slow bowling ethic in common.' Dexter continued: 'Patience, accuracy and persistence are the trademarks of spin bowlers throughout cricket history and these special attributes certainly come across to me when it is my turn to sit at home and watch the box.'

Eavesdropping on the deliberations at one Test match was the actor and writer Colin Welland. In a feature article in the *Daily Mail* in 1979, he expressed his envy at their television lives. 'For a start I now realise how Jim Laker took all those wickets. He *chuckled* them out. He hunches over the microphone in his shirt-sleeves with that confident air of someone who has a new story to tell you. But he's watching, is Jim, analysing, assessing, and, have you noticed, he is completely cliché-free. Because to him each ball is a new experience – and he finds words to fit.'

Welland watched Richie Benaud 'striding through the comfortable cluster of BBC cardigans ... On screen he is the sort of fellow you would find yourself trying to please. In reality he has a generous smile and a warm humour, but he is always ready to crack the whip.' The abiding impression of this onlooker was the complete concentration of the commentary team. 'For you, they pick their words precisely, enhancing the pictures flickering before them. You are well served.'

Peter Walker, in his appraisal of a hugely admired television collaboration, refers to the rapport between Laker and Benaud. 'Jim accepted that Richie was his peer as a cricketer. They were two of a kind, each with a quiet steel, and both private men. They accorded one another a deep respect, which broadened into affection.' Benaud himself confirms the bond with Laker. 'I found Jim quiet but a very good conversationalist, dogmatic to a degree, but then so was I; an excellent raconteur and possessed of a very dry sense of humour. Above all, he had a great enthusiasm for his work and for people. Jim's enthusiasm was, though, quiet, something that I appreciated.'

Laker's humour, says Benaud, could be sharp and this also pervaded his fairly expressed observations on television. 'Jim was always supporting England but it is difficult to recall any time when he was parochial.' Nick Hunter adds the rider on the patriotic allegiances. 'If a match between England and Australia had reached the "whites of their knuckles", there was no way that Benaud and Laker would agree with each other.'

Through the broad sweep of televised cricket, Laker demonstrated his expertise. 'Jim was outstanding in the actual commentaries where economy of words and the ability to fit the story into a space are so important,' says Benaud. He remembers Laker as a level-headed cricketer who carried this attribute into television. 'Jim had a wonderful knowledge of the game which he was able to impart in an interesting fashion, whether in conversation, or on the box.'

The disarming raconteur was, considered Peter West, underused. He remembers a 'remarkably detailed memory' of the games in which Laker had played. 'Jim, with his mentally wry and nimble humour, could produce an anecdote at the drop of a hat.' West believes that Laker should have lightened the 'winter of a cricketer's discontent' with his reminiscences on television.

Nick Hunter remembers the occasions, all too infrequent because of pressures of time, when Laker described the techniques of spin bowling in talks on television. 'Jim received many letters on all aspects of cricket. But after these informative sessions there was a deluge of mail from viewers.' Laker's television world, says Richie Benaud, was based in part on talks with the viewers. 'The other aspect, and a very important one, is that I never once heard him talk down to viewers when on television.'

It was one of the keys to Benaud's own discipline as a broadcaster. 'Never under any circumstances', he wrote, 'talk down to the camera lens. Behind that lens are a million viewers and they know there is nothing worse than a pompous cricketer, a pompous sporting official, or an overbearing cricket commentator.'

Laker's fairness in commentary, alluded to by Benaud, is endorsed by Nick Hunter, who earns the Australian's approval as a producer with a wonderful feel for the game and an unerring editorial sense. 'Jim was completely honest in his commentaries,' says Hunter. 'He had his opinions but they were not dated.' There was a realisation that he was a generation on from the players under his microscope and allowances were made for the disparity.

Laker was, though, scathing when he detected a less than full commitment by cricketers. His discomfort with those he considered playboys produced a rift between him and others in the BBC commentary team and the England team of 1981. Relations between the two ranks gathered a heavy frost after Ian Botham was severely criticised during his brief reign as England captain. Botham, after two noughts in the Test at Lord's, was subjected to intense pressures. He reluctantly surrendered the captaincy to Mike Brearley at Headingley. The barrage of criticism was unrelenting and Laker, in his own column in the *Daily Express*, did not mince his words.

Amid the dissension the England players, perhaps under-standably, took up a stance of isolation from their critics. Botham, with awesome vengeance, hit a magnificent 149 in his famous innings which retrieved an apparently hopeless cause at Headingley. 'It just shows', he said, 'that the media should never have written us off.' Laker had held his watching brief at home after an illness. He revelled in an epic exploit, which led to England's rally, as much as anyone. 'It wasn't that Jim didn't like Botham, or any of the England players,' comments Nick Hunter. 'He had criticised the team for their lack of application.'

Generally, though, Laker and Benaud eschewed extravagant criticism. They were loath to weigh in too heavily because they had experienced traumas of their own in Test combat. They would express their disapproval in a kind of verbal shorthand, a series of one-liners, such as Benaud's 'Goodness gracious me' in his response to the issue of ball-tampering. Off camera, matters were different. 'Jim could be quite peremptory and dismissive at times,' says Nick Hunter. He would have liked a leavening of vitriol on air. It was a vain hope. 'Both Jim and Richie bent over backwards to be fair.'

The star quality which surrounds household names in broadcasting was disdained by Jim Laker. As a shy man, he did not court recognition. His daughter Angela does, though, remember the grumpy snort when it was withdrawn. She and her sister Fiona would often accompany their father when he was commentating on Sunday League games. 'We would huddle together, cringing, in the back seat of the car if the stew-ard in the press car park failed to instantly recognise Dad.' It was a rare occurrence. The exception was when a 'gawky young man, with trailing blond hair', standing in for the regu-lar attendant, was neglectful in this duty. Impatience would prevail as their father wound down the car window. '*Jim Laker*,' he would brusquely call out, and then drive on to his appointed place.

Jim Laker never wavered in his admiration for John Arlott as a broadcaster without peer. This reverence for a commentator, who achieved esteem on both radio and television, was slightly muted for others who felt that Arlott was constrained by pictures. As a poet, he could paint scenes of imaginative design on radio. This remarkable facility did not have the same impact on television. Arlott, throughout his distinguished life, maintained an affinity with those who played cricket. He was especially close to the journeyman professionals in and beyond his beloved Hampshire. His concern for their welfare was best demonstrated by his diligence as the president of the Professional Cricketers' Association.

The friendship with Laker blossomed in their twin commentating duties on BBC 1 and 2, covering Test and one-day cricket. It had, on Arlott's part, elements of hero-worship, but he was coolly exact in his observations on Laker as a fellow broadcaster. 'He has a deceptively fast reaction to any movement or action on the field,' wrote Arlott. 'Among long-distance observers of a rapid incident, he is more likely than anyone to read it accurately.'

There was also Laker's inheritance from his mother of natural teaching instincts. One member of the family refers to his ability to communicate – and enlighten viewers with a hitherto lukewarm interest in cricket. 'Jim could explain cricket matters in a way which was so understandable. It wasn't just a visual thing. He did actually, with his mathematical mind, frame the symmetry and greater design of the game.'

Tony Lewis, the former Glamorgan and England captain who succeeded Peter West as the BBC presenter, markedly comments on the metamorphosis of Laker behind the microphone. For a man with a diffidence as a cricketer he revealed an unexpectedly strong presence on television. 'Jim spread a great deal of ease in the green huts we broadcast in,' says Lewis. In moments of crisis, Laker would trip quietly around, a whistle on his lips, to relieve the tension.

Lewis presents a study of a broadcaster with the highest standards. 'These did not apply just to himself but also to everybody else, otherwise it would have been difficult to work with him.' He emphasises the importance of a convergence of views in the television box and the 'mix and match' of different accents and personalities in commentary sessions. 'As a team we were extremely close and happy and comfortable with each other's performances.'

Laker's impatience with slipshod cricket was a testament to his own fidelity to the game. The quality of mercy was perhaps strained in one laconic rebuke in the Test against New Zealand at Trent Bridge in 1973. He was the commentator who watched a skied catch elude the clutching hands of the England fieldsman, Tony Lewis. It scarcely entered the category of a chance. As Lewis relates, he had raced about 150 yards around the boundary and snapped two fingernails before plunging into the crowd. Laker phlegmatically remarked: 'Lewis has put down a catch a long-on.' The athleticism of the chase went unreported; the ball had trimmed his nails, so *ipso facto* it was a catch. Afterwards, Lewis gingerly challenged Laker on the lack of gallantry. 'You're a hard man, Jim,' he said.

Nick Hunter has said that the task of a television sports producer is to provide the viewer with 'the best seat in the house'. It is, in fact, a moveable feast since the armchair spectator is now privileged to occupy six or seven seats. He has the choice of two or three replays and, if any statistical information is needed, a computer is instantly available. As the viewer's representative at the ground, the producer aims to provide the correct mix, in the selection not only of close-ups and wide-angles, replays and slow-motions but also of averages and identifications.

The rapid advances in technology have transformed sports coverage. When Laker began his long career as a commentator, there were only three or four, at the most five, cameras available at a Test match. Coverage was from one end only; there were no computers or action replays. Before the installation of computers in the 1970s scorecards were handwritten in copperplate, then compiled in Letraset for greater neatness. Videotape was not used until the mid-1960s; before then you had to watch live action as there were no recordings available.

193

Hunter recalls that when the videodisc – the instant slow-motion replay – was first employed, the Test umpire, Syd Buller, bluntly told him that this facility was not required. It would – shades of other later innovations – undermine the umpire's authority. Hunter, writing in 1986, said there was very little that could be *proved* on television. It was more likely that those behind the cameras would confirm the umpires' verdicts. In his view, the replays had helped viewers – and players – to understand the umpires' problems better. He believed then that the visual and aural aids for decisions to be made by a third umpire in the pavilion should be resisted. Umpires were human and, like batsmen, bowlers and fieldsmen, could make mistakes. 'It would not be the same if computers, cameras and microphones became the arbiters,' he said. There are many experienced umpires, including Dickie Bird, who still insist that the best technology can never offer the perfect decision.

The increase in sophisticated gadgetry, with as many as fourteen cameras bearing down on Test match action today, has a devouring intensity. Like tumbrils at a revolution, they present a threat to the men in white coats. In the fierce spotlight the noose tightens to diminish their independence.

In less beseeching days, Jim Laker exemplified the honour of an impartial judge as a television commentator. S. J. de Lotbiniere ('Lobby', as he was known) was the former head of Outside Broadcasts, first in radio in 1935, and then in television in 1952. He pioneered disciplines which became a byword in the broadcasting lexicon. 'Lobby' set down and insisted upon one golden rule: 'A commentator earns his fee as much by silence as by speech.' Laker subscribed to this tenet of broadcasting. One of his major assets on television was an economy of words. 'As a commentator,' recalls Tony Lewis, 'Jim read the game brilliantly. There was always the right emphasis. He never gave anything more than it was worth. He did not hold back from praise but he would explain exactly how that lay in the firmament.'

Jim Swanton said that Laker talked over the air rather as he bowled – precisely, accurately, shrewdly, with no fanciful flights. As another observer recalled, Laker did not super-impose his own personality on the action. The quiet Yorkshireman stayed in the background, wisely guiding the viewers through the events of the day. He had the happy knack of putting his finger instantly on the nub of any argument.

The consummate broadcaster never did speak until the time was right. At the Laker home in Putney, the silences were as recognisable as any gush of words. 'When you put the telly on,' says his daughter Angela, 'you always knew if it was Dad.' The action flickered on the screen but not a sound was coming out. The kettle would bubble nicely on the kitchen hob. Then, as tea was poured, Angela would summon the attention of the family and announce: 'Dad's on.'

13

COMEDY ON THE HOME FRONT

'A lovely fresh egg on a haddock;
'Eh by gum, but it's good,
Better than sausage and Yorkshire pud.'

There was something endearing about the droll merrymaking of the man with music-hall voices. Jim Laker was top of the bill again with his verses and songs, an entertainer who consorted happily with comedy at home.

The abundant repertoire of the warm-hearted family man included one raptly received monologue, the mournful saga of 'Albert and the Lion'. It was his party piece, rendered in its entirety, on car journeys. The memories of his children are of a father who exuded fun; the milestones of their infancy were decorated with affectionate clowning. There were the risqué songs of George Formby and other show-stopping melodies in Jim's make-believe Palladium. 'Dad was always singing or presenting his recitations in the car,' say his daughters, Fiona and Angela. Their travels gathered speed propelled along by his roguish humour.

The laughter engendered by this special man is a cherished keepsake. Jim, tall and handsome, attained a matinee idol status among his daughters' schoolfriends. They revelled in his twinkling mischief. He was at his most charming with children. The annual deluge of Valentine's Day cards was an amusing instance of the adoration accorded to him.

Jim always rigorously maintained his boyhood allegiance, as a soccer enthusiast, to the claret and amber colours of Bradford

City, whose results were eagerly scanned in the weekend sports pages. As a spectator, though, he joined the throng of Chelsea fans in the more glamorous environs of Stamford Bridge. He was often accompanied to matches by Angela. There was the luxury of the lifting of the bedtime curfew on her first outing to an evening match under floodlights. She was overwhelmed by the tumultuous atmosphere. The beams of lights so exaggerated the pace of the action on the field that the match flashed by in a colourful blur.

Loyalty to the blues of Chelsea became a childhood passion. The soccer ritual was extended to watching the club reserves on first-team away days. Then, on the sparsely populated terraces, Angela would tug impatiently at her father's sleeves at half-time. Before the teams reappeared she would scamper along the steps to gain a view of home attacks at the other end.

Angela remembers, as a 10-year-old, being perched precariously alongside her father in their allotted places in the stand at Stamford Bridge. 'Dad, in his sheepskin coat, would spread his considerable bulk over his own and most of my seat.' Jim watched, taut with concentration, the ebb and flow of play. He was imperturbable and unruffled amid the uproar of the crowd. His earnest gaze would instantly identify the Chelsea goal-scorers.

'Dad was great to be with at a football match,' says Angela. 'He would just look on without emotion and then, with utter conviction, tell me who'd scored.' The message was delivered in staccato style. 'Cooke, Tambling, Venables,' he would declaim in a voice which permitted no argument. It was an example of the fine judgement he displayed on professional duty as a commentator. 'He was never wrong. We would check in the newspaper next morning for confirmation of the scorers and find that he was right.'

There was one unaccountable hitch in their soccer arrangements. It was a bad error. By some mischance in 1970, as Jim recalled, a family holiday had been booked in Majorca which coincided with an important fixture. Chelsea were playing Leeds in the FA Cup final at Wembley. It was a swelteringly hot day in Majorca. Angela was at home in spirit, wearing her Chelsea scarf and flourishing a rattle in her hand as she listened to the radio commentary. Jim, aware of her disappointment, promised his daughter that in the event of a replay he would ensure their presence at the match.

Chelsea did, fortuitously, force a draw at Wembley. Old Trafford, chosen as the venue for the replay, now linked two famous victories. Little more than a six-hit from the soccer arena was Jim's own field of dreams. Fifteen years earlier he had inscribed his name in cricket history with his deeds against Australia. Chelsea, as sporting ambassadors to the north, achieved a notable triumph to delight him as an observer. Leeds, in the first of their three finals in the 1970s, were beaten 2–1 after extra time. Angela's blue scarf was hurled aloft to greet the winning goal, headed in by David Webb.

The celebrations, which coincided with her mother's birthday, continued long after the match. The Lakers spent the night at a hotel in Cheshire. 'I was in cloud cuckoo land,' says Angela. 'We stayed up until the early hours, exchanging yarns, with two other Chelsea fans, actors James Bolam and Tom Courtenay.'

Jim, interviewed in the Chelsea club's 'Stars in the Stand' series, enthused about the pleasures of his soccer outings. 'For me, the fascination about Chelsea over 20 years has been the players of great talent. I'd rather have 20 minutes of the skills of Charlie Cooke, Peter Osgood or Alan Hudson than watch England for a whole match, because I believe that for the customer football is all about entertainment ... This is how cricket used to be. Cricketers weren't well paid in my time. But we'd have 20,000 at The Oval to watch a county match. Today, players are better paid but play to empty grounds, and I don't envy them a bit. They can't get the satisfaction out of the game as we did.'

The sporting idylls at Stamford Bridge, the shared experiences of Jim and Angela, were not usually granted to the Lakers' other daughter, Fiona. Yet it was the elder girl, a talented tennis player, who did enjoy a special bond with her father. Jim was immensely proud of her ability and drove her to local tournaments. 'Fiona had a raw, natural talent, while I just enjoyed sport without the special and necessary commitment,' observes Angela.

On family holidays abroad, Fiona and Jim were content to relax on the beach, while Angela and her mother pursued their rounds of sightseeing. Jim, not a great tourist, preferred a less taxing holiday, sleepily floating on his back in the waters by the shore. He never learned to swim properly; nor did he progress as a skier. At one resort he spent fifteen minutes on the slopes before deciding that this was not really his style.

A similar attitude prevailed when his girls went to receive religious instruction at the local Sunday school. Churchgoing had been the pattern of Jim's childhood. Fiona and Angela found their attendances more irksome and only persevered because the lessons were restricted to the winter months; in the summer, cricket took precedence. Homework was a compulsory requirement until the day when Jim discovered that he could not help his daughters. Sunday School and the Lakers thereafter parted company.

The complications of having a famous father rear in the memory of Angela. Explaining his celebrity was necessarily more detailed than with other parents and could invoke charges of immodesty. She remembers cutting job advertisements out of newspapers and urging her father to apply for posts. It would, she thought, make life much easier if he was simply a postman.

Grand National racing days evoke wistful memories of Jim, the 'lucky and astute gambler', within the family. Angela, who has inherited this trait, often longs to hear the advice of her father as to the horse she should bet on. Nick Hunter, the former television producer, recalls one extraordinary example of Jim's intuitive powers as a gambler. It occurred during their visit to a casino in Leeds. 'Jim was wandering around the tables, hovering at each in turn, for about twenty minutes.' Hunter watched this survey with keen interest and asked: 'What are you doing, Jim?' There was a hushed reply: 'I'm just waiting.' Suddenly Jim moved swiftly to one table. He selected no. 7, his usual batting position, for the wager. 'I'll have a few quid on this number,' he told his companion. The wheel spun and came to rest on the number. Hunter remembers that another half-hour elapsed before Jim thoughtfully stopped at another table. It was another successful venture. His winnings amounted to around £700. Jim did not linger to squander his riches; he pocketed the money and left the club.

The prowess in public speaking, peppered with funny asides and with seemingly little more than mental preparation, always left his audiences wanting more. His discourses were invested with the spontaneity of a born raconteur. Away from the bigger lecture stages, as at local cricket clubs, Jim rarely asked for a fee. He made so many appearances at one venue, the Brighton Brunswick Club, that he decided one day to introduce another speaker. 'You must be getting bored of me,' he told his hosts. His suggested replacement was Don Wilson. 'He's another Yorkshireman, but he's quite good,' was his lavish recommendation.

Discourtesy did arouse anger, which was only barely concealed, when he was invited to speak at one function in Leeds. The diners were frustrated by the tedious marathons of two barristers preceding Jim on the toast list. They listened with mounting impatience to talks lasting for one and a half hours. At 12.30 a.m., Jim at last rose to address the assembly. His brief remarks were calculated to admonish his fellow speakers on their ill manners. 'I was contracted to speak on August 23,' he announced. 'It is now August 24. It has been very nice to meet you all. Thank you and good night.'

Jim was an assiduous supporter of charitable organisations, such as SPARKS, the children's charity of which he was a founder member, and the Lord's Taverners, once amusingly described as 'a group of cricketing actors or acting cricketers'. He gave generously of his time on an honorary basis, playing cricket and golf and speaking at dinners. Anthony Swainson was the Director of the Lord's Taverners for nearly twenty years. 'In my early days as Director, it was a great help to me in my work to include Jim Laker among my friends,' he says. Jim served on the Taverners' cricket committee and their joint activities included the launch of a cricket coaching scheme to aid young black cricketers in inner London.

At Swainson's invitation, Jim later joined a panel of experts, which included Trevor Bailey, as chairman, Colin Cowdrey and Richie Benaud. They were brought together during a Test match at Edgbaston to select the fifty greatest cricketers since the Second World War. The product of a wide-ranging debate was a handsome illustrated book, with a foreword by the Duke of Edinburgh. The royalties of the book were donated to the Taverners' charity.

Jim's charity cricket appearances included a match between the Taverners and a women's eleven in whose ranks was the former England captain, Rachel Heyhoe Flint. Arthur Phebey, fielding at first slip, witnessed a bruising confrontation between Jim and the renowned batswoman, known for her broadly fashioned humour. The first ball she received was a gentle half-volley, which was imperiously dispatched to the boundary.

'Jim looked down the wicket and gave me a sly wink,' recalls Phebey. The next ball, floated teasingly outside the off-stump, carried a menacing spin. Rachel was deceived into attempting another aggressive shot. She missed it, was struck a fierce blow in the nether regions, and collapsed on the ground in some distress. Commiserations were expressed before one Taverner ventured a bold query. 'I've often wondered,' he said, 'do you ladies wear a box?' Rachel, having regained her breath, replied: 'No, we wear a manhole cover!'

There was a further delightful instance of her repartee in another match against the Taverners at The Oval. Jim was the captain on this occasion and he put Billy Wright, the Wolves and England footballer, on to bowl. Wright was later given a rest but, after a few more overs, Jim tossed the ball to him again. 'Have you got the strength for another spell, Billy?' he asked. Rachel, by now at the batting crease, overheard the request. 'If he's got the strength,' she responded, 'tell him I've got the time.'

David Frost, the television interviewer, had flown in from Tahiti to play in this match. He was 'talked out' first ball by the audacious Rachel. Having taken guard, he watched the bowler retreating to the start of her run-up. Rachel, from first slip, whispered: 'David, your flies are undone.' Tears of laughter streamed down his face at the sally. It wrecked his concentration and his innings was summarily concluded as he was comprehensively bowled.

The affection for Jim Laker grew irresistibly over the years. Peter Walker, welcomed into the Laker household, was able to re-assess the kindly personality of a man whose austere facade had presented a misleading impression in the early stages of their relationship. 'My initial judgement of Jim was proved to be hopelessly inaccurate and incorrect. I was proud to regard myself as his friend.' On one visit to the Laker home in Putney, he was privileged to view Jim's collection of cricket trophies. Walker remembers Jim's quiet pride during the inspection of the memorabilia. 'I rejoiced in it, too, because I was in the presence of sporting history.' Six months later, many priceless objects were stolen in a burglary. 'Jim, I'm so sorry,' said Walker, when he visited him after a match at The Oval. Jim was hurt but undaunted by the offence. He did not lose his sense of proportion. 'Does it really matter?' he replied.

Two important souvenirs escaped the attention of the intruders. They were two inscribed cricket balls, presented by the Lancashire County Cricket Club to Laker to commemorate his 19 wickets at Old Trafford in 1956. These were donated to the MCC by his widow and are available for inspection in the Memorial Gallery at Lord's.

It is also appropriate, befitting Laker's renown as a broadcaster, that other memorable exploits are featured in the television room at The Oval. The Laker Room was opened by Mrs Laker during the Test against Pakistan in August 1996. The display cases contain items donated by her and others from the Surrey archives. They include Laker's MCC tour blazer (South Africa, 1956–57) and his Surrey blazer from the 1950s. Another memento is the 8 for 2 cricket ball presented by Yorkshire CCC to mark his feat for England against the Rest in the Test trial at Bradford in 1950. Laker's great achievements in 1956 dominate the collection. A cartoon by Roy Ullyett, including the match scorecard, and a poem by Alan de Silva pay tribute to his record-breaking figures against Australia at Old Trafford. A painting of Laker by the distinguished artist Jocelyn Galsworthy is another highlight of this impressive assembly.

Jim Laker always rejoiced in his Yorkshire heritage. The allegiance to his roots was apparent in every sentence he uttered. While not betraying his birthright, he was by no means a misfit in his adopted Surrey; the exile won ease and assurance in gentler climes. His daughter Angela remembers the 'king in his palace' at Kennington. 'Dad was a big man, holding my little hand, as we went on a promenade around the Oval. Everybody would stop to greet him and say hello. I really felt that he was extra special on those days.'

Yorkshire – and especially his boyhood surroundings at Saltaire – still beckoned. In later years Jim began to renew his contacts with old friends. He attended Bradford League matches at the riverside setting of Roberts Park when he had a free weekend, or on the Sundays of Tests at Headingley. Pat McKelvey, the former Surrey slow left-arm bowler, had by this time moved north to play for Saltaire. He recalls one visit by his old colleague. The match was against local rivals, Salts, whose ground is situated on the opposite bank of the River Aire. Jim watched McKelvey bowling from the river end and applauded the fall of early wickets. The Saltaire bowler did, however, subsequently find one tail-ender in obdurate mood. He was twice hit for sixes and, each time, the ball had to be retrieved from the river.

Between the innings, after this late assault, he took a stroll with Jim around the ground. 'I'm glad to see you're still taking a few wickets,' remarked Jim. 'But when I played here, I always bowled from the other end.' McKelvey innocently sought an explanation. 'Well,' said Jim, 'I was never much good with a wet ball!'

In the early 1980s, McKelvey enlisted Jim's support when the Saltaire club was threatened by the government's proposals for the construction of the Aire Valley trunk road. This dual carriageway was to have swept eastwards from Skipton and Bingley and then straight along the valley bottom. It would have engulfed the Saltaire ground and other sports fields in the vicinity. A protest group against the development, which came to be known as SCAR (Sports Clubs against the Road) was set up, and Jim readily agreed to act as their celebrity patron. McKelvey recalls: 'Jim needed no second bidding when he heard of our plight. He immediately expressed his horror at the effect and extent of the road proposals. He then fired off a letter to the press, making clear his personal objection to the scheme.' The sequel was the decision, yet to be implemented, of the government to divert the new road away from the valley bottom and through a tunnel beneath the Shipley town centre.

It was his faithfulness in friendship which earned Jim Laker esteem and regard. This was particularly true in relations, lasting over fifty years, with fellow pupils at Salts High School. Bill Burgess, Jim Sutton and Fred Robinson are three members of this ensemble; they shared with Jim what were described as 'junior blokeish activities'. Fred Robinson remembers a 'reliable and conscientious' friend with whom he maintained a closeness all his life. There was, as an example of their comradeship, an ease in picking up threads, however much time had elapsed between their meetings. 'We always felt comfortable with each other,' says Bill Burgess.

All of them recall Jim's nice, dry humour, which was accompanied by an enigmatic smile. The ambiguity of his cunning asides carried the challenge of a crossword clue. 'Work that one out' was the unspoken substance of his jests. They were often delivered as parting shots after a television commentary stint. His fellow broadcasters were left to ponder on the import of the ad-libs.

Jim's humour was also reflected in his response to happenings which fitted his sense of the ridiculous. For instance, a reunion was once arranged at a favourite pub rendezvous between the Strand and Waterloo Bridge in London. It was probably, to paraphrase the words of the song, 'one of the places that Hitler had knocked about a bit'. The three friends, and Jim most of all, dissolved into laughter when they arrived at the appointed meeting place only to find it was no longer there.

Conviviality was the keynote of the friendships. Jim was only too glad to escape attention after the cut and thrust of his cricket duels. One evening, after a Test match at Headingley, all were present again at the pleasing retreat of the Bankfield Hotel. It was a time of shared reminiscences. Cricket, or more particularly Jim's exploits in the Test, did not dominate the conversation. 'He was such a modest man; he had bowled well that day,' says Bill Burgess. 'But I always got the impression that success embarrassed him.'

As in the best of relations, differing status did not impose barriers. These were labels of pretence against which Jim would have recoiled with disdain. Burgess staunchly expresses the tone of his regard: 'I wanted to keep in touch and availed myself of every opportunity to do so.' Fame never deflected Jim in his loyalty to trusted companions. 'He was, with the passing of the years, still a nice man,' comments Burgess. 'There was never any question that he wanted something from you.'

In a letter, which prefaced his saddening illness, Jim issued an invitation into the television commentary box. 'Don't forget the next match at Lord's. Do come up and make contact with me.'

Epilogue
FAREWELL TO A MASTER

'His genuine and friendly voice has been so close to us for so many years.'

Cliff Morgan

The indulgences which greet the passing of great men would have brought a hefty sigh from one of their number, Jim Laker. A portrait of pride was drawn by Richie Benaud at the memorial service at Southwark Cathedral in July 1986. As Benaud put it, Jim would have wondered what was going on 'with the gates full, the sun out, and no one going out'.

The blessings of their broadcasting comradeship were recalled by Benaud in a calm and laconic manner which Jim would have appreciated. 'After the English season,' said Benaud, 'we went our separate ways, Jim to drive up and down the country in snow and ice, making speeches at cricket dinners, I back to Australia for the southern summer. The next time we'd meet would be at the start of a new season. Jim would just glance up from what he was reading and say: "Mornin' Richie." No more was needed.'

The ease of the annual reunion was an expression of the accord which existed between the two men. The thanksgiving at Southwark was also free of affectation. It did not linger in mournful tidings, or swoop into a sea of sentiment. But as one writer said, there would have been a twinkle in Laker's eyes and a tremble of his lips when he realised it was all for him.

The first symptoms of an illness which was to lead to his death had beset Jim on a March day five years earlier. They occurred on the eve of his departure to Barbados to watch the latter stages of the England tour of the West Indies. 'It's an old story,' said Jim, after he had fought and won a battle for his life. 'It could never happen to me, especially when everyone kept saying how fit and well I looked.'

His widow, Lilly, remembers how Jim was laid low with severe pains and a high temperature. A series of tests at a local hospital yielded the diagnosis of a virus infection. Three days later, although still feeling weak and unwell, Jim declared himself fit to leave for the Caribbean. Before their departure they switched on the television at home. The one o'clock news bulletin contained one shocking announcement. Ken Barrington, Jim's former Surrey colleague and the MCC assistant manager, was dead. Barrington, at the age of 50, had died of a heart attack in his hotel room in Barbados. 'Jim was terribly upset about Kenny; we had a very bad trip,' recalls Lilly. Laker himself remembered his grief-stricken state and how their visit to the West Indies took on the proportions of a nightmare.

On his return home, he appeared for some weeks to have turned the corner. It was a brief respite; the fever and pains flared again to compel a hasty retreat from the Surrey Old Players' dinner at The Oval in mid-May. Lilly remembers that Jim was in such acute distress that all he could do was to lie on the floor, or a hard surface. At the time the muscular spasms seemed to indicate a form of fibrositis.

Fortunately, in this hour of need, Lilly was able to enlist the help of Lance Bromley, a family friend and a leading surgeon at St Mary's Hospital in Paddington. 'Suddenly, I dialled his number and Lance himself answered the phone. It was a miracle.' Bromley was at Jim's bedside within three hours of Lilly's call. His diagnosis was a life-threatening aortic aneurism (an excessive enlargement of the artery). His prompt intervention came not a moment too soon. On the following day, Jim underwent a five-hour operation performed by Mr Eastcott, a top surgeon specialising in diseases of the main artery.

Laker recalled the skills of the hospital team which drew him out of the shadows of death. 'Instead of driving up the M1 to Birmingham for the start of the new BBC season, I found the venue had been abruptly changed to an intensive-care unit in a London hospital. Instead of a microphone covering my mouth there was an oxygen mask, and replacing a producer testing my eardrums were ever-attentive nurses searching for virgin territory to implant their needles.'

He had been unaware of the severity of his illness. It was only later, when he emerged from intensive care, that he realised what a close call it had been. 'After three days of magnificent attention, some of the trappings, wires and drips, thankfully disappeared and the first thimbleful of water slipped down my throat. It tasted as delicate as a drop of Richie Benaud's favourite champagne.'

The convalescence was protracted but Jim made an excellent recovery. By June he was back home and watching the television coverage of the series between England and Australia. For the first time in more than ten years he had to vacate his commentary position. From the comfort of his armchair he followed the course of a fluctuating contest which might have been choreographed as a tonic for him. This was the series which reached its crescendo in the dramatic events at Headingley.

In his last book, *Cricket Contrasts*, published in 1985, Laker dwelt upon the dethronement of Ian Botham as England captain. 'I had felt all along that it was a mistake to saddle such a splendid all-rounder with the added problems of captaincy. There was always the worrying thought that it would affect his own performances. We needed him at his brilliant best to beat Australia.'

It was a perceptive judgement on a cricketer who had been imprisoned by other responsibilities. At Headingley, Botham attacked with the zeal of an archer directing his arrows against superior forces at Agincourt. Christopher Martin-Jenkins was Laker's deputy in the commentary box. He watched a resplendent Botham summon conquest with his own brand of audacity. Bob Willis, with match-winning figures of eight wickets for 43 runs, caught the infection of Botham's rage. England were the victors by 18 runs in an astonishing somersault in fortunes. It was only the second time in Test history that a side had won after being forced to follow on.

Two days after these thrilling events, Laker pronounced himself fit to return to the commentary box. He was at Edgbaston to witness another exceptional performance by Botham. Australia, set a target of 151, were victory-bound until Botham once again confounded the odds. He took five wickets for one run in 28 deliveries. For Laker, never an observer to accentuate the past at the expense of the present, the deeds of 1981 established Botham as a cricketer who would have shone in any era. In the fifth Test at Old Trafford, where England retained the Ashes, there was another explosive feat to crown his glorious summer. Botham's century off 102 balls included six sixes. Before tea, when Lillee and Alderman took the new ball, he bludgeoned 66 off eight overs.

Jim Laker had surmounted his own more fraught assault course. His health was not good but he was now leading a normal life, if quieter than before his perilous illness. Tony Lewis remembers how Jim began to pace himself on the broadcasting round. It was a fine balance because dovetailing the demands of Test and Sunday League cricket clearly put an extra strain on his resources. Increasingly, it became his custom to spend the night following a match with the television crew.

There was evidence of this care, as Lewis reflects, in the advice he received from Jim on negotiating the pressures of a frantic circuit. 'Don't drive above 60mph on the motorway,' instructed Jim. 'And don't rush home; your wife won't thank you. Pick a little hotel and rest awhile before your next assignment.' The wisdom communicated to the younger man demonstrated Jim's awareness of the need to conserve his own energies.

Jim and Lilly spent the Christmas of 1985 with their daughter Fiona at her Wiltshire home. They returned home on New Year's Day. Jim became ill in the car on the journey and his condition worsened to such an extent that he was hospitalised for three weeks in January. He was a heavy smoker but moderate in his drinking. The problem was diagnosed as pancreatitis. There were more tests and, in order to avoid a recurrence, the decision was taken to remove his gall bladder. Jim did not want to have the operation; but the medical verdict pointed to a successful outcome. It did not occur to them, to Lilly's abiding regret, to engage a second opinion on the projected operation.

There were, at the time, few worries in the Laker household. The consultant surgeon had offered complete reassurance in the preliminary discussions with Jim and Lilly. Jim's next television commitment was scheduled for early May; it was agreed that he should undergo the operation at the end of March. He would spend two weeks in hospital and then take a holiday before resuming his commentary duties. These post-operative expectations were sadly unfulfilled. What was, in truth, a minor and possibly unnecessary operation had an agonising sequel. Jim grew increasingly ill and contracted septicaemia. He died at Parkside Clinic, Wimbledon on the evening of 23 April. He was 64.

The grief in cricket circles was compounded within twenty-four hours by the death of another gallant champion, Bill Edrich, of Middlesex and England. As one writer said, two mighty trees had fallen in cricket's memory lane. The rivalry between Laker and Edrich – and their fiercely competitive duels – is enshrined in the folklore of the game. The ice was always broken off the field. One of their contemporaries said: 'Bill used to rejoice in his battles with Jim. He will be delighted that Jim is going to bowl at him up there.'

Celebrities from the cricket and broadcasting worlds were among the congregation of 800 people who gathered to pay tribute to a great bowler at Southwark Cathedral in July 1986. They included two of Jim's England captains, Sir Len Hutton and Peter May; and old Surrey colleagues Alec Bedser and Alf Gover. Raman Subba Row, another former county partner, was there in his capacity as chairman of the Test and County Cricket Board. Subba Row has one striking memory of this occasion of thanksgiving. Walking alongside him into the church was the tennis star, Fred Perry, who echoed the feelings of respect which dominated the minds of all in attendance on that day. 'I had to come to Jim's memorial service,' he said. 'It was essential that I was present here today.'

Two other old friends from The Oval – Sir George Edwards, the former county president, and Micky Stewart, the Surrey cricket manager – read the lessons. The tribute to Jim was presented by the Rev. Alan Sirman, the vicar of Holy Trinity Church, Putney. 'For millions throughout the world his quiet and knowledgeable broadcasts brought the action and subtleties of the game he loved into their homes. His family life was a source of warmth and joy to him.'

The high art form which cricket represented for Jim had also been marked by gentlemanly behaviour and honesty both on and off the field. It would, he hoped, be an inspiration and example to everyone. 'Most especially, we pray that the young people of our nation should see his way of life as a standard by which to measure their own.'

One of those younger men was Grahame Clinton, who had found Jim the kindliest of benefactors when he moved from Kent to The Oval in the late 1970s. 'Jim's early death was a great disappointment for Surrey,' he said. 'His passing left a tremendous void at The Oval and had a fundamental effect on the fortunes of the club. Jim was very highly respected by the senior members of the committee, and his views were always carefully noted.'

Clinton tellingly dwelt upon Jim's ability to span the generations in cricket. 'He did not live in the past and tended to make light of his own achievements and those of others during his career.' 'We weren't all *that* good,' Jim had modestly declared. 'There are as many good players now as there were then.'

From one long-standing friend and devotee, John Arlott, came an eloquent and moving tribute. 'His daughters loved him, and his wife, Lilly, adored him. If he took a quizzical look at the world, he missed very little. To work with him, and to be accepted by him, was something of an accolade. It was an admission to a school of cricketing thought that was often quite bewildering in its depth.' Arlott added: 'The off-break is not merely the bowler's bread and butter, it is the staff of his life. And in that school Jim Laker was the past master.'

The oration at Jim's funeral had earlier referred to the lustre of his achievements in the 1950s when he had restored pride to his country. The cricketing father figure of other years was besieged by one perennial question. The legions of admirers constantly urged him to recall his Old Trafford command performance in 1956. Jim reacted to the chorus, as one writer said, with mixed feelings. 'There he would stand, hands thrust deep into his trouser pockets, powerful shoulders sloping, a sad face with a suspicion of a smile, the voice distinctive and deep.'

Micky Stewart was given the sad task of scattering Jim's ashes at The Oval. He pondered for some time on the proper area for his mission. Then, smiling at the remembrance, he chose the region of long-on beneath the Laker Stand. 'Batsmen would try to get out of jail by slogging Jim over to cow-shot corner,' he recalled. Jim always insisted on a fielding patrol there to guard against the aggressors. He did not take kindly to such indignities. If his captain refused to give him this security, Jim would place the ball on the ground and say: 'All right then, let someone else bowl.'

There was a poignant sequel on this same stretch of turf. Witnessing the event was Lilly Laker and her daughter, Angela. In the summer of 1996 they watched Jim's grandson, 10-year-old Patrick, in the final round of a schools' cricket competition at The Oval. Patrick had earlier scored a half-century to enable his school to reach the final. The match was played directly underneath the Laker stand in which they were seated. Patrick struck two sixes and, each time, the balls landed unerringly by their feet.

It was a quite uncanny experience. The batsman, with the sweet bliss of youth, provided a lovely and moving cameo. It was, in a way, although the boy did not realise it, a farewell salute to his grandfather, a man he had scarcely known.

BIBLIOGRAPHY

John Arlott: *Jim Laker* (monograph, privately printed).

A. J. Arnold: *A Game That Would Pay: Professional Football in Bradford* (Duckworth, 1988).

Trevor Bailey: *The Greatest of My Time* (Eyre & Spottiswoode, 1968); with Fred Trueman: *The Spinners' Web* (Willow Books, Collins, 1988).

Alex Bannister: *Cricket Cauldron* (Stanley Paul, 1954).

Alec Bedser: *Cricket Choice* (Pelham, 1981).

Richie Benaud: *On Reflection* (Willow Books, Collins, 1984).

Catford Cyphers Cricket Club, Centenary booklet (1990).

Ted Dexter, with Ralph Dellor: *Ted Dexter's Little Cricket Book* (Bloomsbury, 1996).

Alan Hill: *The Family Fortune: A Saga of Sussex Cricket* (Scan Books, 1978); *Johnny Wardle: Cricket Conjuror* (David and Charles, 1988); *Bill Edrich* (André Deutsch, 1994); *Peter May* (André Deutsch, 1996).

Sir Leonard Hutton and Alex Bannister: *Fifty Years in Cricket* (Stanley Paul, 1984).

Brian Johnston: *Chatterboxes* (Star, W. H. Allen, 1984); (ed.) *Armchair Cricket, 1968* (British Broadcasting Corporation, 1968).

Jim Laker: *Spinning Round the World* (Muller, 1957); *Over to Me* (Muller, 1960); *The Australian Tour of 1961* (Muller, 1961); *A Spell from Laker* (Hamlyn, 1979); *Cricket Contrasts* (Stanley Paul, 1985).

Tony Lock: *For Surrey and England* (Hodder & Stoughton, 1957).

Jack McHarg: *Arthur Morris: An Elegant Genius* (ABC Books, Sydney, 1995).

Sir Michael Marshall: *Gentlemen and Players* (Grafton Books, 1987).

Peter May: *A Game Enjoyed* (Stanley Paul, 1985).

Gordon Ross: *The Surrey Story* (Stanley Paul, 1958); *Surrey* (Arthur Barker, 1971).

Saltaire Cricket Club: *Saltaire CC: 1869–1969* (centenary booklet, Shipley, 1969).

E. W. Swanton: *West Indian Adventure* (Museum Press, 1954); *Swanton in Australia: with MCC 1946–1975* (Collins, 1975); (ed.) *Barclays World of Cricket* (Collins, 1986).

Hedley Verity: *Bowling 'em out* (Hutchinson, 1936).

Peter West: *Flannelled Fool and Muddied Oaf* (W. H. Allen, 1986).

Wilfrid S. White: *Sydney Barnes* (E. F. Hudson, 1937).

Contemporary reports and articles in the *Daily Telegraph*; *The Times*; the *Sunday Times*; *Evening Standard*, London; *Evening News*, London; *Daily Mail*; *Daily Express*; *Sunday Express*; *Daily Mirror*; *Daily Herald*; *News of the World*; *Empire News*; *Manchester Guardian*; *Picture Post*; *Yorkshire Post*; *Telegraph & Argus* (Bradford); *Bradford Observer*; *Egyptian Gazette* (Cairo); *Mail in Egypt*; *Auckland Herald*; *New Zealand Cricket Almanack*; *Sydney Morning Herald*; *Jamaica Gleaner*; *Surrey CCC Yearbooks*; *The Cricketer*; *Playfair Cricket Monthly*; *Wisden Cricket Monthly*; and various editions of the *Wisden Cricketers' Almanack*.

STATISTICAL APPENDIX

Compiled by Paul E. Dyson

James Charles Laker
in First-Class Cricket

Born: Frizinghall, Bradford   Died: Putney, London
9 February 1922   23 April 1986

First-class debut: Surrey v. Combined Services at The Oval.
17 July 1946.

County Cap: Surrey v. Middlesex at Lord's. 26 August 1947.

England debut: v. West Indies at Bridgetown, Barbados.
21 January 1948.

Final day of Test cricket: England v. Australia at Melbourne.
18 February 1959.

Final day of first-class cricket: Cavaliers v. Barbados at
Bridgetown.
27 February 1965.

Batting and Fielding, season by season

	M	I	NO	Runs	HS	Avge	100	50	Ct
1946	3	3	1	3	3	1.50	–	–	1
1947	18	26	4	408	60	18.54	–	1	13
1947–48	8	12	2	212	55	21.20	–	1	4
1948	29	44	10	828	99	24.35	–	3	16
1949	28	39	7	548	100	17.12	1	–	26
1950	30	42	6	589	53	16.36	–	1	22
1950–51	10	10	1	171	61	19.00	–	1	5
1951	28	38	6	624	89	19.50	–	4	22
1951–52	4	4	0	77	35	19.25	–	–	3
1952	30	34	5	310	26	10.68	–	–	16
1953	31	34	3	502	81	16.19	–	1	25
1953–54	7	9	1	123	33	15.37	–	–	4
1954	29	33	9	607	113	25.29	1	1	29
1955	30	38	6	706	78*	22.06	–	4	26
1956	25	34	5	320	43*	11.03	–	–	8
1956–57	14	16	6	79	17	7.90	–	–	3
1957	28	28	11	210	44	12.35	–	–	9
1958	28	29	6	325	59	14.13	–	1	10
1958–59	10	13	3	107	22*	10.70	–	–	1
1959	24	30	7	301	28	13.08	–	–	15
1962	12	11	2	43	13	4.77	–	–	5
1963	10	12	5	95	24*	13.57	–	–	4
1963–64	2	1	1	0	0*	–	–	–	1
1964	8	6	1	110	28	22.00	–	–	2
1964–65	4	2	0	6	5	3.00	–	–	1
Total	450	548	108	7304	113	16.60	2	18	271

Bowling, season by season

	Ovrs	Mdns	Runs	Wkts	Avge	5WI	10WM	BB
1946	60	12	169	8	21.12	–	–	3–43
1947	575.5	135	1420	79	17.97	5	–	8–69
1947–48	388.5	117	973	36	27.02	3	–	7–103
1948	1058.4	250	2903	104	27.91	4	–	8–55
1949	1192.1	419	2422	122	19.85	8	1	8–42
1950	1399.5	522	2544	166	15.32	12	5	8–2
1950–51	315.2	131	579	36	16.08	3	–	6–23
1951	1301.3	400	2681	149	17.99	13	5	7–36
1951–52	228.1	88	379	24	15.79	3	1	5–44
1952	1071	342	2219	125	17.75	9	1	7–57
1953	1155.5	382	2366	135	17.52	7	1	6–25
1953–54	333.5	113	756	22	34.36	–	–	4–47
1954	966.2	315	2048	135	15.17	13	5	8–51
1955	1093.1	362	2382	133	17.90	9	3	7–95
1956	959.3	364	1906	132	14.43	8	3	10–53
1956–57	+387.7	122	875	50	17.50	2	–	6–47
1957	1016.5	393	1921	126	15.24	5	–	7–16

1958	882.5	330	1651	116	14.23	7	2	8–46
1958–59	+282.1	63	655	38	17.23	3	1	5–31
1959	797.2	246	1920	78	24.61	5	2	7–38
1962	390.5	96	962	51	18.86	5	1	7–73
1963	374	128	828	43	19.25	2	1	7–89
1963–64	72	13	221	5	44.20	–	–	2–50
1964	226	55	577	17	33.94	–	–	4–41
1964–65	133.4	23	434	14	31.00	1	–	5–54
Total	15993.3	5236	35791	1944	18.41	127	32	10–53
	+670	185						

+ 8-ball overs

Batting and Fielding for each team

	M	I	NO	Runs	HS	Avge	100	50	Ct
Surrey (in County Championship)	259	326	59	4719	113	17.67	1	15	189
Surrey (in other matches)	50	61	11	812	100	16.24	1	–	35
A Surrey XI	1	2	1	25	17*	25.00	–	–	–
Total for Surrey	310	389	71	5556	113	17.47	2	15	224
Essex (all in CC)	30	29	8	248	28	11.80	–	–	11
England (Tests)	46	63	15	676	63	14.08	–	2	12
MCC (overseas)	22	22	5	266	41	15.64	–	–	7
MCC (in UK)	6	7	3	68	17	17.00	–	–	2
Total for MCC	28	29	8	334	41	15.90	–	–	9
Commonwealth	10	10	1	171	61	19.00	–	1	5
An England XI	7	9	3	76	18	12.66	–	–	3
Cavaliers	6	3	1	6	5	3.00	–	–	2
Auckland	4	4	0	77	35	19.25	–	–	3
Players	3	4	0	25	8	6.25	–	–	1
South/South of England	3	4	1	106	33	35.33	–	–	–
Leveson Gower's XI	2	2	0	17	10	8.50	–	–	1
P. F. Warner's XI	1	2	0	12	10	6.00	–	–	–
Total	450	548	108	7304	113	16.60	2	18	271

Summary

	M	I	NO	Runs	HS	Avge	100	50	Ct
County Championship	289	355	67	4967	113	17.24	1	15	200
Test Matches	46	63	15	676	63	14.08	–	2	12
Other Matches	115	130	26	1661	100	15.97	1	1	59
Total	450	548	108	7304	113	16.60	2	18	271

Bowling

	Overs	Mdns	Runs	Wkts	Avge	5WI	10WM	BB
Surrey (in County Championshlp)	9870.3	3297	20528	1203	17.06	82	19	8–42
Surrey (in other matches)	1720.3	515	3708	192	19.31	11	5	10–88
A Surrey XI	31	7	69	1	69.00	–	–	1–42
Total for Surrey	11622	3819	24305	1396	17.41	93	24	10–88
Essex (all in CC)	990.5	279	2367	111	21.32	7	2	7–73
England (Tests)	1640.4 +272.7	604 70	4101	193	21.24	9	3	10–53
MCC (overseas)	314.5 +397.1	98 115	1600	88	18.18	6	1	6–47
MCC (in UK)	235.4	76	506	24	21.08	1	–	7–35
Total for MCC	550.3 +397.1	174 115	2106	112	18.80	7	1	7–35
Commonwealth	315.2	131	579	36	16.08	3	–	6–23
An England XI	157.4	38	473	20	23.65	1	1	8–2
Cavaliers	205.4	36	655	19	34.47	1	–	5–54
Auckland	228.1	88	379	24	15.79	3	1	5–44
Players	107.1	35	242	14	17.28	1	–	6–48
South/South of England	50	6	138	4	34.50	–	–	2–5
Leveson Gower's XI	59.1	8	264	7	37.71	1	–	5–97
P. F. Warner's XI	66.2	18	182	8	22.75	1	–	6–109
Total	15993.3 +670	5236 185	35791	1944	18.41	127	32	10–53

Summary

	Overs	Mdns	Runs	Wkts	Avge	5WI	10WM	BB
County Championship	10861.2	3576	22895	1314	17.42	89	21	8–42
Test Matches	1640.4 +272.7	604 70	4101	193	21.24	9	3	10–53
Other Matches	3491.3 +397.1	1056 115	8795	437	20.12	29	8	10–88
Total	15993.3 +670	5236 185	35791	1944	18.41	127	32	10–53

Against each team
(excluding Test matches)

Batting and Fielding
In United Kingdom

	M	I	NO	Runs	HS	Avge	100	50	Ct
Derbyshire	13	17	1	157	38	9.81	–	–	13
Essex	22	32	9	345	56*	15.00	–	1	14
Glamorgan	22	31	5	531	61	20.42	–	2	15
Gloucestershire	19	26	3	416	113	18.08	1	–	12
Hampshire	18	20	6	301	81	21.50	–	2	9
Kent	20	24	5	437	99	23.00	–	1	14
Lancashire	15	16	2	218	55	15.57	–	1	10
Leicestershire	21	20	3	337	59	19.82	–	2	17
Middlesex	23	31	4	455	60	16.85	–	1	13
Northamptonshire	18	25	6	510	89	26.84	–	2	13
Nottinghamshire	25	23	6	299	42*	18.68	–	–	16
Somerset	15	15	3	177	39	14.75	–	–	18
Sussex	12	14	5	248	78*	27.55	–	2	6
Warwickshire	14	18	3	180	35	12.00	–	–	10
Worcestershire	17	19	5	107	20*	7.64	–	–	15
Yorkshire	20	29	2	331	66	12.25	–	1	8
Cambridge University	13	9	2	285	100	40.71	1	–	12
Oxford University	2	3	0	19	17	6.33	–	–	1
MCC	12	17	6	159	43*	14.45	–	–	9
The Rest (of England)	8	10	4	118	26	19.66	–	–	1
Gentlemen	3	4	0	25	8	6.25	–	–	1
Combined Services	2	2	0	3	3	1.50	–	–	1
South of England	1	2	0	12	10	6.00	–	–	–
Australians	7	10	2	125	43	15.62	–	–	4
Indians	5	6	0	44	16	7.33	–	–	2
New Zealanders	5	6	2	61	15*	15.25	–	–	2
Pakistanis	2	3	0	29	13	9.66	–	–	1
South Africans	1	2	0	7	7	3.50	–	–	1
West Indians	4	6	0	127	30	21.16	–	–	2
Commonwealth	3	6	2	45	18	11.25	–	–	2

Overseas

	M	I	NO	Runs	HS	Avge	100	50	Ct
Combined/ Australian XI	2	2	0	10	8	5.00	–	–	–
Queensland	1	1	0	0	0	0.00	–	–	1
Tasmania	1	1	1	11	11*	–	–	–	–
South Australia	1	1	0	12	12	12.00	–	–	–
Victoria	1	1	0	12	12	12.00	–	–	–
Baroda	1	1	0	1	1	1.00	–	–	1

Bombay	1	1	0	3	3	3.00	–	–	–
Bombay Governor's XI	1	0	0	–	–	–	–	–	–
Cricket Club of India	1	1	0	26	26	26.00	–	–	1
India (unofficial Test)	1	1	0	37	37	37.00	–	–	1
Indian Services XI	1	2	0	61	61	30.50	–	1	–
Patiala	1	1	1	17	17*	–	–	–	1
Raja of Jath's XI	1	1	0	14	14	14.00	–	–	–
Saurashtra	1	1	0	6	6	6.00	–	–	–
Uttar Pradesh Governor's XI	1	1	0	6	6	6.00	–	–	1
Canterbury	1	2	0	35	24	17.50	–	–	1
Central District	1	0	0	–	–	–	–	–	–
Otago	1	1	0	7	7	7.00	–	–	1
Wellington	1	1	0	35	35	35.00	–	–	1
Border	1	0	0	–	–	–	–	–	–
Combined SA Universities	1	1	1	4	4*	–	–	–	1
Griqualand West	1	1	0	6	6	6.00	–	–	1
Natal	2	2	2	15	13*	–	–	–	–
Orange Free State	1	0	0	–	–	–	–	–	–
Rhodesia	1	1	0	0	0	0.00	–	–	–
Transvaal	1	1	0	4	4	4.00	–	–	–
Western Province	1	1	0	10	10	10.00	–	–	–
Barbados	4	4	0	58	38	14.50	–	–	1
British Guiana	1	2	0	61	41	30.50	–	–	2
Jamaica/Jamaican XI	8	6	2	69	33	17.25	–	–	3

Summary

Against British teams	335	407	80	5670	113	17.33	2	15	228
Against Overseas teams	69	78	13	958	61	14.73	–	1	31
Test Matches	46	63	15	676	63	14.08	–	2	12
Total	450	548	108	7304	113	16.60	2	18	271

Bowling

In United Kingdom

	Overs	Mdns	Runs	Wkts	Avge	5WI	10WM	BB
Derbyshire	418.4	133	895	55	16.27	2	–	5–57
Essex	869.4	243	1913	113	16.92	9	3	7–36
Glamorgan	825.3	274	1638	84	19.50	5	1	6–67
Gloucestershire	761.4	293	1382	112	12.33	8	3	8–45
Hampshire	699.2	198	1662	88	18.88	6	–	8–69
Kent	857.4	282	1744	112	15.57	10	2	7–47
Lancashire	512	174	983	50	19.66	1	1	6–41
Leicestershire	895.4	338	1565	90	17.38	5	–	7–89
Middlesex	851.3	232	2070	107	19.34	9	2	8–57
Northamptonshire	698.3	227	1560	79	19.74	7	2	7–57
Nottinghamshire	854.1	315	1815	90	20.16	5	–	7–16
Somerset	526.3	186	1092	69	15.82	7	1	7–59

	Overs	Mdns	Runs	Wkts	Avge	5WI	10WM	BB
Sussex	492.5	155	1068	67	15.94	3	2	8–46
Warwickshire	429.4	111	1090	60	18.16	5	1	8–42
Worcestershire	604	213	1270	83	15.30	5	2	7–61
Yorkshire	734.4	253	1512	76	19.89	3	1	6–23
Cambridge University	494.2	181	907	39	23.25	1	–	5–54
Oxford University	62.1	18	127	11	11.54	1	–	5–24
MCC	376.1	88	919	67	13.71	6	3	8–51
The Rest (of England)	188	51	429	24	17.87	1	1	8–2
Gentlemen	107.1	35	242	14	17.28	1	–	6–48
Combined Services	42	9	121	6	20.16	–	–	3–43
South of England	66.2	18	182	8	22.75	1	–	6–109
Australians	229	59	665	23	28.91	1	1	10–88
Indians	171	42	394	16	24.62	1	1	6–64
New Zealanders	186	61	374	14	26.71	1	–	6–112
Pakistanis	61	20	123	3	41.00	–	–	3–63
South Africans	46	12	127	6	21.16	1	–	5–56
West Indians	147	46	301	9	33.44	–	–	4–48
Commonwealth	80.4	12	307	9	34.11	–	–	3–43

Overseas

	Overs	Mdns	Runs	Wkts	Avge	5WI	10WM	BB
Baroda	33	9	59	6	9.83	1	–	5–52
Bombay	30	10	52	1	52.00	–	–	1–52
Bombay Governor's XI	35.5	11	103	5	20.60	–	–	4–61
Cricket Club of India	26	11	37	3	12.33	–	–	3–37
India (unofficial Test)	80.5	41	120	8	15.00	1	–	5–88
Indian Services XI	23	14	35	4	8.75	–	–	4–32
Patiala	44.4	19	71	6	11.83	1	–	6–23
Raja of Jath's XI	18	6	50	1	50.00	–	–	1–16
Saurashtra	11	3	27	1	27.00	–	–	1–27
Uttar Pradesh Gvrnr's XI	13	7	25	1	25.00	–	–	1–0
Canterbury	45	16	94	1	94.00	–	–	1–70
Central Districts	54	20	72	5	14.40	–	–	3–24
Otago	68.1	31	92	8	11.50	1	–	5–44
Wellington	61	21	121	10	12.10	2	1	5–53
Border	+12	5	26	5	5.20	–	–	4–16
Combined SA Univs	+33	6	84	6	14.00	–	–	3–34
Griqualand West	+21.3	8	40	2	20.00	–	–	2–24
Natal	+56	17	127	8	15.87	1	–	5–53
Orange Free State	+22	8	38	1	38.00	–	–	1–18
Rhodesia	+23	8	66	3	22.00	–	–	3–63
Transvaal	+36.3	9	81	6	13.50	–	–	4–40
Western Province	+39	15	89	8	11.12	1	–	6–47
Combined/Australian XI	+61.6	16	137	8	17.12	–	–	4–52
Queensland	+17.4	4	27	4	6.75	–	–	4–27
South Australia	+43.1	11	101	10	10.10	2	1	5–31
Tasmania	+6	1	11	0	–	–	–	–
Victoria	+26	7	61	1	61.00	–	–	1–61
Barbados	177.1	43	518	21	24.66	1	–	5–76
British Guiana	37	12	84	5	16.80	1	–	5–74
Jamaica/Jamaican XI	306.2	79	765	19	40.26	1	–	5–54

Summary

Against British teams	12368.1	4027	26186	1504	17.41	101	25	8–2
Against Overseas teams	1984.4 +397.1	605 115	5504	247	22.28	17	4	10–88
Test Matches	1640.4 +272.7	604 70	4101	193	21.24	9	3	10–53
Total	15993.3 +670	5236 185	35791	1944	18.41	127	32	10–53

On each ground
(including Test matches)

Batting and Fielding
In United Kingdom
(listed by county)

	M	I	NO	Runs	HS	Avge	100	50	Ct
Chesterfield	3	3	0	10	4	3.33	–	–	2
Derby	2	3	0	21	12	7.00	–	–	3
Derbyshire	5	6	0	31	12	5.16	–	–	5
Brentwood	5	4	0	41	22	10.25	–	–	1
Chelmsford	2	3	0	54	33	18.00	–	–	1
Clacton	2	3	2	18	13*	18.00	–	–	1
Colchester	2	2	0	20	19	10.00	–	–	1
Ilford	7	10	3	153	56*	21.85	–	1	3
Leyton	2	3	0	16	12	5.33	–	–	1
Romford	3	4	2	22	14	11.00	–	–	2
Southend	2	2	0	37	34	18.50	–	–	2
Essex	25	31	7	361	56*	15.04	–	1	12
Cardiff	5	8	0	110	61	13.75	–	1	4
Llanelli	1	1	0	20	20	20.00	–	–	–
Pontypridd	1	1	0	13	13	13.00	–	–	2
Swansea	6	10	4	262	53	43.66	–	1	2
Glamorgan	13	20	4	405	61	31.15	–	2	8
Bristol	4	3	0	76	39	25.33	–	–	2
Cheltenham	3	5	1	96	32*	24.00	–	–	3
Gloucester	3	6	1	28	16	5.60	–	–	–
Gloucestershire	10	14	2	200	39	16.66	–	–	5
Bournemouth	3	4	1	69	43	23.00	–	–	2
Portsmouth	4	6	3	56	19	18.66	–	–	2
Southampton	3	2	1	54	51	54.00	–	1	–
Hampshire	10	12	5	179	51	25.57	–	1	4

Blackheath	8	11	4	155	40	22.14	–	–	3
Dover	1	–	–	–	–	–	–	–	1
Kent	9	11	4	155	40	22.14	–	–	4
Liverpool	1	–	–	–	–	–	–	–	1
Old Trafford	10	13	0	188	55	14.46	–	–	1	3
Lancashire	11	13	0	188	55	14.46	–	1	4
Hinckley	1	1	0	0	0	0.00	–	–	–
Leicester	9	10	1	134	53	14.88	–	1	7
Loughborough	1	1	0	42	42	42.00	–	–	1
Leicestershire	11	12	1	176	53	16.00	–	1	8
Lord's (Middlesex)	36	50	13	559	60	15.10	–	1	17
Kettering	1	2	1	51	33*	51.00	–	–	1
Northampton	5	9	2	188	43*	26.85	–	–	3
Peterborough	2	1	0	25	25	25.00	–	–	2
Rushden	1	2	0	27	17	13.50	–	–	–
Northamptonshire	9	14	3	291	43*	26.45	–	–	6
Trent Bridge (Notts)	16	15	6	248	63	27.55	–	1	6
Bath	1	1	1	6	6*	–	–	–	2
Taunton	3	2	0	31	19	15.50	–	–	3
Wells	1	1	0	26	26	26.00	–	–	1
Weston–super–Mare	2	3	2	43	39	43.00	–	–	1
Somerset	7	7	3	106	39	26.50	–	–	7
Guildford	13	11	2	282	100	31.33	1	1	9
Kingston	3	5	2	45	18	15.00	–	–	–
The Oval	160	197	27	2541	113	14.94	1	5	129
Surrey	176	213	31	2868	113	15.75	2	6	138
Hastings	8	12	4	131	26	16.37	–	–	2
Hove	4	6	2	98	53*	24.50	–	1	2
Worthing	1	–	–	–	–	–	–	–	–
Sussex	13	18	6	229	53*	19.08	–	1	4
Coventry	1	2	0	32	16	16.00	–	–	1
Edgbaston	6	5	2	35	17*	11.66	–	–	1
Warwickshire	7	7	2	67	17*	13.40	–	–	2
Dudley	1	1	0	8	8	8.00	–	–	2
Kidderminster	1	1	0	7	7	7.00	–	–	–
Worcester	7	9	2	41	11*	5.85	–	–	6
Worcestershire	9	11	2	56	11*	6.22	–	–	8
Bradford	4	4	1	38	14	12.66	–	–	3
Headingley	8	11	1	196	66	19.60	–	1	1
Scarborough	3	3	1	34	17*	17.00	–	–	1
Sheffield	3	5	1	42	16	10.50	–	–	1
Yorkshire	18	23	4	310	66	16.31	–	1	6
Fenner's (Camb. U.)	6	4	1	100	44	33.33	–	–	5

Overseas
(listed by country)

	M	I	NO	Runs	HS	Avge	100	50	Ct
Adelaide	1	1	0	12	12	12.00	–	–	–
Brisbane	2	3	0	28	15	9.33	–	–	1
Hobart	1	1	1	11	11*	–	–	–	–
Melbourne	3	5	2	44	22*	14.66	–	–	–
Perth	1	1	0	2	2	2.00	–	–	–
Sydney	2	2	0	10	8	5.00	–	–	–
Australia	10	13	3	107	22*	10.70	–	–	1
Baroda	1	1	0	1	1	1.00	–	–	1
Bombay	4	3	0	66	37	22.00	–	–	2
Dehra Dun	1	2	0	61	61	61.00	–	1	–
Lucknow	1	1	0	6	6	6.00	–	–	1
Patiala	1	1	1	17	17*	–	–	–	1
Poona	1	1	0	14	14	14.00	–	–	–
Rajkot	1	1	0	6	6	6.00	–	–	–
India	10	10	1	171	61	19.00	–	1	5
Auckland	2	1	0	35	35	35.00	–	–	1
Christchurch	1	2	0	35	24	17.50	–	–	1
Dunedin	1	1	0	7	7	7.00	–	–	1
New Zealand	4	4	0	77	35	19.25	–	–	3
Bloemfontein	1	–	–	–	–	–	–	–	–
Cape Town	3	3	1	14	10	7.00	–	–	1
Durban	2	3	2	19	13*	19.00	–	–	1
East London	1	–	–	–	–	–	–	–	–
Johannesburg	3	5	1	29	17	7.25	–	–	–
Kimberley	1	1	0	6	6	6.00	–	–	1
Pietermaritzburg	1	1	1	2	2*	–	–	–	–
Port Elizabeth	1	2	1	9	6	9.00	–	–	–
Salisbury	1	1	0	0	0	0.00	–	–	–
Rhodesia and South Africa	14	16	6	79	17	7.90	–	–	3
Bridgetown	6	7	0	61	38	8.71	–	–	1
Georgetown	3	5	0	104	27	20.80	–	–	2
Kingston	7	7	2	55	33	11.00	–	–	5
Melbourne Park	2	2	1	35	31	17.50	–	–	1
Montego Bay	1	–	–	–	–	–	–	–	–
Port of Spain	2	3	1	86	55	43.00	–	1	1
West Indies	21	24	4	341	55	17.05	–	1	10

Summary

	M	I	NO	Runs	HS	Avge	100	50	Ct
In United Kingdom	391	481	94	6529	113	16.87	2	16	249
Overseas	59	67	14	775	61	14.62	–	2	22
Total	450	548	108	7304	113	16.60	2	18	271

Bowling

In United Kingdom
(listed by county)

	Overs	Mdns	Runs	Wkts	Avge	5WI	10WM	BB
Chesterfield	118.1	32	257	18	14.27	1	–	5–64
Derby	61.3	16	140	9	15.55	–	–	4–64
Derbyshire	179.4	48	397	27	14.70	1	–	5–64
Brentwood	199.1	46	442	13	34.00	1	–	5–46
Chelmsford	109.2	32	227	18	12.61	2	1	7–94
Clacton	67	12	189	11	17.18	–	–	4–42
Colchester	44	8	143	8	17.87	1	–	6–52
Ilford	278.2	73	716	28	25.57	1	–	7–84
Leyton	21	5	46	3	15.33	–	–	2–13
Romford	98	39	203	12	16.91	1	1	6–49
Southend	86	30	163	10	16.30	1	–	5–32
Essex	902.5	245	2129	103	20.66	7	2	7–84
Cardiff	222.2	74	441	23	19.17	1	–	5–86
Llanelli	44	17	67	6	11.16	1	–	6–67
Pontypridd	24.2	11	34	3	11.33	–	–	3–19
Swansea	248	70	563	24	23.45	2	1	5–53
Glamorgan	538.4	172	1105	56	19.73	4	1	6–67
Bristol	170	73	262	18	14.55	1	1	8–45
Cheltenham	93.2	39	166	15	11.06	1	–	5–30
Gloucester	122	39	275	25	11.00	2	1	6–27
Gloucestershire	385.2	151	703	58	12.12	4	2	8–45
Bournemouth	132	42	306	10	30.60	–	–	3–57
Portsmouth	158.4	37	465	20	23.25	1	–	8–69
Southampton	157.3	49	328	19	17.26	2	–	6–53
Hampshire	448.1	128	1099	49	22.42	3	–	8–69
Blackheath	352.4	132	645	37	17.43	2	–	6–60
Dover	57.4	12	159	13	12.23	2	1	7–73
Kent	410.2	144	804	50	16.08	4	1	7–73
Liverpool	55	15	128	5	25.60	–	–	4–81
Old Trafford	325.1	100	643	41	15.68	2	1	10–53
Lancashire	380.1	115	771	46	16.76	2	1	10–53
Hinckley	28.1	9	61	7	8.71	–	–	4–22
Leicester	378.1	141	681	40	17.02	3	–	7–89
Loughborough	42	18	43	1	43.00	–	–	1–19
Leicestershire	448.2	168	785	48	16.35	3	–	7–89
Lord's (Middlesex)	1257.2	376	2896	169	17.06	13	4	8–51

Kettering	38.5	15	94	11	8.54	2	1	6–58
Northampton	164.3	46	404	13	31.07	–	–	3–86
Peterborough	46.4	9	124	7	17.71	1	–	6–55
Rushden	49.2	16	99	9	11.00	1	–	7–57
Northamptonshire	299.2	86	721	40	18.02	4	1	7–57
Trent Bridge (Notts)	702	258	1471	62	23.72	3	–	7–16
Bath	61.5	23	122	9	13.55	1	–	7–59
Taunton	69	24	137	11	12.45	1	–	5–22
Wells	45.5	16	70	7	10.00	–	–	4–24
Weston–super–Mare	78.4	25	186	10	18.60	1	–	6–66
Somerset	255.2	88	515	37	13.91	3	–	7–59
Guildford	472.2	148	916	54	16.96	4	1	7–38
Kingston	83.4	19	222	9	24.66	–	–	3–43
The Oval	5788.4	1932	11929	687	17.36	44	12	10–88
Surrey	6344.4	2099	13067	750	17.42	48	13	10–88
Hastings	212.2	43	637	20	31.85	1	–	6–109
Hove	143.5	45	369	28	13.17	1	1	8–46
Worthing	52.5	12	128	7	18.28	1	–	6–49
Sussex	409	100	1134	55	20.61	3	1	8–46
Coventry	51	6	185	10	18.50	1	1	7–95
Edgbaston	227.5	81	528	17	31.05	–	–	4–119
Warwickshire	278.5	87	713	27	26.40	1	1	7–95
Dudley	59.3	15	144	8	18.00	1	–	6–66
Kidderminster	42.2	14	86	4	21.50	–	–	3–30
Worcester	279.3	104	571	37	15.43	2	1	7–61
Worcestershire	381.2	133	801	49	16.34	3	1	7–61
Bradford	182.1	85	304	24	12.66	2	1	8–2
Headingley	309.2	118	616	32	19.25	3	1	6–55
Scarborough	89.1	16	332	11	30.18	1	–	5–97
Sheffield	85	30	178	6	29.66	–	–	4–56
Yorkshire	665.4	249	1430	73	19.58	6	2	8–2
Fenner's (Camb. U.)	234.4	104	378	20	18.90	–	–	4–38

Overseas

(listed by country)

	Overs	Mdns	Runs	Wkts	Avge	5WI	10WM	BB
Adelaide	+43.1	11	101	10	10.10	2	1	5–31
Brisbane	+44.5	10	81	7	11.57	–	–	4–27
Hobart	+6	1	11	0	–	–	–	–
Melbourne	+72.5	13	208	6	34.66	–	–	4–93

Perth	+26	7	55	2	27.50	–	–	2–55
Sydney	+89.6	21	199	13	15.30	1	–	5–107
Australia	+282.1	63	655	38	17.23	3	1	5–31
Baroda	33	9	59	6	9.83	1	–	5–52
Bombay	172.4	73	312	17	18.35	1	–	5–88
Dehra Dun	23	14	35	4	8.75	–	–	4–32
Lucknow	13	7	25	1	25.00	–	–	1–0
Patiala	44.4	19	71	6	11.83	1	–	6–23
Poona	18	6	50	1	50.00	–	–	1–16
Rajkot	11	3	27	1	27.00	–	–	1–27
India	315.2	131	579	36	16.08	3	–	6–23
Auckland	115	41	193	15	12.86	2	1	5–53
Christchurch	45	16	94	1	94.00	–	–	1–70
Dunedin	68.1	31	92	8	11.50	1	–	5–44
New Zealand	228.1	88	379	24	15.79	3	1	5–44
Bloemfontein	+22	8	38	1	38.00	–	–	1–18
Cape Town	+114.1	38	245	17	14.41	1	–	6–47
Durban	+71	21	159	7	22.71	1	–	5–53
East London	+12	5	26	5	5.20	–	–	4–16
Johannesburg	+81.3	24	194	10	19.40	–	–	4–40
Kimberley	+21.3	8	40	2	20.00	–	–	2–24
Pietermaritzburg	+15	4	44	3	14.66	–	–	2–33
Port Elizabeth	+28	6	63	2	31.50	–	–	1–26
Salisbury	+23	8	66	3	22.00	–	–	3–63
South Africa and Rhodesia	+387.7	122	875	50	17.50	2	–	6–47
Bridgetown	304.2	83	859	34	25.26	2	–	7–103
Georgetown	139	53	300	13	23.07	1	–	5–74
Kingston	280.4	77	700	16	43.75	–	–	4–71
Melbourne Park	82	29	171	5	34.20	–	–	2–40
Montego Bay	36.2	6	92	5	18.40	1	–	5–54
Port of Spain	86	18	262	4	65.50	–	–	2–108
West Indies	928.2	266	2384	77	30.96	4	–	7–103

Summary

In United Kingdom	14521.4	4751	30919	1719	17.98	112	30	10–53
Overseas	1471.5 +670	485 185	4872	225	21.65	15	2	7–103
Total	15993.3 +670	5236 185	35791	1944	18.41	127	32	10–53

+ 8-ball overs

Season-by-season record at The Oval
Batting and Fielding

	M	I	NO	Runs	HS	Avge	100	50	Ct
1947	10	12	1	143	39	13.00	–	–	8
1948	9	13	3	305	99	30.50	–	1	7
1949	14	17	3	158	40	11.28	–	–	13
1950	13	19	1	243	44	12.78	–	–	9
1951	12	19	3	266	89	15.56	–	1	14
1952	13	17	3	132	23	9.42	–	–	9
1953	16	16	2	237	81	16.92	–	1	14
1954	13	15	3	291	113	24.25	1	–	21
1955	16	20	1	312	78*	16.42	–	1	13
1956	12	16	0	119	43	7.43	–	–	6
1957	10	10	3	70	24	10.00	–	–	4
1958	11	10	1	145	59	16.11	–	1	3
1959	11	13	3	120	17*	12.00	–	–	8
Total	160	197	27	2541	113	14.94	1	5	129

Bowling

	Ovrs	Mdns	Runs	Wkts	Avge	5WI	10WM	BB
1947	218.3	44	549	33	16.63	–	–	4–40
1948	275.4	60	709	32	22.15	1	–	8–55
1949	574.4	208	1171	74	15.82	5	1	8–42
1950	624.1	240	1103	64	17.23	5	1	8–57
1951	584.4	180	1166	63	18.50	7	4	7–65
1952	412.5	128	853	52	16.40	4	1	6–64
1953	627.3	216	1347	81	16.62	4	1	6–25
1954	490.2	156	978	62	15.77	6	2	6–16
1955	529	187	1090	59	18.47	4	–	6–5
1956	434	149	990	61	16.22	3	1	10–88
1957	330.4	133	553	35	15.80	–	–	4–31
1958	333.4	121	634	48	13.20	4	1	7–53
1959	353	110	786	23	34.17	1	–	5–11
Total	5788.4	1932	11929	687	17.36	44	12	10–88

TEST CRICKET
Series-by-Series
Batting and Fielding

Date and opponents		M	I	NO	Runs	HS	Avge	100	50	Ct
1947–48	West Indies	4	7	1	109	55	18.16	–	1	1
1948	Australia	3	6	1	114	63	22.80	–	1	–
1949	New Zealand	1	1	0	0	0	0.00	–	–	–
1950	West Indies	1	2	0	44	40	22.00	–	–	–

1951	South Africa	2	3	1	46	27	23.00	–	–	1
1952	India	4	4	2	44	23*	22.00	–	–	3
1953	Australia	3	4	0	64	48	16.00	–	–	–
1953–54	West Indies	4	5	1	44	27	11.00	–	–	3
1954	Pakistan	1	1	1	13	13*	–	–	–	–
1955	South Africa	1	2	0	14	12	7.00	–	–	–
1956	Australia	5	6	1	37	12	7.40	–	–	–
1956–57	South Africa	5	9	3	40	17	6.66	–	–	1
1957	West Indies	4	3	1	18	10*	9.00	–	–	1
1958	New Zealand	4	3	1	27	15	13.50	–	–	2
1958–59	Australia	4	7	2	62	22*	12.40	–	–	–
TOTALS		**46**	**63**	**15**	**676**	**63**	**14.08**	**–**	**2**	**12**

Bowling

		Overs	Mdns	Runs	Wkts	Avge	Balls per wkt	5WI	10WM	BB
1947–48	West Indies	186.4	48	548	18	30.44	62.22	1	–	7–103
1948	Australia	155.2	42	472	9	52.44	103.55	–	–	4–138
1949	New Zealand	32	6	89	4	22.25	48.00	–	–	4–78
1950	West Indies	31	9	86	1	86.00	186.00	–	–	1–43
1951	South Africa	111	30	208	14	14.85	47.57	1	1	6–55
1952	India	90.3	33	189	8	23.62	67.87	–	–	4–39
1953	Australia	58.5	11	212	9	23.55	39.22	–	–	4–75
1953–54	West Indies	221.1	84	469	14	33.50	94.78	–	–	4–71
1954	Pakistan	32.2	17	39	2	19.50	97.00	–	–	1–17
1955	South Africa	60.4	31	84	7	12.00	52.00	1	–	5–56
1956	Australia	283.5	127	442	46	9.60	37.02	4	2	10–53
1956–57	South Africa	+145.1	46	324	11	29.45	105.54	–	–	2–7
1957	West Indies	246.2	99	448	18	24.88	82.11	–	–	4–119
1958	New Zealand	131	67	173	17	10.17	46.23	1	–	5–17
1958–59	Australia	+127.6	24	318	15	21.20	68.13	1	–	5–107
Total		1640.4 +272.7	604 70	4101	193	21.24	62.31	9	3	10–53

+ 8-ball overs

Record against each opponent
Batting and Fielding

	M	I	NO	Runs	HS	Avge	100	50	Ct
Australia	15	23	4	277	63	14.57	–	1	–
India	4	4	2	44	23*	22.00	–	–	3
New Zealand	5	4	1	27	15	9.00	–	–	2
Pakistan	1	1	1	13	13*	–	–	–	–
South Africa	8	14	4	100	27	10.00	–	–	2
West Indies	13	17	3	215	55	15.35	–	1	5
Total	46	63	15	676	63	14.08	–	2	12

JIM LAKER

Bowling

	Overs	Mdns	Runs	Wkts	Avge	Balls per wkt	5WI	10WM	BB
Australia	498 +127.6	180 24	1444	79	18.27	50.75	5	2	10–53
India	90.3	33	189	8	23.62	67.87	–	–	4–39
New Zealand	163	73	262	21	12.47	46.57	1	–	5–17
Pakistan	32.2	17	39	2	19.50	97.00	–	–	1–17
South Africa	171.4 +145.1	61 46	616	32	19.25	68.46	2	1	6–55
West Indies	685.1	240	1551	51	30.41	80.60	1	–	7–103
Total	1640.4 +272.7	604 70	4101	193	21.24	62.31	9	3	10–53

Half-centuries
63 v Australia   Trent Bridge   1948
55 v West Indies   Port of Spain 1947–48

Five-wickets in an innings
10–53 v Australia   Old Trafford   1956
9–37   v Australia   Old Trafford   1956
7–103 v West Indies   Bridgetown   1947–48
6–55   v South Africa   The Oval   1951
6–55   v Australia   Headingley   1956
5–17   v New Zealand   Headingley   1958
5–56   v South Africa   The Oval   1955
5–58   v Australia   Headingley   1956
5–107 v Australia   Sydney   1958–59

Ten wickets in a match
19–90   v Australia   Old Trafford   1956
11–113 v Australia   Headingley   1956
10–119 v South Africa   The Oval   1951

Record on each ground
(listed by country)

Batting and Fielding

	M	I	NO	Runs	HS	Avge	100	50	Ct
Edgbaston	2	2	1	18	11*	18.00	–	–	1
Headingley	6	7	1	98	48	16.33	–	–	1
Lord's	5	7	2	81	28	16.20	–	–	2
Old Trafford	5	6	0	79	40	13.16	–	–	1
The Oval	8	10	3	69	15	9.85	–	–	1
Trent Bridge	3	3	1	76	63	38.00	–	1	1
Total	29	35	8	421	63	15.59	–	1	7

Brisbane	1	2	0	28	15	14.00	–	–	–
Melbourne	2	4	2	32	22*	16.00	–	–	–
Sydney	1	1	0	2	2	2.00	–	–	–
Total	4	7	2	62	22*	12.40	–	–	–
Cape Town	1	1	0	0	0	0.00	–	–	–
Durban	1	2	1	6	6	6.00	–	–	1
Johannesburg	2	4	1	25	17	8.33	–	–	–
Port Elizabeth	1	2	1	9	6	9.00	–	–	–
Total	5	9	3	40	17	6.66	–	–	1
Bridgetown	2	3	0	3	3	1.00	–	–	–
Georgetown	2	3	0	43	27	14.33	–	–	–
Kingston	2	3	1	21	9	10.50	–	–	3
Port of Spain	2	3	1	86	55	43.00	–	1	1
Total	8	12	2	153	55	15.30	–	1	4
Total overseas	17	28	7	255	55	12.14	–	1	5

Bowling

	Overs	Mdns	Runs	Wkts	Avge	Balls per wkt	5WI	10WM	BB
Edgbaston	92	43	155	8	19.37	69.00	–	–	4–119
Headingley	260.2	103	509	30	16.96	52.06	3	1	6–55
Lord's	182.5	73	391	16	24.43	68.56	–	–	4–13
Old Trafford	173	54	325	27	12.03	38.44	2	1	10–53
The Oval	305.3	114	638	40	15.95	45.82	2	1	6–55
Trent Bridge	219.1	85	424	14	30.28	93.92	–	–	4–58
Total	1232.5	472	2442	135	18.08	54.79	7	3	10–53
Brisbane	+27.1	6	54	3	18.00	72.33	–	–	2–15
Melbourne	+46.5	6	147	5	29.40	74.60	–	–	4–93
Sydney	+54	12	117	7	16.71	61.71	1	–	5–107
Total	+127.6	24	318	15	21.20	68.13	1	–	5–107
Cape Town	+42.1	17	72	3	24.00	112.33	–	–	2–7
Durban	+30	8	76	2	38.00	120.00	–	–	2–29
Johannesburg	+45	15	113	4	28.25	90.00	–	–	1–5
Port Elizabeth	+28	6	63	2	31.50	112.00	–	–	1–26
Total	+145.1	46	324	11	29.45	105.54	–	–	2–7
Bridgetown	127.1	40	341	13	26.23	58.69	1	–	7–103
Georgetown	102	41	216	8	27.00	76.50	–	–	2–32
Kingston	92.4	33	198	7	28.28	79.42	–	–	4–31
Port of Spain	86	18	262	4	65.50	129.00	–	–	2–108
Total	407.5	132	1017	32	31.78	76.46	1	–	7–103
Total overseas	407.5 +272.7	132 70	1659	58	28.60	79.82	2	–	7–103

Methods of Dismissal

Caught	99	51.29%
Bowled	52	26.94%
Lbw	32	16.58%
Stumped	10	5.18%
Total	193	100.00%

Batsmen most frequently dismissed by Laker

11 C. L. Walcott (West Indies)
10 K. R. Miller (Australia)
 7 J. W. Burke, I. W. Johnson, K. D. Mackay (all Australia)
 6 R. Benaud, C. C. McDonald (both Australia)
 5 R. A. McLean (South Africa)

Most fielding dismissals from Laker's bowling
(all caught unless otherwise stated)

15 T. G. Evans (6ct, 9st)
12 G. A. R. Lock
10 M. C. Cowdrey
 7 A. S. M. Oakman, F. S. Trueman
 6 J. C. LAKER
 5 T. E. Bailey

Note: Lock also took one catch as a substitute.

Most wickets in a series

		Tests	Balls	Runs	Wkts	Avge	Balls per wkt	5WI	10WM	BB
S. F. Barnes 1913–14	E v. SA	4	1356	536	49	10.93	27.67	7	3	9–103
J. C. LAKER 1956	E v. A	5	1703	442	46	9.60	37.02	4	2	10–53
C. V. Grimmett 1935–36	A v. SA	5	2077	642	44	14.59	47.20	5	3	7–40
T. M. Alderman 1981	A v. E	6	1950	893	42	21.26	46.42	4	–	6–135

Best bowling figures in an innings

10–53	J. C. LAKER	England v Australia	Old Trafford	1956
9–28	G. A. Lohmann	England v South Africa	Johannesburg	1895–96
9–37	J. C. LAKER	England v Australia	Old Trafford	1956
9–52	R. J. Hadlee	New Zealand v Australia	Brisbane	1985–86
9–56	Abdul Qadir	Pakistan v England	Lahore	1987–88
9–57	D. E. Malcolm	England v South Africa	The Oval	1994

Best bowling figures in a match

19–90	J. C. LAKER	England v Australia	Old Trafford	1956
17–159	S. F. Barnes	England v South Africa	Johannesburg	1913–14
16–136	N. D. Hirwani	India v West Indies	Madras	1987–88
16–137	R. A. L. Massie	Australia v England	Lord's	1972

Best bowling figures for England in first innings of debut Test

7–46	J. K. Lever	v India	Delhi	1976–77
7–49	A. V. Bedser	v India	Lord's	1946
7–103	J. C. LAKER	v West Indies	Bridgetown	1947–48

Ten or more wickets in a Test for England by lowest average since 1946

4.36	11–48	G. A. R. Lock	v West Indies	The Oval	1957
4.73	19–90	J. C. LAKER	v Australia	Old Trafford	1956
5.46	13–71	D. L. Underwood	v Pakistan	Lord's	1974
5.90	11–65	G. A. R. Lock	v New Zealand	Headingley	1958

Highest wicket aggregates by English spin bowlers

	Tests	Balls	Runs	Wkts	Avge	Balls per wkt	5WI	10WM	BB
D. L. Underwood 1966–81/2	86	21862	7674	297	25.83	73.60	17	6	8–51
J. C. LAKER 1947/8–58/9	46	12027	4101	193	21.24	62.31	9	3	10–53
G. A. R. Lock 1952–67/8	49	13147	4451	174	25.58	75.55	9	3	7–35
F. J. Titmus 1955–74/5	53	15118	4931	153	32.22	98.81	7	–	7–79
H. Verity 1931–39	40	11173	3510	144	24.37	77.59	5	2	8–43
J. E. Emburey 1978–93	60	14227	5105	138	36.99	103.09	6	–	7–78
W. Rhodes 1899–1929/30	58	8231	3425	127	26.96	64.81	6	1	8–68
P. H. Edmonds 1975–87	51	12028	4273	125	34.18	96.22	2	–	7–66
D. A. Allen 1959/60–66	39	11297	3779	122	30.97	92.59	4	–	5–30
R. Illingworth 1958–73	61	11934	3807	122	31.20	97.81	3	–	6–29

Laker and Lock appeared in 24 Test matches together and are one of only four pairs of English spin bowlers who have played in at least 20 Tests together. The four are:

W. Rhodes and F. E. Woolley	29 Tests	1909–26
J. C. Laker and G. A. R. Lock	24 Tests	1952–58/59
R. Illingworth and D. L. Underwood	24 Tests	1966–73
P. H. Edmonds and J. E. Emburey	21 Tests	1978–87

Their records are compared below:

	Runs	Wkts	Avge		Runs	Wkts	Avge	Runs	Wkts	Avge
									Totals	
Rhodes	899	23	39.08	Woolley	1499	51	29.39	2398	74	32.40
LAKER	1810	114	15.87	LOCK	1877	92	20.40	3687	206	17.89
Illingworth	1714	53	32.33	Underwood	2291	109	21.01	4005	162	24.72
Edmonds	1348	36	37.44	Emburey	1436	37	38.81	2784	73	38.13

J. C. Laker and G. A. R. Lock
Season by Season
(matches in which both played)

		Laker			Lock			Totals		
	M	Overs	Wkts	Avge	Overs	Wkts	Avge	Overs	Wkts	Avge
1949	19	814.3	98	16.67	532.4	41	27.10	1347.1	139	19.75
1950	20	1027.4	112	16.34	727	53	26.57	1754.4	165	19.62
1951	24	1085.1	127	17.75	775.5	686	21.09	1861	195	18.91
1952	23	829.2	102	16.59	769.3	93	17.26	1598.5	195	16.91
1953	16	561.3	63	20.12	615.3	91	14.47	1177	154	16.78
1953/54	6	295.5	20	34.25	357.2	20	43.55	653.1	40	38.90
1954	23	793.4	115	14.56	812.4	103	15.00	1606.2	218	14.77
1955	25	848	99	18.54	1039.4	170	12.54	1887.4	269	14.75
1956	19	754.5	112	13.20	765.1	95	15.00	1520	207	14.02
1956/57	8	+212.3	34	14.55	+173.3	22	17.59	+385.6	56	15.75
1957	24	822.5	109	13.93	914.4	160	12.39	1737.3	269	13.01
1958	23	759.5	103	13.53	769.5	127	11.40	1529.4	230	12.35
1958/59	6	+202	28	16.75	+202.1	22	19.59	+404.1	50	20.66
1959	19	587.2	52	26.61	690.4	74	21.72	1278	126	23.74
Total	255	9180.3	1174	16.52	8770.3	1139	16.43	17951	2313	16.60
		+414.3			+375.4			+789.7		

Note: Laker bowled 51.21% of the balls and took 50.75% of the wickets.

Surrey's Bowlers in the County Championship 1952–58

	Laker and Lock			A. Bedser and Loader			Others			Totals		
	Overs	Wkts	Avge	Overs	Wkts	Avge	Overs	Wkts	Avge	Overs	Wkts	Avge
1952	1672.3	202	16.67	895.4	118	16.88	1722.3	155	27.29	4290.4	475	20.19
1953	1231.1	160	14.90	1183.1	151	16.94	1709.5	143	27.31	4124.1	454	19.49
1954	1553.3	213	13.95	1140.1	162	14.54	671.2	60	27.26	3365	435	16.00
1955	1751.4	251	14.70	1290.1	171	16.80	880.1	106	20.14	3922	528	16.47
1956	1101.5	174	12.98	1409.5	185	16.78	929	87	23.25	3440.4	446	16.56
1957	1373.3	238	11.88	1455.5	210	15.17	578.5	83	16.27	3408.1	531	13.87
1958	1380.4	207	13.19	1042.1	119	18.00	1279	118	25.60	3701.5	444	17.77
	10064.5	1445	14.00	8417	1116	16.32	7770.4	752	24.33	26252.3	3313	17.12

Note: During this period Laker and Lock bowled 38% of the overs but took 44% of the wickets. A. Bedser and Loader had figures of 32% and 34%, respectively.

Season-by-season home record in County Championship 1952–58
(matches in which both played)

		Laker				Lock				Totals		
	M	O	W	Avge	WPM	O	W	Avge	WPM	O	W	Avge	WPM
1952	11	375	42	17.73	3.81	353.1	52	12.76	4.72	728.1	94	14.98	8.54
1953	7	279.3	36	16.58	5.14	254	44	11.93	6.28	533.3	80	14.02	11.42
1954	9	322.3	44	14.06	4.88	302.4	50	11.78	5.55	625.1	94	12.85	10.44
1955	12	332.4	40	16.67	3.33	422.4	68	10.86	5.66	755.2	108	13.01	9.00
1956	8	250	34	18.82	4.25	251.2	37	13.02	4.62	501.2	71	15.80	8.87
1957	7	208.4	24	13.70	3.42	234.5	53	8.71	7.57	443.3	77	10.27	11.00
1958	9	278.4	45	12.62	5.00	269.4	48	11.60	5.33	548.2	93	12.09	10.33
	63	2047	265	15.71	4.20	2088.2	352	11.41	5.58	4135.2	617	13.26	9.79

Season-by-season away record in County Championship 1952–58
(matches in which both played)

		Laker				Lock				Totals		
	M	O	W	Avge	WPM	O	W	Avge	WPM	O	W	Avge	WPM
1952	7	355.2	44	16.04	6.28	334.2	33	23.18	4.71	689.4	77	19.10	11.00
1953	2	83.3	7	22.14	3.50	100	18	9.66	9.00	183.3	25	13.16	12.50
1954	10	348.5	52	14.25	5.20	387	44	13.77	4.40	735.5	96	14.03	9.60
1955	8	316.5	34	22.47	4.25	410.5	62	15.14	7.75	727.4	96	17.73	12.00
1956	2	87.1	11	14.00	5.50	115.4	20	11.75	10.00	202.5	31	12.54	15.50
1957	10	334.2	56	12.14	5.60	381.1	60	15.71	6.00	715.3	116	15.71	11.60
1958	8	307.1	38	14.78	4.75	342.5	47	14.40	5.87	650	85	14.57	10.62
	47	1833.1	242	15.54	5.14	2071.5	284	15.27	6.04	3905	526	15.40	11.19

Season-by-season record in County Championship 1952–58
(matches in which both played)

		Laker				Lock				Totals		
	M	O	W	Avge	WPM	O	W	Avge	WPM	O	W	Avge	WPM
1952	18	730.2	86	16.87	4.77	687.3	85	16.81	4.72	1417.5	171	16.84	9.50
1953	9	363	43	17.48	4.77	354	62	11.27	6.88	717	105	13.81	11.66
1954	19	671.2	96	14.16	5.05	689.4	94	12.71	4.94	1361	190	13.44	10.00
1955	20	649.3	74	19.33	3.70	833.3	130	12.90	6.50	1483	204	15.24	10.20
1956	10	337.1	45	17.64	4.50	367	57	12.57	5.70	704.1	102	14.81	10.20
1957	17	543	80	12.61	4.70	616	113	12.43	6.64	1159	193	12.50	11.35
1958	17	585.5	83	13.61	4.88	612.3	95	12.98	5.58	1198.2	178	13.28	10.47
	110	3880.1	507	15.63	4.60	4160.1	636	13.13	5.78	8040.2	1143	14.24	10.39

Miscellany

Batting

Centuries

113	Surrey v Gloucestershire	The Oval	1954
100	Surrey v Cambridge University	Guildford	1949

Score of 99

Run out Surrey v Kent	The Oval	1948

Pairs

Surrey v Gloucestershire	The Oval	1949
Surrey v Yorkshire	The Oval	1950

Note: the pair against Yorkshire was followed by another duck – against Worcestershire at Worcestershire.

Century Partnerships

2nd	P. B. H. May	MCC v Jamaica	Melbourne Park	1953–54
7th	R. Subba Row	Surrey v Hampshire	The Oval	1953
7th	A. J. W. McIntyre	Surrey v Northamptonshire	Guildford	1955
7th	A. J. W. McIntyre	Surrey v Hampshire	Southampton	1951
7th	A. J. W. McIntyre	Surrey v Middlesex	The Oval	1950
8th	B. Constable	Surrey v Camb. Univ.	Guildford	1949
8th	K. F. Barrington	Surrey v Gloucestershire	The Oval	1954
8th	A. J. W. McIntyre	Surrey v Leicestershire	The Oval	1958
8th	A. V. Bedser	Surrey v Glamorgan	Cardiff	1951

Bowling

Eight or more wickets in an innings

10–53	England v Australia	Old Trafford	1956
10–88	Surrey v Australians	The Oval	1956
9–37	England v Australia	Old Trafford	1956
8–2	England v The Rest	Bradford	1950
8–42	Surrey v Warwickshlre	The Oval	1949
8–45	Surrey v Gloucestershire	Bristol	1950
8–46	Surrey v Sussex	Hove	1958
8–51	Surrey v MCC	Lord's	1954
8–55	Surrey v Gloucestershire	The Oval	1948
8–57	Surrey v Middlesex	The Oval	1950
8–69	Surrey v Hampshire	Portsmouth	1947

Twelve or more wickets in a match

19–90	England v Australia	Old Trafford	1956
15–97	Surrey v MCC	Lord's	1954
13–159	Essex v Kent	Dover	1962

12–78	Surrey	v	Sussex	Hove	1958
12–86	Surrey	v	Gloucestershire	Bristol	1950
12–98	Surrey	v	Kent	The Oval	1949
12–130	Surrey	v	Australians	The Oval	1956
12–144	Surrey	v	Worcestershire	The Oval	1951

Fifty or more wickets in a month

	Inns	Overs	Maidens	Runs	Wkts	Avge	5WI	10WM	BB
May 1951	16	437.4	146	812	60	13.53	7	3	7–36
July 1950	16	484.1	207	759	55	13.80	4	3	8–45

Note: The feat in 1950 included 22 wickets (av. 8.36) in two matches against Gloucestershire.

Conceding less than one run per over in an innings
(minimum 20 overs)

figures	runs per over	match			venue	
24-20-13-2	0.54	England	v	West Indies	Edgbaston	1957
36–23–27–3	0.75	England	v	New Zealand	Headingley	1958
22–11–17–5	0.77	England	v	New Zealand	Headingley	1958
30.2–17–25–6	0.82	Surrey	v	Leicestershire	The Oval	1953
28–12–24–0	0.85	Surrey	v	Leicestershire	Loughborough	1953
21–13–20–1	0.95	Surrey	v	Nottinghamshire	The Oval	1957

Also of note:	14–12–2–8	0.14	England v The Rest	Bradford	1950
	13–10–3–1	0.23	Surrey v Notts	Trent Bridge	1958
	16–11–5–6	0.31	Surrey v Notts	The Oval	1955
	18–14–8–3	0.44	England v Australia	The Oval	1956
	+14.1–9–7–2	0.49	England v South Africa	Cape Town	1956–57

Note: In two matches against Leicestershire in 1953, Laker conceded 104 runs from 96.2 overs.

Conceding less than one run per over in a match
(minimum 30 overs)

figures	runs	match	venue	
58-34-44-8	0.75	England v New Zealand	Headingley	1958
49-28-45-3	0.91	Surrey v Cambridge University	Fenner's	1953

1000th first-class wicket

C. L. Walcott lbw b Laker 26   England v West Indies   Georgetown 1953–54

100th Test wicket

R. Benaud c Oakman b Laker 30   England v Australia   Headingley   1956

237

Methods of dismissal

Caught	1065	54.78%
Bowled	557	28.65%
Lbw	246	12.65%
Stumped	72	3.70%
Hit wicket	4	0.21%
Total	1944	100.00%

Batsmen most frequently dismissed by Laker

14 W. J. Edrich, C. A. Milton
13 C. L. Walcott
12 D. J. Insole, K. R. Miller, R. Smith
11 J. F. Crapp, R. G. Marlar, C. C. McDonald
10 T. E. Bailey, L. H. Compton, R. T. Simpson, F. J. Titmus, J. J. Warr

Most fielding dismissals from Laker's bowling

122 G. A. R. Lock
110 A. J. McIntyre (77ct, 33st)
107 W. S. Surridge
 68 J. C. LAKER
 64 M. J. Stewart
 43 A.V. Bedser
 32 E. A. Bedser
 30 P. B. H. May
 29 J. F. Parker
 28 K. F. Barrington
 27 D. G. W. Fletcher
 25 B. Constable

Best position in national first-class averages

4th 1950, 1957; 6th 1956, 1958, 1962

Best position amongst season's leading wicket aggregates

3rd 1950, 1951; 6th 1954

Best position in own county's championship averages

1st 1947, 1949, 1950, 1962, 1963
2nd 1948, 1951, 1952, 1953, 1954, 1957, 1958

1000 wickets for Surrey in County Championship

This feat has been achieved by eleven bowlers, the highest aggregate being that of T. Richardson; the following table shows the five who have the best average.

238

	Seasons	Runs	Wkts	Avge
J. C. LAKER	1947–59	20528	1203	17.06
G. A. R. Lock	1946–63	25255	1458	17.32
T. Richardson	1892–1904	27371	1531	17.87
W. H. Lockwood	1890–1904	18395	1001	18.37
A. V. Bedser	1946–60	23753	1241	19.14

Ten wickets in an innings twice in same season

J. C. Laker   1956
(the only instance in the history of first-class cricket)

Ten wickets in an innings against Australian teams

10–43	E.Barratt	Players	v	Australians	The Oval	1878
10–88	J. C. LAKER	Surrey	v	Australians	The Oval	1956
10–53	J. C. LAKER	England	v	Australia	Old Trafford	1956

Note: The feat has also been achieved four times against Australian teams in Australia.

Acknowledgements

Edgar Appleby, Jeff Hancock (Librarian, Surrey CCC), David Seymour, and the Staff of the City of York Central Library.

Bibliography

Bailey, P., Thorn, P., and Wynne-Thomas, P.: *Who's Who of Cricketers*
Brooke, R.: *The Collins Who's Who of English First-Class Cricket; A History of the County Championship*
Frindall, W.: *England Test Cricketers; The Wisden Book of Test Cricket; The Wisden Book of Cricket Records*
Mosey, D.: *Laker: Portrait of a Legend*
Woolgar, J.: *England's Test Cricketers*
Wynne-Thomas, P.: *The Complete History of Cricket Tours.*

Also various editions of *The Cricket Statistician, The Cricketer, Playfair Cricket Monthly* and *Wisden Cricketers' Almanack.*

INDEX